# Oracle8™ DBA: Performance Tuning

Michael R. Ault

Josef M. Brinson

The Coriolis Group, LLC
14455 N. Hayden Road
Suite 220
Scottsdale, Arizona 85260

480/483-0192
FAX 480/483-0193
http://www.coriolis.com

Library of Congress Cataloging-in-Publication Data
Ault, Michael R.
   Oracle8 DBA : performance tuning exam cram / by Michael R. Ault and Josef Brinson.
      p.  cm.
   Includes index.
   ISBN 1-57610-602-0
   1. Electronic data processing personnel--Certification.   2. Database management--Examinations--Study guides.   3. Oracle (Computer file)  I. Brinson, Josef.  II. Title.
QA76.3.A93   2000
005.75'85--dc21
                               00-022932
                               CIP

**President, CEO**
Keith Weiskamp

**Publisher**
Steve Sayre

**Acquisitions Editor**
Jeff Kellum

**Marketing Specialist**
Cynthia Caldwell

**Project Editor**
Toni Zuccarini Ackley

**Technical Reviewer**
Pete Sharman

**Production Coordinator**
Wendy Littley

**Cover Designer**
Jesse Dunn

**Layout Designer**
April Nielsen

Printed in the United States of America
10 9 8 7 6 5 4 3 2 1

14455 North Hayden Road • Suite 220 • Scottsdale, Arizona 85260

## Coriolis: The Smartest Way To Get Certified™

To help you reach your goals, we've listened to readers like you, and we've designed our entire product line around you and the way you like to study, learn, and master challenging subjects.

In addition to our highly popular *Exam Cram* and *Exam Prep* books, we offer several other products to help you pass certification exams. Our *Practice Tests* and *Flash Cards* are designed to make your studying fun and productive. Our *Audio Reviews* have received rave reviews from our customers—and they're the perfect way to make the most of your drive time!

The newest way to get certified is the *Exam Cram Personal Trainer*—a highly interactive, personalized self-study course based on the best-selling *Exam Cram* series. It's the first certification-specific product to completely link a customizable learning tool, exclusive *Exam Cram* content, and multiple testing techniques so you can study what, how, and when you want.

*Exam Cram Insider*—a biweekly newsletter containing the latest in certification news, study tips, and announcements from Certification Insider Press—gives you an ongoing look at the hottest certification programs. (To subscribe, send an email to **eci@coriolis.com** and type "subscribe insider" in the body of the email.) We also sponsor the Certified Crammer Society and the Coriolis Help Center—two other resources that will help you get certified even faster!

Help us continue to provide the very best certification study materials possible. Write us or email us at **cipq@coriolis.com** and let us know how our books have helped you study. Tell us about new features that you'd like us to add. Send us a story about how we've helped you; if we use it in one of our books, we'll send you an official Coriolis shirt!

Good luck with your certification exam and your career. Thank you for allowing us to help you achieve your goals.

Keith Weiskamp
President and CEO

# Look For These Other Books From The Coriolis Group:

## Oracle8 DBA: SQL and PL/SQL Exam Cram
by Michael R. Ault

## Oracle8 DBA: Backup and Recovery Exam Cram
by Debbie Wong

## Oracle8 DBA: Database Administration Exam Cram
by Paul Collins

## Oracle8 DBA: Network Administration Exam Cram
by Barbara Ann Pascavage

## Oracle DBA 7.3 to 8 Upgrade Exam Cram
by Robert Freeman

## Oracle8 and Windows NT Black Book
by Mike Curtis and Jacqueline King

## Oracle8 Black Book
by Michael R. Ault

*As with all my other books, I want to dedicate this to my loving family: Susan, my wife; Marie, my eldest daughter; and Michelle, my youngest. I also want to dedicate this book to my mother and father, who were the pillars upon which I stood to reach adulthood. My love and thanks go out to all of them.*
*—Michael R. Ault*


*To my wife and family, who patiently waited for me to finish this book so we could resume a normal evening and weekend life and have some fun again.*
*—Josef M. Brinson*

ᏘᏘ

# About The Authors

**Michael R. Ault** has been working in the data processing field since 1974 and with Oracle since 1990. Mike holds five Oracle masters certificates. Mike began his certification history with the Oracle Corporation test-based Oracle6 certification, continued it as one of the developers and recipients of the Chauncey Oracle7 certification, and is currently an Oracle8 and Oracle8i OCP. Mike has written several books, including *Oracle 7.0 Administration and Management, Oracle8 Administration & Management, Oracle DBA Test 1 and Test 2 Exam Cram, Oracle DBA Test 3 and Test 4 Exam Cram*, and *Oracle8 Black Book*. Mike has also written numerous articles for *Oracle* magazine, *DBMS Magazine*, and *OREVIEW* magazine, and is a frequent presenter at ECO, IOUG-A, and Oracle Open World conferences. Mike also SYSOPS for the CompuServe ORAUSER forum and the RevealNet, Inc., Web page's DBA Pipeline. Mike is also the primary author for the Oracle Administrator Knowledge Base product from RevealNet, Inc. Currently, Mike is the part owner and Chief Technical Officer for DBMentors International, Inc., an Oracle consulting and training company.

**Josef M. Brinson** is an OCP-certified Oracle DBA. He has worked in the industry for 14 years, leading many projects involving database design and development with several top corporations. Josef has also provided leadership in the migration of mainframe-based systems to client/server installations. Currently, he is Chief Operations Officer for DBMentors International, Inc., a consulting firm providing expertise in Oracle-related projects.

# Acknowledgments

As an author, I sometimes fail to see all the hands that the manuscript passes through on its way to becoming a real book. I would be remiss if I cannot thank these folks personally, not to thank them here in the acknowledgements. To that end I would like to thank: Wendy Littley, Production Coordinator; Pete Sharman, Technical Editor; Bart Reed, Copyeditor; and last but not least, Jeff Kellum, Acquisitions Editor. Of course, Toni Zuccarini Ackley deserves thanks for all of her hard work to make the book come out somewhere near on time. I especially want to thank Josef Brinson for all his hard work in upgrading this book to Oracle8. My deepest gratitude to you all.

—*Michael R. Ault*

I first want to thank my partner, Michael Ault, who agreed to be my co-founder of DBMentors International, Inc., and who dangled the "carrot" in front of me throughout my effort to publish this book. Then along came the team from The Coriolis Group, who used their talents, and much patience, to guide me through the process of writing the book. My heartfelt thanks to Jeff Kellum, Acquisitions Editor, who kept me focused on the task. My thanks also go to the various editors, Toni Zuccarini Ackley, Bart Reed, and Pete Sharman, without whose help I would not have been able to complete the task.

—*Josef M. Brinson*

# Contents At A Glance

# Table Of Contents

# Introduction

Welcome to *Oracle8 DBA: Performance Tuning Exam Cram*! This book will help you get ready to take—and pass—the fourth of the five-part series of exams for Oracle Certified Professional-Oracle8 Certified Database Administrator (OCP-DBA) certification. In this Introduction, we talk about Oracle's certification programs in general and how the *Exam Cram* series can help you prepare for Oracle8's certification exams.

*Exam Cram* books help you understand and appreciate the subjects and materials you need to pass Oracle certification exams. The books are aimed strictly at test preparation and review. They do not teach you everything you need to know about a topic. Instead, we present and dissect the questions and problems that you're likely to encounter on a test.

Nevertheless, to completely prepare yourself for any Oracle test, we recommend that you begin by taking the Self-Assessment included in this book immediately following this Introduction. This tool will help you evaluate your knowledge base against the requirements for an OCP-DBA under both ideal and real circumstances.

Based on what you learn from that exercise, you might decide to begin your studies with some classroom training or by reading one of the many DBA guides available from Oracle and third-party vendors. We also strongly recommend that you install, configure, and fool around with the software or environment that you'll be tested on, because nothing beats hands-on experience and familiarity when it comes to understanding the questions you're likely to encounter on a certification test. Book learning is essential, but hands-on experience is the best teacher of all!

# The Oracle Certified Professional (OCP) Program

The OCP program for DBA certification currently includes five separate tests. A brief description of each test follows, and Table 1 shows the required exams for the OCP-DBA certification:

# Table 1 OCP-DBA Requirements*

| All 5 of these tests are required | | |
|---|---|---|
| Test 1 | Exam 1Z0-001 | Introduction to Oracle: SQL and PL/SQL |
| Test 2 | Exam 1Z0-013 | Oracle8: Database Administration |
| Test 3 | Exam 1Z0-015 | Oracle8: Backup and Recovery |
| Test 4 | Exam 1Z0-014 | Oracle8: Performance Tuning |
| Test 5 | Exam 1Z0-016 | Oracle8: Network Administration |

\* If you are currently an OCP certified in Oracle7.3, you need take only the upgrade exam (Oracle8: New Features for Administrators, Exam 1Z0-010) to be certified in Oracle8.

➤ *Introduction to Oracle: SQL And PL/SQL (Exam 1Z0-001)*—Test 1 is the base test for the series. Knowledge tested in Test 1 will also be used in all other tests in the DBA series. Besides testing knowledge of SQL and PL/SQL language constructs, syntax, and usage, Test 1 covers Data Definition Language (DDL), Data Manipulation Language (DML), and Data Control Language (DCL). Also covered in Test 1 are basic data modeling and database design.

➤ *Oracle8: Database Administration (Exam 1Z0-013)*—Test 2 deals with all levels of database administration in Oracle8 (primarily version 8.0.5 and above). Topics include architecture, startup and shutdown, database creation, managing database internal and external constructs (such as redo logs, rollback segments, and tablespaces), and all other Oracle structures. Database auditing, use of National Language Support (NLS) features, and use of SQL*Loader and other utilities are also covered.

➤ *Oracle8: Backup And Recovery (Exam 1Z0-015)*—Test 3 covers one of the most important parts of the Oracle DBA's job: database backup and recovery operations. Test 3 tests knowledge in backup and recovery motives, architecture as it relates to backup and recovery, backup methods, failure scenarios, recovery methodologies, archive logging, supporting 24x7 shops, troubleshooting, and use of Oracle8's standby database features. The test also covers the use of the Recovery Manager (RMAN) product from Oracle, new in Oracle8.

➤ *Oracle8: Performance Tuning (Exam 1Z0-014)*—Test 4 covers all aspects of tuning an Oracle8 database. Topics in both application and database tuning are covered. The exam tests knowledge in diagnosis of tuning problems, database optimal configuration, shared pool tuning, buffer cache tuning, Oracle block usage, tuning rollback segments and redo mechanisms, monitoring and detecting lock contention, tuning sorts, tuning in OLTP, DSS, and mixed environments, and load optimization.

➤ *Oracle8: Network Administration (Exam 1Z0-016)*—Test 5 covers all parts of the Net8 product: Net8, Oracle Names Server, the listener process, lsnrctl (the listener control utility), and the Net8 configuration files sqlnet.ora, tnsnames.ora, and listener.ora.

To obtain an OCP certificate in database administration, an individual must pass all five exams. You do not have to take the tests in any particular order. However, it is usually better to take the examinations in order because the knowledge tested builds from each exam. The core exams require individuals to demonstrate competence with all phases of Oracle8 database lifetime activities. If you already have your Oracle7.3 certification, you need to take only one exam—Oracle8: New Features for Administrators (Exam 1Z0-010)—to upgrade your status.

It's not uncommon for the entire process to take a year or so, and many individuals find that they must take a test more than once to pass. The primary goal of the *Exam Cram* series is to make it possible, given proper study and preparation, to pass all of the OCP-DBA tests on the first try.

Finally, certification is an ongoing activity. Once an Oracle version becomes obsolete, OCP-DBAs (and other OCPs) typically have a six-month time frame in which they can become recertified on current product versions. (If an individual does not get recertified within the specified time period, his certification becomes invalid.) Because technology keeps changing and new products continually supplant old ones, this should come as no surprise.

The best place to keep tabs on the OCP program and its various certifications is on the Oracle Web site. The current root URL for the OCP program is at **http://education.oracle.com/certification**. Oracle's certification Web site changes frequently, so if this URL doesn't work, try using the Search tool on Oracle's site (**www.oracle.com**) with either "OCP" or the quoted phrase "Oracle Certified Professional Program" as the search string. This will help you find the latest and most accurate information about the company's certification programs.

# Taking A Certification Exam

Alas, testing is not free. You'll be charged $125 for each test you take, whether you pass or fail. In the United States and Canada, tests are administered by Sylvan Prometric. Sylvan Prometric can be reached at 1-800-891-3926, any time from 7:00 A.M. to 6:00 P.M., Central Time, Monday through Friday. If you can't get through at this number, try 1-612-896-7000 or 1-612-820-5707.

To schedule an exam, call at least one day in advance. To cancel or reschedule an exam, you must call at least one day before the scheduled test time (or you may be charged the $125 fee). When calling Sylvan Prometric, please have the following information ready for the telesales staffer who handles your call:

➤ Your name, organization, and mailing address.

➤ The name of the exam you want to take.

➤ A method of payment. (The most convenient approach is to supply a valid credit card number with sufficient available credit. Otherwise, payments by check, money order, or purchase order must be received before a test can be scheduled. If the latter methods are required, ask your order-taker for more details.)

An appointment confirmation will be sent to you by mail if you register more than five days before an exam, or it will be sent by fax if less than five days before the exam. A Candidate Agreement letter, which you must sign to take the examination, will also be provided.

On the day of the test, try to arrive at least 15 minutes before the scheduled time slot. You must supply two forms of identification, one of which must be a photo ID.

All exams are completely closed book. In fact, you will not be permitted to take anything with you into the testing area. We suggest that you review the most critical information about the test you're taking just before the test. (*Exam Cram* books provide a brief reference—The Cram Sheet, located inside the front of this book—that lists the essential information from the book in distilled form.) You will have some time to compose yourself, to mentally review this critical information, and even to take a sample orientation exam before you begin the real thing. We suggest you take the orientation test before taking your first exam; they're all more or less identical in layout, behavior, and controls, so you probably won't need to do this more than once.

When you complete an Oracle8 certification exam, the testing software will tell you whether you've passed or failed. Results are broken into several topical areas. Whether you pass or fail, we suggest you ask for—and keep—the detailed report that the test administrator prints for you. You can use the report to help you prepare for another go-round, if necessary, and even if you pass, the report shows areas you may need to review to keep your edge. If you need to retake an exam, you'll have to call Sylvan Prometric, schedule a new test date, and pay another $125.

# Tracking OCP Status

Oracle generates transcripts that indicate the exams you have passed and your corresponding test scores. After you pass the necessary set of five exams, you'll be certified as an Oracle8 DBA. Official certification normally takes anywhere from four to six weeks (generally within 30 days), so don't expect to get your credentials overnight. Once certified, you will receive a package with a Welcome Kit that contains a number of elements:

➤ An OCP-DBA certificate, suitable for framing.

➤ A license agreement to use the OCP logo. Once it is sent in to Oracle and your packet of logo information is received, the license agreement allows you to use the logo for advertisements, promotions, documents, letterhead, business cards, and so on. An OCP logo sheet, which includes camera-ready artwork, comes with the license.

Many people believe that the benefits of OCP certification go well beyond the perks that Oracle provides to newly anointed members of this elite group. We're starting to see more job listings that request or require applicants to have an OCP-DBA certification, and many individuals who complete the program can qualify for increases in pay and/or responsibility. As an official recognition of hard work and broad knowledge, OCP certification is a badge of honor in many IT organizations.

# How To Prepare For An Exam

At a minimum, preparing for OCP-DBA exams requires that you obtain and study the following materials:

➤ The Oracle8 Server version 8.0.5 Documentation Set on CD-ROM.

➤ The exam preparation materials, practice tests, and self-assessment exams on the Oracle certification page (**http://education.oracle.com/ certification**). Find the materials, download them, and use them!

➤ This *Exam Cram* book. It's the first and last thing you should read before taking the exam.

In addition, you'll probably find any or all of the following materials useful in your quest for Oracle8 DBA expertise:

➤ *OCP resource kits*—Oracle Corporation has a CD-ROM with example questions and materials to help with the exam; generally, these are provided free by requesting them from your Oracle representative. They have also been offered free for the taking at most Oracle conventions, such as IOUGA-Alive! and Oracle Open World.

➤ *Classroom training*—Oracle, TUSC, LearningTree, and many others offer classroom and computer-based training-type material that you will find useful to help you prepare for the exam. But a word of warning: These classes are fairly expensive (in the range of $300 per day of training). However, they do offer a condensed form of learning to help you brush up on your Oracle knowledge. The tests are closely tied to the classroom training provided by Oracle, so we would suggest taking at least the introductory classes to get the Oracle-specific (and classroom-specific) terminology under your belt.

➤ *Other publications*—You'll find direct references to other publications and resources in this book, and there's no shortage of materials available about Oracle8 DBA topics. To help you sift through some of the publications out there, we end each chapter with a "Need To Know More?" section that provides pointers to more complete and exhaustive resources covering the chapter's subject matter. This section tells you where to look for further details.

➤ *The Oracle Support CD-ROM*—Oracle provides a Support CD-ROM on a quarterly basis. This CD-ROM contains useful white papers, bug reports, technical bulletins, and information about release-specific bugs, fixes, and new features. Contact your Oracle representative for a copy.

➤ *The Oracle Administrator and PL/SQL Developer*—These are online references from RevealNet, Inc., an Oracle and database online reference provider. These online references provide instant lookup on thousands of database and developmental topics and are an invaluable resource for study and learning about Oracle. Demo copies can be downloaded from **www.revealnet.com**. Also available at the RevealNet Web site are the DBA and PL/SQL Pipelines, online discussion groups where you can obtain expert information from Oracle DBAs worldwide. The costs of these applications run about $400 each (current pricing is available on the Web site) and are worth every cent.

These required and recommended materials represent a nonpareil collection of sources and resources for Oracle8 DBA topics and software. In the section that follows, we explain how this book works and give you some good reasons why this book should also be on your required and recommended materials list.

# About This Book

Each topical *Exam Cram* chapter follows a regular structure, along with graphical cues about especially important or useful material. Here's the structure of a typical chapter:

➤ *Opening hotlists*—Each chapter begins with lists of the terms, tools, and techniques that you must learn and understand before you can be fully conversant with the chapter's subject matter. We follow the hotlists with one or two introductory paragraphs to set the stage for the rest of the chapter.

➤ *Topical coverage*—After the opening hotlists, each chapter covers a series of topics related to the chapter's subject. Throughout this section, we highlight material most likely to appear on a test using a special Exam Alert layout, like this:

 This is what an Exam Alert looks like. Normally, an Exam Alert stresses concepts, terms, software, or activities that will most likely appear in one or more certification test questions. For that reason, any information found offset in Exam Alert format is worthy of unusual attentiveness on your part. Indeed, most of the facts appearing in The Cram Sheet appear as Exam Alerts within the text.

Even if material isn't flagged as an Exam Alert, *all* the contents of this book are associated, at least tangentially, to something test-related. This book is tightly focused for quick test preparation, so you'll find that what appears in the meat of each chapter is critical knowledge.

We have also provided tips that will help build a better foundation of data administration knowledge. Although the information may not be on the exam, it is highly relevant and will help you become a better test-taker.

 This is how tips are formatted. Keep your eyes open for these, and you'll become a test guru in no time!

➤ *Practice questions* —A section at the end of each chapter presents a series of mock test questions and explanations of both correct and incorrect answers. We also try to point out especially tricky questions by using a special icon, like this:

Ordinarily, this icon flags the presence of an especially devious question, if not an outright trick question. Trick questions are calculated to "trap"

you if you don't read them carefully, and more than once at that. Although they're not ubiquitous, such questions make regular appearances in the Oracle8 exams. That's why exam questions are as much about reading comprehension as they are about knowing DBA material inside out and backward.

➤ *Details and resources*—Every chapter ends with a section titled "Need To Know More?". This section provides direct pointers to Oracle and third-party resources that offer further details on the chapter's subject matter. In addition, this section tries to rate the quality and thoroughness of each topic's coverage. If you find a resource you like in this collection, use it, but don't feel compelled to use all these resources. On the other hand, we recommend only resources we use on a regular basis, so none of our recommendations will be a waste of your time or money.

The bulk of the book follows this chapter structure slavishly, but there are a few other elements that we would like to point out. Chapter 11 includes a sample test that provides a good review of the material presented throughout the book to ensure you're ready for the exam. Chapter 12 provides an answer key to the sample test. In addition, you'll find a handy glossary and an index.

Finally, look for The Cram Sheet, which appears inside the front of this *Exam Cram* book. It is a valuable tool that represents a condensed and compiled collection of facts, figures, and tips that we think you should memorize before taking the test. Because you can dump this information out of your head onto a piece of paper before answering any exam questions, you can master this information by brute force—you need to remember it only long enough to write it down when you walk into the test room. You might even want to look at it in the car or in the lobby of the testing center just before you walk in to take the test.

# How To Use This Book

If you're prepping for a first-time test, we've structured the topics in this book to build on one another. Therefore, some topics in later chapters make more sense after you've read earlier chapters. That's why we suggest you read this book from front to back for your initial test preparation.

If you need to brush up on a topic or you have to bone up for a second try, use the index or table of contents to go straight to the topics and questions that you need to study. Beyond the tests, we think you'll find this book useful as a tightly focused reference to some of the most important aspects of topics associated with being a DBA, as implemented under Oracle8.

Given all the book's elements and its specialized focus, we've tried to create a tool that you can use to prepare for—and pass—the Oracle OCP-DBA set of examinations. Please share your feedback on the book with us, especially if you have ideas about how we can improve it for future test-takers. We'll consider everything you say carefully, and we try to respond to all suggestions. You can reach us via email at **mikerault@compuserve.com**. Or you can send your questions or comments to **cipq@coriolis.com**. Please remember to include the title of the book in your message; otherwise, we'll be forced to guess which book you're making a suggestion about. Also, be sure to check out the Web pages at **www.coriolis.com**, where you'll find information updates, commentary, and certification information.

Thanks, and enjoy the book!

# Self-Assessment

We've included a Self-Assessment in this *Exam Cram* to help you evaluate your readiness to tackle Oracle Certified Professional-Oracle8 Certified Database Administrator (OCP-DBA) certification. It should also help you understand what you need to master the topic of this book—namely, Exam 1Z0-014 (Test 4), "Performance Tuning." But before you tackle this Self-Assessment, let's talk about the concerns you may face when pursuing an Oracle8 OCP-DBA certification, and what an ideal Oracle8 OCP-DBA candidate might look like.

## Oracle8 OCP-DBAs In The Real World

In the next section, we describe an ideal Oracle8 OCP-DBA candidate, knowing full well that only a few actual candidates meet this ideal. In fact, our description of that ideal candidate might seem downright scary. But take heart; although the requirements to obtain an Oracle8 OCP-DBA may seem pretty formidable, they are by no means impossible to meet. However, you should be keenly aware that it does take time, requires some expense, and consumes a substantial effort.

You can get all the real-world motivation you need from knowing that many others have gone before you. You can follow in their footsteps. If you're willing to tackle the process seriously and do what it takes to obtain the necessary experience and knowledge, you can take—and pass—the certification tests. In fact, the *Exam Crams* and the companion *Exam Preps* are designed to make it as easy as possible for you to prepare for these exams. But prepare you must!

The same, of course, is true for other Oracle certifications, including:

➤ Oracle7.3 OCP-DBA, which is similar to the Oracle8 OCP-DBA certification but requires only four core exams

➤ Application Developer, Oracle Developer Rel 1 OCP, which is aimed at software developers and requires five exams

➤ Application Developer, Oracle Developer Rel 2 OCP, which is aimed at software developers and requires five exams

➤ Oracle Database Operators OCP, which is aimed at database operators and requires only one exam

➤ Oracle Java Technology Certification OCP, which is aimed at Java developers and requires five exams

# The Ideal Oracle8 OCP-DBA Candidate

Just to give you some idea of what an ideal Oracle8 OCP-DBA candidate is like, here are some relevant statistics about the background and experience such an individual might have. Don't worry if you don't meet these qualifications (or if you don't even come close), because this world is far from ideal, and where you fall short is simply where you'll have more work to do. The ideal candidate will have:

➤ Academic or professional training in relational databases, Structured Query Language (SQL), performance tuning, backup and recovery, and Net8 administration

➤ Three-plus years of professional database administration experience, including experience installing and upgrading Oracle executables, creating and tuning databases, troubleshooting connection problems, creating users, and managing backup and recovery scenarios

We believe that well under half of all certification candidates meet these requirements. In fact, most probably meet less than half of these requirements (that is, at least when they begin the certification process). But, because all those who have their certifications already survived this ordeal, you can survive it, too—especially if you heed what this Self-Assessment can tell you about what you already know and what you need to learn.

## Put Yourself To The Test

The following series of questions and observations is designed to help you figure out how much work you'll face in pursuing Oracle certification and what kinds of resources you may consult on your quest. Be absolutely honest in your answers, or you'll end up wasting money on exams you're not ready to take. There are no right or wrong answers, only steps along the path to certification. Only you can decide where you really belong in the broad spectrum of aspiring candidates.

Two things should be clear from the outset, however:

➤ Even a modest background in computer science will be helpful.

➤ Hands-on experience with Oracle products and technologies is an essential ingredient to certification success.

# Educational Background

1. Have you ever taken any computer-related classes? [Yes or No]

   If Yes, proceed to question 2; if No, proceed to question 4.

2. Have you taken any classes on relational databases? [Yes or No]

   If Yes, you will probably be able to handle Oracle's architecture and network administration discussions. If you're rusty, brush up on the basic concepts of databases and networks. If the answer is No, consider some basic reading in this area. We strongly recommend a good Oracle database administration book such as *Oracle8 Administration and Management* by Michael Ault (Wiley, 1998). Or, if this title doesn't appeal to you, check out reviews for other, similar titles at your favorite online bookstore.

3. Have you taken any networking concepts or technologies classes? [Yes or No]

   If Yes, you will probably be able to handle Oracle's networking terminology, concepts, and technologies (but brace yourself for frequent departures from normal usage). If you're rusty, brush up on basic networking concepts and terminology. If your answer is No, you might want to check out the Oracle Technology Network Web site (**http://technet. oracle.com**) and read some of the white papers on Net8. If you have access to the Oracle MetaLink Web site or the Technology Network Web site, download the Oracle Net8 Administration manual.

4. Have you done any reading on relational databases or networks? [Yes or No]

   If Yes, review the requirements from questions 2 and 3. If you meet those, move to the next section, "Hands-On Experience." If you answered No, consult the recommended reading for both topics. This kind of strong background will be of great help in preparing you for the Oracle exams.

# Hands-On Experience

Another important key to success on all of the Oracle tests is hands-on experience. If we leave you with only one realization after taking this Self-Assessment, it should be that there's no substitute for time spent installing, configuring, and using the various Oracle products upon which you'll be tested repeatedly and in depth.

5. Have you installed, configured, and worked with Net8? [Yes or No]

If Yes, make sure you understand basic concepts as covered in Exam 1Z0-013, "Oracle8: Database Administrator" (Test 2) and advanced concepts as covered in Exam 1Z0-014, "Oracle8: Performance Tuning" (Test 4). You should also study the Net8 configuration and administration for Exam 1Z0-016, "Oracle8: Network Administration" (Test 6).

 You can download the candidate certification guide, objectives, practice exams, and other information about Oracle exams from the company's Training and Certification page on the Web at **http://education.oracle.com/certification**.

If you haven't worked with Oracle, you must obtain a copy of Oracle8 or Personal Oracle8. Then, learn about the database and Net8.

 For any and all of these Oracle exams, the candidate guides for the topics involved are a good study resource. You can download them free from the Oracle Web site (**http://education. oracle.com**). You can also download information on purchasing additional practice tests ($99 per exam).

If you have the funds or your employer will pay your way, consider taking a class at an Oracle training and education center.

Before you even think about taking any Oracle exam, make sure you've spent enough time with Net8 to understand how it may be installed and configured, how to maintain such an installation, and how to troubleshoot that software when things go wrong. This will help you in the exam—as well as in real life.

## Testing Your Exam-Readiness

Whether you attend a formal class on a specific topic to get ready for an exam or use written materials to study on your own, some preparation for the Oracle certification exams is essential. At $125 a try, pass or fail, you want to do everything you can to pass on your first try. That's where studying comes in.

We have included in this book several practice exam questions for each chapter and a sample test, so if you don't score well on the chapter questions, you can study more and then tackle the sample test at the end of the book. If you don't earn a score of at least 79 percent after this test, you'll want to investigate the other practice test resources we mention in this section.

For any given subject, consider taking a class if you've tackled self-study materials, taken the test, and failed anyway. If you can afford the privilege, the opportunity to interact with an instructor and fellow students can make all the difference in the world. For information about Oracle classes, visit the Training and Certification page at **http://education.oracle.com**.

If you can't afford to take a class, visit the Training and Certification page anyway, because it also includes free practice exams that you can download. Even if you can't afford to spend much, you should still invest in some low-cost practice exams from commercial vendors, because they can help you assess your readiness to pass a test better than any other tool.

6. Have you taken a practice exam on your chosen test subject? [Yes or No]

   If Yes—and you scored 79 percent or better—you're probably ready to tackle the real thing. If your score isn't above that crucial threshold, keep at it until you break that barrier. If you answered No, obtain all the free and low-budget practice tests you can find (or afford) and get to work. Keep at it until you can comfortably break the passing threshold.

There is no better way to assess your test readiness than to take a good-quality practice exam and pass with a score of 79 percent or better. When we're preparing, we shoot for 85-plus percent, just to leave room for the "weirdness factor" that sometimes shows up on Oracle exams.

# Assessing Your Readiness For Exam 1Z0-014 (Test 4)

In addition to the general exam-readiness information in the previous section, other resources are available to help you prepare for the Oracle8: Performance Tuning exam. For starters, visit the RevealNet pipeline (**www.revealnet.com**) or **http://technet.oracle.com**. These are great places to ask questions and get good answers, or simply to observe the questions that others ask (along with the answers, of course).

Oracle exam mavens also recommend checking the Oracle Knowledge Base from RevealNet. You can get information on purchasing the RevealNet software at **www.revealnet.com**.

For Oracle8: Performance Tuning preparation in particular, we'd also like to recommend that you check out one or more of these books as you prepare to take the exam:

➤ Aronoff, Eyal, Kevin Loney, and Noorali Sonawalla. *Oracle8 Advanced Tuning and Administration*. Oracle Press, 1998.

➤ Ault, Michael. *Oracle8 Administration and Management*. Wiley, 1998.

➤ Loney, Kevin. *Oracle8 DBA Handbook*. Oracle Press, 1998.

➤ Kreines, David C., and Brian Laskey. *Oracle Database Administration*. O'Reilly, 1999.

➤ Toledo, Hugo. *Oracle Networking*. Oracle Press, 1996.

Stop by your favorite bookstore or online bookseller to check out one or more of these books. In our opinion, the second and third books are the best general all-around references on Oracle8 available, and the fourth complements the contents of this *Exam Cram* very nicely. The fifth book provides excellent basic information on networking.

One last note: Hopefully, it makes sense to stress the importance of hands-on experience in the context of the Oracle8: Performance Tuning exam. As you review the material for this exam, you'll realize that hands-on experience with Oracle8 commands, tools, and utilities is invaluable.

# Onward, Through The Fog!

Once you've assessed your readiness, undertaken the right background studies, obtained the hands-on experience that will help you understand the products and technologies at work, and reviewed the many sources of information to help you prepare for a test, you'll be ready to take a round of practice tests. When your scores come back positive enough to get you through the exam, you're ready to go after the real thing. If you follow our assessment regime, you'll not only know what you need to study, but when you're ready to make a test date at Sylvan. Good luck!

# Oracle OCP
# Certification Exams

### Terms you'll need to understand:

√ Radio button

√ Checkbox

√ Fxhibit

√ Multiple-choice question formats

√ Careful reading

√ Process of elimination

### Techniques you'll need to master:

√ Assessing your exam-readiness

√ Preparing to take a certification exam

√ Practicing (to make perfect)

√ Making the best use of the testing software

√ Budgeting your time

√ Saving the hardest questions until last

√ Guessing (as a last resort)

As experiences go, test taking is not something that most people anticipate eagerly, no matter how well they're prepared. In most cases, familiarity helps ameliorate test anxiety. In plain English, this means you probably won't be as nervous when you take your fourth or fifth Oracle certification exam as you will be when you take your first one.

But no matter whether it's your first test or your tenth, understanding the exam-taking particulars (how much time to spend on questions, the setting you'll be in, and so on) and the testing software will help you concentrate on the material rather than on the environment. Likewise, mastering a few basic test-taking skills should help you recognize—and perhaps even outfox—some of the tricks and gotchas you're bound to find in some of the Oracle test questions.

In this chapter, we'll explain the testing environment and software, as well as describe some proven test-taking strategies you should be able to use to your advantage.

# Assessing Exam-Readiness

Before you take any Oracle exam, we strongly recommend that you read through and take the Self-Assessment included with this book (it appears just before this chapter, in fact). This will help you compare your knowledge base to the requirements for obtaining an OCP, and it will also help you identify parts of your background or experience that may be in need of improvement, enhancement, or further learning. If you get the right set of basics under your belt, obtaining Oracle certification will be that much easier.

Once you've gone through the Self-Assessment, you can remedy those topical areas where your background or experience may not measure up to an ideal certification candidate. But you can also tackle subject matter for individual tests at the same time, so you can continue making progress while you're catching up in some areas.

Once you've worked through an *Exam Cram*, have read the supplementary materials, and have taken the practice test at the end of the book, you'll have a pretty clear idea of when you should be ready to take the real exam. Although we strongly recommend that you keep practicing until your scores top the 79 percent mark, 85 percent would be a good goal to give yourself some margin for error in a real exam situation (where stress will play more of a role than when you practice). Once you hit that point, you should be ready to go. But if you get through the practice exam in this book without attaining that score, you should keep taking practice tests and studying the materials until you get there. You'll find more pointers on how to study and prepare in the Self-Assessment. But now, on to the exam itself!

# The Testing Situation

When you arrive at the Sylvan Prometric Testing Center where you scheduled your test, you'll need to sign in with a test coordinator. He or she will ask you to produce two forms of identification, one of which must be a photo ID. Once you've signed in and your time slot arrives, you'll be asked to leave any books, bags, or other items you brought with you, and you'll be escorted into a closed room. Typically, that room will be furnished with anywhere from one to half a dozen computers, and each workstation is separated from the others by dividers designed to keep you from seeing what's happening on someone else's computer.

You'll be furnished with a pen or pencil and a blank sheet of paper, or in some cases, an erasable plastic sheet and an erasable felt-tip pen. You're allowed to write down any information you want on this sheet, and you can write stuff on both sides of the page. We suggest that you memorize as much as possible of the material that appears on The Cram Sheet (inside the front of this book), and then write that information down on the blank sheet as soon as you sit down in front of the test machine. You can refer to the sheet any time you like during the test, but you'll have to surrender it when you leave the room.

Most test rooms feature a wall with a large window. This allows the test coordinator to monitor the room, to prevent test-takers from talking to one another, and to observe anything out of the ordinary that might go on. The test coordinator will have preloaded the Oracle certification test you've signed up for, and you'll be permitted to start as soon as you're seated in front of the machine.

All Oracle certification exams permit you to take up to a certain maximum amount of time (usually 90 minutes) to complete the test (the test itself will tell you, and it maintains an on-screen counter/clock so that you can check the time remaining any time you like). Each exam consists of between 60 and 70 questions, randomly selected from a pool of questions.

 The passing score varies per exam and the questions selected. For Exam 1Z0-014, the passing score is 79 percent.

All Oracle certification exams are computer generated and use a multiple-choice format. Although this might sound easy, the questions are constructed not just to check your mastery of basic facts and figures about Oracle8 DBA topics, but also require you to evaluate one or more sets of circumstances or requirements. Often, you'll be asked to give more than one answer to a question; likewise, you may be asked to select the best or most effective solution to a problem from a range of choices, all of which technically are correct. The tests are quite an adventure, and they involve real thinking. This book will show you what to expect and how to deal with the problems, puzzles, and predicaments you're likely to find on the tests—in particular, Exam 1Z0-014, "Oracle8: Performance Tuning."

# Test Layout And Design

A typical test question is depicted in Question 1. It's a multiple-choice question that requires you to select a single correct answer. Following the question is a brief summary of each potential answer and why it was either right or wrong.

## Question 1

---

> If SQL statements are not performing well, what can sometimes be done to improve performance?
>
> ○ a.   Create larger redo log files
>
> ○ b.   Resize the shared pool to a smaller value
>
> ○ c.   Create indexes where appropriate

The correct answer is c. Creating indexes can improve performance, provided that they're created on the appropriate columns. Improperly sized redo logs affect the database as a whole, not just specific SQL statements. Therefore, answer a is incorrect. Resizing the shared pool to a smaller value usually has a negative effect on performance. Therefore, answer b is incorrect.

This sample question corresponds closely to those you'll see on Oracle certification tests. To select the correct answer during the test, you would position the cursor over the radio button next to answer c and click the mouse to select that particular choice. The only difference between the certification test and this question is that the real questions are not immediately followed by the answers.

Next, we'll examine a question where one or more answers are possible. This type of question provides checkboxes, rather than radio buttons, for marking all appropriate selections.

# Question 2

> Which of the following items can you track using the **DBMS_ APPLICATION_INFO** package provided by Oracle8? [Choose two]
>
> ❑ a.  User information
>
> ❑ b.  Performance
>
> ❑ c.  Resource usage
>
> ❑ d.  Network information
>
> ❑ e.  Database files
>
> ❑ f.  Error information

The correct answers are b and c. The built-in **DBMS_APPLICATION_INFO** package is provided by Oracle to obtain information specifically on performance and resource consumption and does not provide information for any of the other choices. A variety of tables are provided for user information and database files, but the information is not found in **DBMS_APPLICATION_ INFO**. Therefore, answers a and e are incorrect. Because **DBMS_ APPLICATION_INFO** is an Oracle-stored package, it does not trace network information. Therefore, answer d is incorrect. For error information, the log and trace files are very useful, but not **DBMS_APPLICATION_INFO**. Therefore, answer f is incorrect.

For this type of question, one or more answers must be selected to answer the question correctly. For Question 2, you would have to position the cursor over the checkboxes next to items b and c to obtain credit for a correct answer.

These two basic types of questions can appear in many forms. They constitute the foundation on which all the Oracle certification exam questions rest. More complex questions may include so-called "exhibits," which are usually tables or data-content layouts of one form or another. You'll be expected to use the information displayed in the exhibit to guide your answer to the question.

Other questions involving exhibits may use charts or diagrams to help document a workplace scenario that you'll be asked to troubleshoot or configure. Paying careful attention to such exhibits is the key to success—be prepared to toggle between the picture and the question as you work. Often, both are complex enough that you might not be able to remember all of either one.

# Using Oracle's Test Software Effectively

A well-known test-taking principle is to read over the entire test from start to finish, but to answer only those questions that you feel absolutely sure of on the first pass. On subsequent passes, you can dive into more complex questions, knowing how many such questions you have to deal with.

Fortunately, Oracle test software makes this approach easy to implement. At the bottom of each question, you'll find a checkbox that permits you to mark that question for a later visit. (Note that marking questions makes review easier, but you can return to any question by clicking the Forward and Back buttons repeatedly until you get to the question.) As you read each question, if you answer only those you're sure of and mark for review those that you're not, you can keep going through a decreasing list of open questions as you knock the trickier ones off in order.

There's at least one potential benefit to reading the test over completely before answering the trickier questions: Sometimes, you find information in later questions that sheds more light on earlier ones. Other times, information you read in later questions might jog your memory about Oracle8 DBA facts, figures, or behavior that also will help with earlier questions. Either way, you'll come out ahead if you defer those questions about which you're not absolutely sure of the answer(s).

Keep working on the questions until you are absolutely sure of all your answers or until you know you'll run out of time. If there are still unanswered questions, you'll want to zip through them and guess. No answer guarantees no credit for a question, and a guess has at least a chance of being correct. (Oracle scores blank answers and incorrect answers as equally wrong.)

At the very end of your test period, you're better off guessing than leaving questions blank or unanswered.

# Taking Testing Seriously

The most important advice we can give you about taking any Oracle test is this: Read each question carefully. Some questions are deliberately ambiguous; some use double negatives; others use terminology in incredibly precise ways. We've taken numerous practice tests and real tests, and in nearly every test we've missed at least one question because we didn't read it closely or carefully enough.

Here are some suggestions on how to deal with the tendency to jump to an answer too quickly:

➤ Make sure you read every word in the question. If you find yourself jumping ahead impatiently, go back and start over.

➤ As you read, try to restate the question in your own terms. If you can do this, you should be able to pick the correct answer(s) much more easily.

➤ When returning to a question after your initial read-through, reread every word again—otherwise, the mind falls quickly into a rut. Sometimes seeing a question afresh after turning your attention elsewhere lets you see something you missed before, but the strong tendency is to see what you've seen before. Try to avoid that tendency at all costs.

➤ If you return to a question more than twice, try to articulate to yourself what you don't understand about the question, why the answers don't appear to make sense, or what appears to be missing. If you chew on the subject for a while, your subconscious might provide the details that are lacking, or you may notice a "trick" that will point to the right answer.

Above all, try to deal with each question by thinking through what you know about being an Oracle8 DBA—utilities, characteristics, behaviors, facts, and figures involved. By reviewing what you know (and what you've written down on your information sheet), you'll often recall or understand things sufficiently to determine the answer to the question.

# Question-Handling Strategies

Based on the tests we've taken, a couple of interesting trends in the answers have become apparent. For those questions that take only a single answer, usually two or three of the answers will be obviously incorrect, and two of the answers will be plausible. But, of course, only one can be correct. Unless the answer leaps out at you (and if it does, reread the question to look for a trick; sometimes those are the ones you're most likely to get wrong), begin the process of answering by eliminating those answers that are obviously wrong.

Things to look for in the "obviously wrong" category include spurious command choices or table or view names, nonexistent software or command options, and terminology you've never seen before. If you've done your homework for a test, no valid information should be completely new to you. In that case, unfamiliar or bizarre terminology probably indicates a totally bogus answer. As long as you're sure what's right, it's easy to eliminate what's wrong.

Numerous questions assume that the default behavior of a particular Oracle utility (such as SQL*Trace and TKPROF) is in effect. It's essential, therefore, to know and understand the default settings for SQL*Trace, TKPROF, and other utilities like UTLBSTAT/ULTESTAT. If you know the defaults and understand what they mean, this knowledge will help you cut through many Gordian knots.

Likewise, when dealing with questions that require multiple answers, you must know and select all of the correct options to get credit. This, too, qualifies as an example of why careful reading is so important.

As you work your way through the test, another counter that Oracle thankfully provides will come in handy—the number of questions completed and questions outstanding. Budget your time by making sure that you've completed one-fourth of the questions one-quarter of the way through the test period (about 15 questions in the first 22 or 23 minutes). Check again three-quarters of the way through (about 45 questions in the first 66 to 69 minutes).

If you're not through after 85 minutes, use the last five minutes to guess your way through the remaining questions. Remember, guesses are potentially more valuable than blank answers, because blanks are always wrong, but a guess might turn out to be right. If you haven't a clue with any of the remaining questions, pick answers at random, or choose all a's, b's, and so on. The important thing is to submit a test for scoring that has an answer for every question.

# Mastering The Inner Game

In the final analysis, knowledge breeds confidence, and confidence breeds success. If you study the materials in this book carefully and review all of the questions at the end of each chapter, you should be aware of those areas where additional studying is required.

Next, follow up by reading some or all of the materials recommended in the "Need To Know More?" section at the end of each chapter. The idea is to become familiar enough with the concepts and situations that you find in the sample questions to be able to reason your way through similar situations on a real test. If you know the material, you have every right to be confident that you can pass the test.

Once you've worked your way through the book, take the practice test in Chapter 11. The test will provide a reality check and will help you identify areas you need to study further. Make sure you follow up and review materials related to the questions you miss before scheduling a real test. Only when you've covered all the ground and feel comfortable with the whole scope of the practice test, should you take a real test.

 If you take the practice test (Chapter 11) and don't score at least 79 percent correct, you'll want to practice further. At a minimum, download the practice tests and the self-assessment tests from the Oracle Education Web site's download page (its location appears in the next section). If you're more ambitious or better funded, you might want to purchase a practice test from one of the third-party vendors that offers them.

Armed with the information in this book and with the determination to augment your knowledge, you should be able to pass the certification exam. But if you don't work at it, you'll spend the test fee more than once before you finally do pass. If you prepare seriously, the exam should go flawlessly. Good luck!

# Additional Resources

By far, the best source of information about Oracle certification tests comes from Oracle itself. Because its products and technologies—and the tests that go with them—change frequently, the best place to go for exam-related information is online.

If you haven't already visited the Oracle certification pages, do so right now. As we're writing this chapter, the certification home page resides at **http://education.oracle.com/certification/** (see Figure 1.1).

> *Note: It might not be there by the time you read this, or it may have been replaced by something new and different, because things change regularly on the Oracle site. Should this happen, please read the section titled "Coping With Change On The Web," later in this chapter.*

The menu options in the left column of the page point to the most important sources of information in the certification pages. Here's what to check out:

➤ *FAQs*—Frequently Asked Questions, yours may get answered here.

➤ *What's New*—Any new tests will be described here.

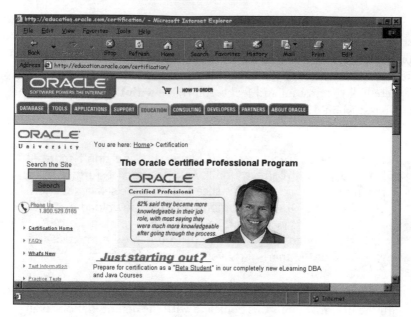

**Figure 1.1** The Oracle certification page should be your starting point for further investigation of the most current exam and preparation information.

➤ *Test Information*—This is a detailed section that provides many jump points to detailed test descriptions for the several OCP certifications.

➤ *Practice Tests*—This section is a source for practice tests.

➤ *Test Registration*—This section provides information for phone registration and a link to the Prometric web page for online registration. Also, this section provides a list of testing sites outside of the USA.

➤ *Candidate Agreement*—Just what are you agreeing to be by becoming Oracle certified?

➤ *OCP Logo*—After you receive your certification, you can go to this page to download OCP graphics.

➤ *Oracle Partners*—This link provides information about test discounts and other offers for Oracle Partner companies.

Of course, these are just the high points of what's available in the Oracle certification pages. As you browse through them—and we strongly recommend that you do—you'll probably find other things we didn't mention here that are every bit as interesting and compelling.

# Coping With Change On The Web

Sooner or later, all the specifics we've shared with you about the Oracle certification pages, and all the other Web-based resources we mention throughout the rest of this book, will go stale or be replaced by newer information. In some cases, the URLs you find here might lead you to their replacements; in other cases, the URLs will go nowhere, leaving you with the dreaded "404 File not found" error message.

When that happens, please don't give up. There's always a way to find what you want on the Web—if you're willing to invest some time and energy. To begin with, most large or complex Web sites—and Oracle's qualifies on both counts—offer a search engine. As long as you can get to Oracle's home page (and we're sure that it will stay at **www.oracle.com** for a long while yet), you can use this tool to help you find what you need.

The more particular or focused you can make a search request, the more likely it is that the results will include information you can use. For instance, you can search the string "training and certification" to produce a lot of data about the subject in general, but if you're looking for the Preparation Guide for the Oracle DBA tests, you'll be more likely to get there quickly if you use a search string such as this:

```
"DBA" AND "preparation guide"
```

Likewise, if you want to find the training and certification downloads, try a search string such as this one:

```
"training and certification" AND "download page"
```

Finally, don't be afraid to use general search tools such as **www.search.com**, **www.altavista.com**, or **www.excite.com** to search for related information. Even though Oracle offers the best information about its certification exams online, there are plenty of third-party sources of information, training, and assistance in this area that do not have to follow a party line like Oracle does. The bottom line is this: If you can't find something where the book says it lives, start looking around. If worse comes to worse, you can always email us! We just might have a clue. Our email addresses are **mikerault@compuserve.com** and **josefbrinson@mindspring.com**.

# Business Requirements And Tuning: An Overview

**2**

## Terms you'll need to understand:

√ OLTP systems

√ DSS systems

√ OLAP systems

√ Hybrid systems

## Techniques you'll need to master:

√ Data design

√ Application design

√ Logical structure design

√ Database operations

√ Memory allocation

√ Tuning I/O and physical structure

√ Tuning resource contention

√ Tuning underlying platforms

The Oracle server is a complex, highly tunable software system. Because performance is a key issue at most sites, one of the many responsibilities of the database administrator (DBA) is to address performance issues at each phase of the system's life cycle. Performance tuning should be viewed as an iterative process that never ends.

Although the DBA is the most important resource involved in the tuning process, he is by no means the only one. The complexity of the Oracle system makes it impossible for one person to be solely responsible for the entire process. Tuning the Oracle system requires the input of designers, analysts, application developers, and administrators, as well as the DBA. However, the DBA must take an active role in each phase of the tuning process.

# The Tuning Process: A Structured Approach

The tuning process should be proactive rather then reactive. The DBA cannot wait until users complain about performance; it's too late at that point to take advantage of some of the most effective tuning strategies. The earlier in the life cycle performance issues are identified, the less it costs in time and resources to resolve the problem.

Quantifiable tuning goals must be established to help identify the reasons for tuning and to help gauge the success or failure of the tuning process. These goals should be kept in mind during the tuning process and used to determine the feasibility of new tuning projects. Also, the goals should be specific rather then generic. The goal should not be "I want the system to run faster" but rather "The system needs to process X number of records in Y amount of time." Defining specific goals is also crucial to determining when to stop tuning. Many DBAs waste significant effort by continuing to tune long after the tuning requirements have been meet.

Before you begin the tuning process, be sure the operating system is functioning at peak performance levels. First, determine whether any paging or swapping is occurring, and if so, seek the system administrator's assistance in correcting the situation. Also, check whether any non-Oracle applications are having an adverse effect on system resources. Oracle is an application that uses system resources just like any other application, and if the system resources are taxed, the performance of Oracle will be directly affected.

# Steps For Tuning An Oracle8 Database

Tuning the Oracle8 database is not just a matter of knowing what to tune but also of knowing when to tune. The database should be tuned in a specific order to derive the optimal benefit and performance. Oracle recommends you follow these steps when tuning an Oracle database (each step is discussed in detail in the following sections):

1. Tune the business rules.

2. Tune the data design.

3. Tune the application design.

4. Tune the logical structure of the database.

5. Tune the database operations.

6. Tune the access paths.

7. Tune the memory allocation.

8. Tune I/O and the physical structure.

9. Tune resource contention.

10. Tune the underlying platforms.

## Tune The Business Rules

The structured approach to tuning begins with the business rules. This is the high-level analysis and design phase of tuning, and it will affect the entire system. The business rules define the requirements of the system and determine the performance goals to be achieved by mapping the business needs to the performance requirements. This is the most critical step in database development and tuning. If this step is overlooked or done incorrectly, it will be impossible to optimally tune the database at a later time.

When the business rules are defined, care should be taken to keep them abstracted from the implementation. Getting bogged down in implementation at this point will not only be time consuming but also counterproductive, leaving the application designer with no leeway in choosing the appropriate implementation.

The requirements of the system will then determine the type of the system—an online transaction processing (OLTP) system, a decision support system (DSS), an online analytical processing (OLAP) system, or a hybrid. The goals and methods for tuning each system are different, and the performance for each is also measured differently.

## OLTP Systems

OLTP systems measure performance based on system throughput. Throughput can be increased by increasing the amount of work a resource does. Looking at wait times is another method used for increasing throughput. If a particular resource has high wait times, you should increase the number of resources. This does not work in all cases, because some resources can't be increased any further. Also, budgetary constraint issues might be involved.

## DSS Systems

DSS systems are measured by their response time. The response time is equal to the amount of time it takes a service to perform, plus the amount of time the user has to wait for the service. In principle, then, the method for increasing response time is simple: Reduce the time it takes a service to perform and/or reduce the wait time for a resource. In practical terms, that's called *tuning*.

## OLAP Systems

OLAP systems are Data Manipulation Language (DML)-intensive systems. In an OLAP system, data is looked at in more than the conventional data joins and views of other systems. Data is presented in summarized and analyzed formats for the user. OLAP systems typically manipulate multi-dimensional blocks and use inverted indexes to map a set of dimension values to a set of pages.

## Hybrid Systems

Hybrid systems are usually the hardest to tune, and naturally they're usually the most common. The difficulty in tuning hybrid systems stems from the conflicting goals you're trying to achieve: throughput and response time. In some cases, the conflicting objectives of these goals are mitigated somewhat in that both goals do not need to be achieved at the same time. Usually the OLTP is done during normal business hours, and DSS processing can be done during off-business hours. You can easily achieve this by using a different init.ora file for each goal. This method will be discussed in more detail in Chapter 3.

# Tune The Data Design

Tuning the data design is the next step in the structured tuning approach. This process begins by determining what data is needed by your application. The relationships between the data and the attributes of the data are determined, and the data is normalized to eliminate redundancies. In practice, this is rarely achieved, and in most cases, it's not desirable from a performance perspective. Redundancy may be required to achieve faster access to the data. In data warehouses, this is quite prevalent.

Next, the primary and foreign key indexes need to be addressed. The type of database will determine the extent of index usage. In a DSS system, the primary focus is reporting and summarization. Indexes for a DSS system should be minimal to reduce the overhead associated with indexes. In an OLTP system, fast retrieval of small pieces of data is the norm. In this type of system, the use of indexes will be greater to achieve the access times required. However, remember that indexes do have overhead associated with them, and overuse can have a negative effect on the system. To avoid the adverse effects of index use, you need to have a thorough understanding of the data usage and access methods of Oracle.

# Tune The Application Design

The developer is an important aspect of tuning as it relates to application design. A poorly designed application can be the single biggest contributor to poor database performance. It is widely believed in the industry that application tuning can account for up to 80 percent of performance gains in a given database.

Guidelines should be set to help developers determine the correct course of action in developing applications. You should make sure that the developers don't override the default Oracle locking mechanisms, which is a prime cause of locking contention. Also, set a standard order for accessing tables for the developers to follow, thereby reducing the risk of deadlocks.

You, as the DBA, should help the developers be aware of the use of indexes and how to construct SQL statements that use the indexes effectively. They should also understand the use of joins and how to construct them for optimal retrieval times. The application developers should have a solid understanding of Oracle's SQL processing, including the following items:

➤ DML (Data Manipulation Language)

➤ DDL (Data Definition Language)

➤ Transaction control

➤ Shared SQL and PL/SQL areas

➤ Optimizer modes

➤ Parallel query

The use of PL/SQL packages is also extremely important, and they should be used as often as possible. PL/SQL packages are stored in parsed format, making execution faster, and the packages can be pinned in the shared pool to further increase performance.

A thorough understanding of the operating system and the Oracle platform being used is essential to the development of a robust database. It's strongly recommended that the people involved in the tuning process be trained adequately on the Oracle version being used to do the development. If the application is designed poorly in the first place, tuning the Oracle instance later will have minimal effect.

Careful consideration to tuning during the design phase gives you the maximum benefit at the lowest cost in the life cycle of the application. You need to avoid any possibility of having to completely revamp the logical design of the database simply because performance is unacceptable and all other tuning options have been exhausted.

# Tune The Logical Structure Of The Database

Now that you know what type of database you're tuning for and have an understanding of the applications that will be running on the database, its time to focus on the logical structure of the database. The logical structure of the database includes tablespaces, schema objects, data blocks, extents, and segments.

The *data block* is the lowest level of logical structure in the database and relates directly to the physical storage of data on disk. The next level of logical structure is the *extent*, which is formed from a specific number of contiguous data blocks. One or more extents then form a *segment*. There are several types of segments, each with a different functional purpose. some of the segment types are:

➤ Data segments

➤ Index segments

➤ Rollback segments

➤ Temporary segments

A *schema* is a logical collection of database objects, such as tables, views, sequences, stored procedures, synonyms, indexes, clusters, and database links. *Tablespaces* are logical storage units that together comprise the database. A tablespace can be used to hold all of an application's objects to make administration easier. In the case of some larger databases, a tablespace can be used to hold a single table or index.

> *Note: There is no direct relationship between a tablespace and a schema. A schema's objects can be scattered over any number of tablespaces, and tablespaces can contain objects from any number of schemas.*

## Tune The Database Operations

Tuning the database operations is the next area of focus. Some of the features provided by Oracle for this phase of tuning include array processing, the optimizer, the row-level lock manager, and PL/SQL.

*Array processing* refers to the execution of a SQL statement by Oracle, and it allows the programmer to specify the number of executions of the statement.

The *optimizer* chooses execution paths for SQL statements based on several conditions:

➤ The **OPTIMIZER_MODE** setting in the init.ora file

➤ Hints in SQL code

➤ Setting the **OPTIMIZER_GOAL** dynamic parameter

➤ Table and index statistics

➤ The SQL statement

The topic of locks and the Oracle locking mechanism are extremely complex. However, at this point, our only interest in row locking is its implementation by transactional locks to maintain data concurrency.

## Tune The Access Paths

The *access path* refers to how Oracle will access the data requested in a SQL statement. You tune the access paths by using clusters, B-tree indexes, and bitmap indexes. Clusters are an excellent option for data that's static. B-tree indexes are the most common type of index used and serve well for normal data needs. The B-tree indexes are exceptionally useful on columns that have unique values, or at least have a high cardinality. Whereas B-tree indexes are useful for unique values, bitmap indexes are at the other end of the spectrum.

Bitmap indexes are best suited for columns that have a very low cardinality, such as true/false fields. Bitmap indexes also offer some other advantages in size and the ability to combine separately defined indexes on the fly.

# Tune The Memory Allocation

Memory tuning begins after the database model has been established and the application has been set in place. Proper memory allocation is one of your primary responsibilities as a DBA and is crucial to performance. The proper allocation of memory resources improves cache performance, reduces parsing of SQL statements, and reduces paging and swapping.

The memory area of Oracle that holds the most frequently requested data is referred to as the *system global area (SGA)*. It is composed of the following memory structures:

➤ Data buffer cache

➤ Shared pool/large pool

➤ Redo log buffers

The database initialization file parameter **PRE_PAGE_SGA** controls the reading of the SGA into memory. If this is set to **YES**, Oracle will read the entire SGA into memory when you start the instance. Setting this parameter will most likely increase the amount of time required for instance startup, but it should decrease the amount of time required for Oracle to reach its full performance capacity after instance startup.

## Data Buffer Cache

The *data buffer cache* is the area of the SGA that stores copies of the data blocks that are read into memory from the physical database files. These data blocks include tables, clusters, rollback segments, and indexes. Each buffer holds a single Oracle data block. In Oracle8, there can be multiple buffer pools—keep, recycle, and default—which are used to hold specific types of data blocks:

➤ *Keep buffer cache*—Used to retain schema objects in memory.

➤ *Recycle buffer cache*—Eliminates data blocks from memory as soon as they're no longer needed.

➤ *Default data buffer cache*—Any data block not specifically assigned to keep or recycle is assigned to the default data buffer cache.

The initialization parameters **BUFFER_POOL_KEEP** and **BUFFER_POOL_RECYCLE** are used to set and manage the keep and recycle data buffers.

## Shared Pool

The *shared pool* is an area of the SGA that contains two major memory areas: the library cache and the dictionary cache. The *library cache* consists of shared and private SQL areas, PL/SQL packages and procedures, and control structures. When there's insufficient memory in the library cache, no space will be available to cache new statements until old statements are removed to make room. Any statements that were removed but are needed again will need to be reparsed. This reparsing procedure requires CPU and I/O resources. Objects can also be pinned in the library cache so that they remain in memory until they're unpinned or the instance is shut down. In Oracle version 7.3 and later, database triggers do not need to be parsed because they're stored in compiled format.

The *dictionary cache* stores information about the database, its structures, and its users. Information in the dictionary cache includes segment names, users, privileges, and locations of extents. Before most operations can take place in the Oracle database, the data dictionary tables must be read; that data is then stored in the dictionary cache. As with the buffer cache and the library cache, the efficiency of the dictionary cache is determined by its hit ratio.

If you're running in a multithreaded server (MTS) environment, user session information, such as private SQL and sort areas, is stored in the shared pool rather than in the memory of user processes. If you're using an MTS, you might need to make your shared pool larger to accommodate the extra memory requirements caused by moving some user session and sort information into the user global area (UGA). The size of the shared pool is determined by the database initialization file parameter **SHARED_POOL_SIZE**. The size of the library cache and dictionary cache is limited by the size of the shared pool. As an alternative to adding overhead to the shared pool, you can configure the large pool area using the **LARGE_POOL_AREA** parameter. The large pool is used by Oracle for session memory for the MTS, I/O server processes, and backup/restore operations. Use of the large pool for these tasks allows Oracle to use the shared pool primarily for shared SQL caching, thus avoiding the performance overhead involved in shrinking the shared pool for MTS operations. Finally, note that the large pool, unlike the shared pool, does not use the least recently used (LRU) list.

## Redo Log Buffer

The redo log buffer is an area of the SGA that records all changes made to the database. Information is periodically written from the redo log buffer to the online redo log files so that they can be applied in a roll-forward action if recovery is needed. The size of the redo log buffer, in bytes, is specified by the database initialization file parameter **LOG_BUFFER**.

Some of the memory structure sizes are set by Oracle, whereas others are set explicitly by the DBA. The memory structures set by Oracle are:

➤ The data dictionary cache

➤ The library cache

➤ Context areas (if you're running a multithreaded server)

Here are the memory structure sizes set explicitly by the DBA:

➤ Buffer cache

➤ Log buffer

➤ Sequence caches

One last caveat concerning memory tuning: Be careful not to allocate such a large percentage of the machine's physical memory to the system global area (SGA) that it causes paging or swapping.

# Tune I/O And The Physical Structure

To obtain maximum performance on your system, I/O distribution should be optimized by spreading the Oracle database files across multiple devices. This is referred to as *striping*. Disk contention can occur when multiple processes try to access the same disk simultaneously. When the maximum number of accesses to a disk has been reached, other processes will need to wait for access to the disk.

Here are some other areas to tune to help I/O:

➤ Free lists

➤ **PCTFREE** and **PCTUSED**

➤ Extents

➤ Raw devices

If processes are trying to insert into the same block, they'll have to wait for each other to write. The use of free lists can help reduce contention. Free lists are used in conjunction with the storage parameters **PCTFREE** and **PCTUSED** by maintaining a list of all data blocks that have free space greater than **PCTFREE**. When free space falls below **PCTFREE**, the data block is removed from the free list. The optimal use of free space helps storage in the data files, which increases the amount of data retrieved on reads.

Extents are dynamically allocated by the Oracle system. If the extents are sized too small, considerable overhead can be involved due to the recursive calls generated by Oracle during extent allocation. Also, extents are contiguous data blocks; therefore, the larger the extent, the larger the contiguous block of data, thus allowing Oracle to read the data from disk with fewer multiblock reads. This does *not* mean you should make each extent as large as possible. There are practical considerations that will limit the size of the extent. The maximum number of extents to allow is in part determined by block size. The general rule is, the smaller the block size, the lower the number of extents.

Raw devices can offer some benefit in performance tuning because of faster access and space considerations. On the other hand, they also have some administrative overhead that normal file systems do not. The benefits and drawbacks of raw devices will need to be determined for the particular needs of your system.

## Tune Resource Contention

Unless you're the only user on your system, contention will occur for some of the Oracle resources at some point. However, when looking at resource contention in Oracle, you need to keep in mind that you're looking at symptoms of problems, not the problems themselves. Some of the resources for which users will be in contention are:

➤ Block contention

➤ Shared pool contention

➤ Lock contention

➤ Pinging (in a parallel server environment)

➤ Latch contention

## Tune The Underlying Platforms

Different platforms have different requirements, and Oracle provides platform-specific documentation you can use to better determine the requirements of your system. Operating system tuning involves the areas of process management, memory management (the system memory), and scheduling. This could involve extending system resources by adding CPUs or making sure there's sufficient swap space available.

It's important to remember that although this facet of tuning is listed last in Oracle's recommended tuning process, this is only the fine-tuning aspect of operating system tuning. Most experts in the field recommend tuning the operating system first. It is impossible to gauge the effectiveness of Oracle instance tuning if you're starting with a poorly performing operating system.

At this stage of development, you can affect the operating system performance more by tuning Oracle than by tuning the operating system directly. For instance, excessive buffer waits will increase the number of system calls, thus degrading the system. By tuning contention in Oracle, you increase system performance without tuning the system directly.

# Practice Questions

## Question 1

Users are experiencing delays in query response time in a database application. Which area should you look at first to resolve the problem?

○ a. Memory

○ b. SGA

○ c. SQL statements

○ d. I/O

The correct answer is c. Generally, SQL statements are the first place you
would want to look in a production environment when investigating response
time.

## Question 2

A mail order system has a DML-intensive order entry system. Which type of
system is this?

○ a. Data warehouse

○ b. DSS

○ c. Hybrid

○ d. OLTP

The correct answer is d. A characteristic of an OLTP system is that it performs
frequent DML operations, such as **INSERT, UPDATE,** and **DELETE.** Data
warehouses by nature are not DML-intensive systems. Therefore, answer a is
incorrect. A DSS system stores large volumes of data that is most frequently
used for reporting (**SELECT**) purposes. Therefore, answer b is incorrect. A
hybrid system is a combination of an OLTP and a DSS system. Therefore,
answer c is incorrect.

# Question 3

---

> The applications have been tuned, but the system still has performance issues. What should you tune now?
>
> ○ a. Memory
>
> ○ b. Data design
>
> ○ c. Operating system
>
> ○ d. Contention
>
> ○ e. I/O

The correct answer is a. Proper tuning of memory structures will reduce the amount of system calls Oracle has to perform. Data design is done prior to the database creation. Therefore, answer b is incorrect. Answers c, d, and e are incorrect because they come later in the Oracle recommended tuning sequence.

# Question 4

---

> The inventory application was installed two years ago, and data files were striped evenly across the file system. Many data files have since been added, and they were placed wherever space was available. You are analyzing the database and see that the new data files are not evenly placed. Which area should you consider tuning because of this condition?
>
> ○ a. Application
>
> ○ b. Memory
>
> ○ c. I/O
>
> ○ d. Contention
>
> ○ e. Design

The correct answer is c. Proper distribution of I/O can dramatically improve database performance. Once you've determined the current I/O, you should consult your hardware documentation to determine the capacity limits of your disks. You might need to move one or more heavily accessed files to a less active disk. You should continue this process until you have an even distribution of I/O on all disks. Application and memory do not affect the placement of files. Therefore, answers a and b are incorrect. Tuning contention refers to contention for system resources. Therefore, answer d is incorrect. The database is already in existence and design happens before the database is created. Therefore, answer e is incorrect.

# Question 5

When you're undertaking a tuning objective, it's usually better at first to explore performance randomly because you have a better chance of finding hidden problems that way.

○ a. True

○ b. False

The correct answer is b. Poking around the system randomly trying to find problems may result in more problems than you had to start with. Always use a structured approach to tuning. This also helps you determine when you should stop tuning.

# Question 6

Which of these choices is a measurable tuning goal that can be used to evaluate system performance?

○ a. Number of concurrent users

○ b. Database size

○ c. Making the system run faster

○ d. Database hit percentages

The correct answer is d. Although the first two choices affect system performance, they're not goals and cannot be used to determine system performance. Therefore, answers a and b are incorrect. Although the option in answer c is a goal, it's too generic to be measurable. Therefore, answer c is also incorrect.

# Question 7

Which type of system uses a combination of OLTP and DSS for the same instance?

○ a. OLTP

○ b. DSS

○ c. Client server

○ d. Hybrid

The correct answer is d. A hybrid system is a combination of an online transaction processing (OLTP) system and a decision support system (DSS), and it might require special configurations to meet the performance needs of both types of systems.

## Question 8

What should your goal be when tuning I/O?

○ a.  To distribute I/O as much as possible

○ b.  To keep Oracle I/O limited to one area of the system

○ c.  To not place any non-Oracle files on the same disks that the Oracle database is on

○ d.  To reduce writes as much as possible

The correct answer is a. Use the **V$FILESTAT** view to identify file I/O distribution since instance startup. Also, use the UTLBSTAT and UTLESTAT scripts to check for file I/O distribution during a specific period of time.

# Need To Know More?

 Aronoff, Eyal, Kevin Loney, and Noorali Sonawalla. *Oracle8 Advanced Tuning and Administration*, Oracle Press, 1998. ISBN 0-07882-534-2.

 Ault, Michael R. *Oracle8 Black Book*. The Coriolis Group, 1998. ISBN 1-57610-187-8. Be sure to read Chapters 9 and 11 carefully.

 Ault, Michael R. *Oracle8i Administration and Management*. Wiley Computer Publishing, 1999. ISBN 0-471-35453-8.

 Corey, Michael, Michael Abbey, and Daniel J. Dechichio, Jr. *Oracle8 Tuning*, Oracle Press, 1997. ISBN 0-07882-390-0.

 The first place to go for more information is the *Oracle8 Tuning Manual* and the *Oracle8 Server Reference Manual*.

# The Tuning Tools And Application Considerations

. . . . . . . . . . . . . . . . . . . . . . . . . . . . . . . . . . . .

### Terms you'll need to understand:

√ Performance Pack

√ **V$** views

√ UTLBSTAT, UTLESTAT, and report.txt

√ Timed statistics

√ OLTP, DSS, and hybrid systems

### Techniques you'll need to master:

√ Understanding the variety of diagnostic tools available
  for database tuning and using them effectively

√ Understanding how to use the **V$** views, UTLBSTAT,
  UTLESTAT, and report.txt for pinpointing performance
  problems

√ Customizing tuning for different application
  environments

This chapter provides an overview of the tuning process and reviews some of the Oracle tools that assist in identifying and addressing performance issues. This chapter also provides a tuning checklist that uses a structured methodology and details the use of UTLBSTAT and UTLESTAT. Finally, this chapter explains how to customize your tuning approach for different application environments.

# Tuning Toolbox

Oracle offers many tools to assist in the tuning process. Table 3.1 lists some tools provided by Oracle for tuning diagnostics. Each tool is discussed in detail in the following sections.

## Performance Pack

In addition to the standard set of applications in the OEM, Oracle offers an optional Performance Pack that consists of integrated monitoring and performance-tuning tools. Performance Pack is a set of tuning diagnostics within Enterprise Manager that provides realtime graphical performance information. The components of Performance Pack include the following:

| Table 3.1    Tools for tuning. | |
| --- | --- |
| Diagnostic Tool | Description |
| Performance Pack | An optional Oracle diagnostic tool for integrated monitoring and tuning of the database. |
| V$ views | Dynamic performance views used for tuning diagnostics. |
| ANALYZE command | A command that provides detailed storage statistics on tables, indexes, and clusters. |
| UTLBSTAT/UTLESTAT | SQL scripts that take a beginning snapshot (UTLBSTAT) and an ending snapshot (UTLESTAT) of database performance statistics and produce a report (report.txt) on system performance. |
| SQL*Trace/TKPROF | Gathers performance information for an SQL statement, including the optimizer access method, CPU utilization, and percentage of logical and physical reads. |
| Explain Plan | Passes an SQL statement through the Oracle optimizer to give an execution plan on how that statement will be executed in the database. |
| Trace files | Provides debugging information for the background processes (for example, LGWR and DBWR). The alert log file records all significant instance events and errors. |

➤ *Oracle Expert*—Assists with initial database configuration and with the collection and evaluation of performance statistics in existing databases. It also provides recommendations for performance improvements on the basis of current database activity and scenarios provided by the DBA.

➤ *Oracle Lock Manager*—Provides lock monitoring for users holding locks or waiting for locks within the database.

➤ *Oracle Performance Manager*—Allows the DBA to monitor database performance in realtime. Provides database statistics regarding through-put, users, tablespaces, redo logs, buffers, caches, and I/O.

➤ *Oracle Tablespace Manager*—Allows the DBA to monitor and manage database storage at the tablespace level. It also provides the ability to drill down to the segment and extent levels.

➤ *Oracle Top Sessions*—Monitors how connected sessions use instance and database resources in realtime. It identifies and isolates the most re-source-intensive sessions and displays the SQL being executed for those sessions.

➤ *Oracle Trace*—Monitors system performance by collecting data about events that occur in an application. The application must contain calls to Oracle Trace routines in order to gather performance statistics.

Any of these Performance Pack tools may be covered on the exam, but the questions will usually just focus on the tool's primary function, and there will rarely be more then one question for any of the tools. Of course, there's always an exception, and in this case it's the Oracle Expert tool. Because it will be covered in more detail than the rest, the following section delves deeper into the operations of Oracle Expert.

## Oracle Expert

The Oracle Expert tuning process begins with data collection. Data is first collected to identify potential tuning opportunities in the database in three major tuning areas:

➤ *Access method tuning*—This includes optimizing database access methods used by an application and searching for redundant SQL in the cache (except for case and spacing).

➤ *Instance parameter tuning*—This includes tuning specific key database initialization parameter categories such as the system global area (SGA), sort operations, I/O, and parallel query.

➤ *Database structure sizing and placement*—This includes evaluating database storage structures for proper placement and sizing, the use of temporary objects, and optimal flexible architecture compliance.

The data for analysis is collected on a session-by-session basis. After collecting the data, Oracle stores the data in the Oracle Expert repository for the analysis phase that's conducted by the rules inference engine. As its name implies, the engine applies a set of rules to the data it's analyzing to identify tuning opportunities. The rules applied to generate the tuning recommendations may be modified by the DBA by adjusting the threshold parameters of the rules. In this way, the rules can be customized to the specific needs of the database.

The amount of data collected can be changed on a session-by-session basis. Data can be collected for any one of the areas listed previously, or data can be collected for any combination of these areas. The data collected can even be refined to a specific object in the database; for example, collected data can be limited to a specific table or index.

> **Note:** *To perform access methods tuning, Oracle Expert requires that schema class data be collected for the schema containing the specific table or index that you want to analyze.*

When finished with its analysis, Oracle Expert provides the DBA with tuning recommendations, implementation scripts, and reports detailing the rationale for each recommendation. In addition, a new init.ora file is generated that reflects all the recommended changes for the initialization parameters. If the DBA determines that he or she does not want to implement the recommendations, changing the parameters for the rule and running a new analysis can override the recommendations.

Although Oracle Expert provides a degree of automation to the tuning process, there is one area of the tuning process that will still require manual intervention to load the data for analysis—the environment. In order to provide recommendations on environment tuning, Oracle Expert must have the data entered manually or imported from an XDL file.

## V$ Views

To tune and troubleshoot the Oracle database, you must familiarize yourself with **V$** dynamic performance views that are commonly used for diagnostics. The *V$ views* are often referred to as *V$ tables*, but the two terms are really synonymous. The **V$** views are created by running the catalog.sql script and are based on **X$** tables, which are memory structures that hold information about the instance. The database user SYS owns the **V$** views, and the DBA can grant **SELECT** on the views to any database user. The **V$** views and the X$ tables are populated at instance startup and are reinitialized each time the instance is restarted. Table 3.2 lists **V$** views that can be used for performance tuning, grouped by the following categories:

➤ Instance/database

➤ Memory

➤ Disk

➤ User/session

➤ Contention

### Table 3.2    V$ views for performance tuning.

| View | Description |
| --- | --- |
| **Instance/Database** | |
| **V$DATABASE** | Database information from the control file |
| **V$INSTANCE** | State of the current instance |
| **V$OPTION** | Options that are installed with the Oracle8 server |
| **V$PARAMETER** | Information about the current parameter values |
| **V$PQ_SYSSTAT** | Session statistics for all parallel queries |
| **V$PROCESS** | Information about currently active processes |
| **V$SESSTAT** | User session statistics |
| **V$WAITSTAT** | Block contention statistics (updated only when timed statistics is enabled) |
| **V$SYSTEM_EVENT** | Information on the total waits for an event |
| **V$EVENT_NAME** | All event names and their parameters |
| **Memory** | |
| **V$DB_OBJECT_CACHE** | Database objects that are cached in the library cache (for example, tables, clusters, indexes, synonym definitions, PL/SQL packages, procedures, and triggers) |
| **V$LIBRARY_CACHE** | Statistics about library cache performance and activity |
| **V$SYSSTAT** | Basic system statistics |
| **V$SGASTAT** | Detailed information on the system global area (SGA) |
| **V$ROWCACHE** | Statistics on data dictionary activity |

*(continued)*

### Table 3.2   V$ views for performance tuning (continued).

| View | Description |
|---|---|
| **Disk** | |
| **V$DATAFILE** | Data file information from the control file |
| **V$FILESTAT** | Information about file read-write statistics |
| **V$LOG** | Log file information from the control file |
| **V$LOG_HISTORY** | Archived log names for all logs in the log history |
| **User/Session** | |
| **V$LOCK** | Information about locks and resources |
| **V$OPEN_CURSOR** | Information about cursors that each session currently has opened and parsed |
| **V$PROCESS** | Information about currently active processes |
| **User/Session** | |
| **V$SESSION** | Session information for each current session |
| **V$SESSTAT** | User session statistics |
| **V$TRANSACTION** | Active transactions in the system |
| **V$SYSTEM_EVENT** | Cumulated statistics of total waits for an event for all sessions since instance startup |
| **V$SESSION_EVENT** | Systemwide waits for an event by a session |
| **V$SESSION_WAIT** | List of resources or events for which active sessions are waiting |
| **Contention** | |
| **V$LOCK** | Locks that are being held and requests for a lock or a latch |
| **V$ROLLNAME** | Names of all online rollback segments |
| **V$ROLLSTAT** | Rollback segment statistics |
| **V$LATCH** | Statistics for non-parent latches and summary statistics for parent latches |
| **V$WAITSTAT** | Block contention statistics (updated only when timed statistics are enabled) |

There are numerous question on the exam regarding the **V$** tables. You need to know what type of data is found in each table and what the data tells you. Pay particular attention to **V$** tables that involve waits, contention, and cache misses.

Some of the columns in the V$ views can store CPU timing information. To populate the views with timing statistics, you must set the **TIMED_STATIS-TICS** parameter to **TRUE**. The **TIMED_STATISTICS** parameter enables and disables the collection of CPU timing statistics for the **V$** views, UTLBSTAT/UTLESTAT, and SQL*Trace.

You can enable **TIMED_STATISTICS** in the database initialization file by adding the following parameter (the instance must then be restarted in order for the change to take effect):

```
TIMED_STATISTICS = TRUE
```

The following database initialization file parameter disables **TIMED_STATISTICS**:

```
TIMED_STATISTICS = FALSE
```

Oracle contains several database initialization parameters that can be changed while the database is running. You can dynamically enable the **TIMED_STATISTICS** value for an instance with the following command:

```
ALTER SYSTEM SET timed_statistics = TRUE;
```

The following command will disable **TIMED_STATISTICS** for an instance:

```
ALTER SYSTEM SET timed_statistics = FALSE;
```

The default for the **TIMED_STATISTICS** parameter is **FALSE**.

# The ANALYZE Command

The **ANALYZE** command is used to gather statistical information or to validate the storage format of a table, index, or cluster. Many of the statistics gathered when the **ANALYZE** command is issued are used by the cost-based optimizer to obtain the optimal execution path for your SQL statements. The **ANALYZE** command also provides statistics on chained and migrated rows for a table or cluster. You can use many of the statistics gathered by the **ANALYZE** command to obtain detailed storage information on a table, cluster, or index. This information helps determine whether the object needs to be rebuilt. You must have the **ANALYZE ANY** system privilege or own the object to analyze a table, cluster, or index. The syntax for the **ANALYZE** command is shown in Figure 3.1.

When you issue the **ANALYZE** command with the **STATISTICS** option, statistics are stored about the physical characteristics of the table, cluster, or

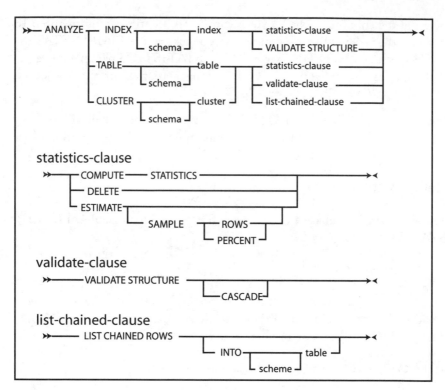

**Figure 3.1** The syntax for the **ANALYZE** command.

index that you analyzed. You can estimate or compute statistics with the **ANALYZE** command. When you use **ESTIMATE STATISTICS**, Oracle collects a representation of information from a portion of the data in an object. When **COMPUTE STATISTICS** is used, Oracle performs a full-table scan on the object to gather the exact statistics. If you are working with a large object, you might want to use **ESTIMATE STATISTICS** first on a specified number of rows or a percentage of the object. When statistics are analyzed on a table or cluster, the indexes for the object are analyzed as well.

The following query is from RevealNet's Oracle Administration product and is used with RevealNet's permission. This query can be executed after tables have been analyzed to produce detailed storage statistics on the tables in the database:

```
rem  FUNCTION: Will show table statistics for a user's
rem  tables or all tables.
rem  File: tab_stat.sql
rem set pages 56 lines 130 newpage 0 verify off echo off
rem feedback off
rem
```

```
column owner              format a12          heading "Owner"
column table_name         format a20          heading "Table"
column tablespace_name    format a20          heading "Tablespace"
column num_rows           format 999,999,999  heading "Rows"
column blocks             format 999,999      heading "Blocks"
column empty_blocks       format 999,999      heading "Empties"
column space_full         format 999.99       heading "% Full"
column chain_cnt          format 999,999      heading "Chains"
column avg_row_len        format 99,999,999,999 heading "Avg Len"
rem
start title132 "Table Statistics Report"
DEFINE OUTPUT = 'rep_out\&db\tab_stat.lis'
spool &output
rem
BREAK ON OWNER SKIP 2 ON TABLESPACE_NAME SKIP 1;
select owner,
       table_name,
       tablespace_name,
       num_rows,
       blocks,
       empty_blocks,
       100*((NUM_ROWS * AVG_ROW_LEN)/
            ((GREATEST(blocks,1) + empty_blocks)
            * 4096)) space_full,
       chain_cnt,
       avg_row_len
from dba_tables
WHERE OWNER NOT IN ('SYS','SYSTEM')
order by owner, tablespace_name;
spool off
pause Press enter to continue
 set pages 22 lines 80 newpage 1 verify on echo on feedback on
clear columns
clear breaks
ttitle off
```

Table 3.3 shows a partial output of the RevealNet query.

The value in the **BLOCKS** column indicates the number of blocks *below* the high-water mark. The high-water mark indicates the highest level of blocks that has been used at any given time in the segment. The high-water mark is reset when the table is truncated but not when rows are deleted from a table. The value in the **EMPTIES** column indicates the number of empty (never used) blocks. The **CHAINS** column indicates the number of chained or migrated rows in a table.

**Table 3.3    Table storage statistics.**

| OWNER | TABLE | TABLE-SPACE | ROWS | BLOCKS | EMPTIES | % FULL | CHAINS | AVG. LENGTH |
|---|---|---|---|---|---|---|---|---|
| SCOTT | CLASS | PDATA1 | 4,746 | 105 | 59 | 52.28 | 0 | 74 |
| | STDENTS | | 20,577 | 350 | 1,189 | 20.89 | 0 | 64 |
| | ACCTS | | 871 | 10 | 4 | 37.97 | 4 | 25 |
| | ZONE | PDATA2 | 494 | 3 | 141 | 1.59 | 0 | 19 |
| | MODELS | | 13 | 1 | 258 | .02 | 0 | 17 |
| APPL | CLASS2 | PDATA1 | 1,338 | 20 | 239 | 6.94 | 7 | 55 |
| | PRICES | | 754 | 10 | 154 | 3.37 | 0 | 30 |

To remove statistics for a table, cluster, or index from the data dictionary, use **DELETE STATISTICS** with the **ANALYZE** command. When statistics are deleted for a table or cluster, the index statistics on the object are also deleted. The following command deletes statistics for the **DEPARTMENT** table:

```
ANALYZE TABLE department DELETE STATISTICS;
```

 Use caution when you delete statistics for tables or clusters. If you are using the cost-based optimizer and there are no statistics for an object, the cost-based optimizer will assume that the object has no rows or 5,000 rows, depending on the release level of the software. You need to understand how the cost-based optimizer will use the information provided by the **ANALYZE** command, and you should keep your statistics current.

## UTLBSTAT And UTLESTAT

If your instance has been running for an extended period of time, the statistics in the **V$** views might not help in your evaluation of the true performance of your system during busy times. If users tell you that the system runs smoothly in the morning but that performance is sluggish in the afternoon, you need to evaluate a time slice of the system performance. To accomplish this, Oracle provides the scripts UTLBSTAT.SQL and UTLESTAT.SQL, which are located in the $ORACLE_HOME/rdbms/admin directory in a Unix environment.

At the beginning of the time period you want to monitor, submit the UTLBSTAT.SQL script from Server Manager while connected as SYSDBA.

The UTLBSTAT script creates tables owned by SYS that store cumulative beginning database statistics. The tables that are created contain the word *begin*, as in **STAT$BEGIN_FILE**. At the end of the monitoring time period, submit the UTLESTAT.SQL script from Server Manager while connected as SYSDBA. The UTLESTAT script creates additional tables and populates them with ending database statistics. The tables created contain the word *end*, as in **STAT$END_STATS**. In addition, UTLESTAT creates the report.txt file, which shows the differences in the statistics from the time that UTLBSTAT was submitted until the time that UTLESTAT was submitted. To obtain time-based statistics from UTLBSTAT and UTLESTAT, the **TIMED_STATISTICS** parameter must be set to **TRUE**.

Before you submit UTLBSTAT, you should ensure that the database has been running for a period of time that is sufficient to populate the V$ tables with dynamic performance statistics. This time period is dependent on the level of activity in your database. Remember that Oracle initializes the dynamic performance tables at instance startup. Information gathered from a recently started database might not reflect true performance statistics. Additionally, if you shut down the database or have an instance crash *after* UTLBSTAT was submitted, but *before* UTLESTAT was submitted, the statistics will not provide a valid picture of the performance on your database. You will need to run both scripts again after the database has been restarted.

UTLESTAT always writes database statistics to the report.txt file in the current directory. If you want to run multiple sets of UTLBSTAT and UTLESTAT to compare statistics for several time slices, remember to rename the report.txt file after each submission of UTLESTAT. If you do not rename the report.txt file, it will be overwritten with the latest statistics gathered by UTLESTAT.

The report.txt file provides information on:

➤ System summary statistics

➤ Systemwide wait statistics

➤ Library cache statistics

➤ Dictionary cache statistics

➤ DBWn statistics

➤ File I/O statistics

➤ Latch statistics

➤ Database initialization parameters

➤ The date and time that UTLBSTAT and UTLESTAT scripts were run

Report.txt includes system statistics on virtually every aspect of database internals. Many of the statistics from report.txt contain truncated statistic names and lines that wrap on the report. Although Oracle's report.txt file provides valuable performance diagnostics, it is not a well-formatted report, and some sections are difficult to read. As with all statistics in report.txt, the period of statistical gathering is from the time UTLBSTAT was submitted until the time UTLESTAT was submitted. Table 3.4 lists some of the system statistics provided in report.txt.

The systemwide events data provided by the report.txt file can also be obtained by querying the V$ tables **V$SESSION_EVENT**, **V$SYSTEM_EVENT**, and **V$SESSION_WAIT**.

### Table 3.4   System statistics reported in report.txt.

| Statistic | Total | Per Transaction |
| --- | --- | --- |
| CPU used by this session | 71,454 | 84.16 |
| CPU used when call started | 71,407 | 84.11 |
| DBWn buffers scanned | 95,686 | 112.7 |
| DBWn checkpoints | 64 | .08 |
| DBWn free buffers found | 30,774 | 36.25 |
| DBWn LRU scans | 274 | .32 |
| DBWn timeouts | 1,065 | 1.25 |
| SQL*Net roundtrips to/from | 76,394 | 89.98 |
| Background timeouts | 3,360 | 3.96 |
| Bytes received via SQL*Net | 14,022,597 | 16,516.6 |
| Calls to get snapshot SCN | 67,798 | 79.86 |
| Calls to kcmgas | 1,072 | 1.26 |
| Calls to kcmgcs | 130 | .15 |
| Calls to kcmgrs | 87,650 | 103.24 |
| Change write time | 606 | .71 |
| Cleanouts and rollbacks | 112 | .13 |
| Cleanouts only: consistent | 38 | .04 |
| Cluster key scan block gets | 20,885 | 24.6 |
| Cluster key scans | 2,191 | 2.58 |
| Commit cleanout failures | 8 | .01 |
| Commit cleanout number | 8,257 | 9.73 |

*(continued)*

**Table 3.4    System statistics reported in report.txt (continued).**

| Statistic | Total | Per Transaction |
|---|---|---|
| Consistent changes | 1,779 | 2.1 |
| Consistent gets | 2,631,477 | 3,099.5 |
| Cursor authentications | 29,690 | 34.97 |
| Data blocks consistent read | 1,779 | 2.1 |
| Database block changes | 178,516 | 210.27 |
| Database block gets | 182,024 | 214.4 |
| Deferred (CURRENT) block | 3,026 | 3.56 |
| Enqueue conversions | 724 | .85 |
| Enqueue releases | 5,927 | 6.98 |
| Enqueue requests | 5,961 | 7.02 |
| Enqueue timeouts | 40 | .05 |
| Enqueue waits | 3 | 0 |
| Execute count | 74,846 | 88.16 |
| Free buffer requested | 28,110 | 33.11 |
| Logons cumulative | 177 | .21 |
| Logons current | 10 | .01 |
| Messages received | 1,388 | 1.63 |
| Messages sent | 1,388 | 1.63 |
| Opened cursors cumulative | 24,804 | 29.22 |
| Opened cursors current | 242 | .29 |
| Parse count | 32,869 | 38.71 |
| Parse time CPU | 18,198 | 21.43 |
| Parse time elapsed | 19,088 | 22.48 |
| Physical reads | 17,181 | 20.24 |
| Physical writes | 6,292 | 7.41 |
| Recursive calls | 483,538 | 569.54 |
| Recursive CPU usage | 12,922 | 15.22 |
| Redo blocks written | 34,045 | 40.1 |
| Redo buffer allocation retr | 5 | .01 |
| Redo entries | 90,139 | 106.17 |
| Redo log space requests | 8 | .01 |

*(continued)*

**Table 3.4  System statistics reported in report.txt (continued).**

| Statistic | Total | Per Transaction |
|---|---|---|
| Redo log space wait time | 418 | .49 |
| Redo size | 16,594,148 | 19,545.52 |
| Redo small copies | 4,668 | 5.5 |
| Redo synch time | 4,457 | 5.25 |
| Redo synch writes | 952 | 1.12 |
| Redo wastage | 271,372 | 319.64 |
| Redo write time | 6,221 | 7.33 |
| Redo writer latching time | 11 | .01 |
| Redo writes | 1,215 | 1.43 |
| Rollback changes | 1,762 | 2.08 |
| Rollbacks only | 1,595 | 1.88 |
| Session logical reads | 2,797,112 | 3,294.6 |
| Session PGA memory | 73,996,476 | 87,157.22 |
| Session PGA memory maximum | 76,544,228 | 90,158.1 |
| Session UGA memory | 1,910,768 | 2,250.61 |
| Session UGA memory maximum | 35,363,760 | 41,653.43 |
| Sorts (disk) | 4 | 0 |
| Sorts (memory) | 10,468 | 12.33 |
| Sorts (rows) | 319,077 | 375.83 |
| Table fetch by **ROWID** | 956,150 | 1,126.21 |
| Table fetch continued row | 4,352 | 5.13 |
| Table scan blocks gotten | 221,624 | 261.04 |
| Table scan rows gotten | 1,485,858 | 1,750.13 |
| Table scans (long tables) | 8 | .01 |
| Table scans (short tables) | 9,285 | 10.94 |
| Total number commit cleanout | 8,300 | 9.78 |
| Transaction rollbacks | 3 | 0 |
| User calls | 72,708 | 85.64 |
| User commits | 849 | 1 |
| User rollbacks | 106 | .12 |
| Write requests | 1,189 | 1.4 |

Library cache statistics are included in the report.txt file. The *library cache* is the portion of the shared pool in the SGA that stores information regarding shared SQL objects. The goal for the library cache is to achieve a high pin ratio and a low number of reloads. Table 3.5 shows library cache statistics in report.txt.

The report.txt file also reports statistics on the dictionary cache, which is the portion of the shared pool that holds information from the data dictionary. The **GET_MISS** and **SCAN_MIS(S)** statistics should be significantly lower than the requests. If the overall ratio of **GET_MISS** to **GET_REQS** is greater than 10 percent, you should consider increasing the **SHARED_POOL_SIZE** parameter in the database initialization file. Table 3.6 shows dictionary cache statistics in report.txt.

**Table 3.5   Library cache statistics in report.txt.**

| LIBRARY | GETS | GET HIT RATIO | PINS | PIN HIT RATIO | RELOADS | INVALIDA-TIONS |
|---|---|---|---|---|---|---|
| BODY | 8 | 1 | 8 | 1 | 0 | 0 |
| CLUSTER | 7 | 1 | 11 | 1 | 0 | 0 |
| INDEX | 0 | 1 | 0 | 1 | 0 | 0 |
| OBJECT | 0 | 1 | 0 | 1 | 0 | 0 |
| PIPE | 0 | 1 | 0 | 1 | 0 | 0 |
| SQL AREA | 434 | .963 | 1432 | .977 | 0 | 9 |
| TABLE/ PROCEDURE | 42 | .905 | 104 | .942 | 0 | 0 |
| TRIGGER | 0 | 1 | 0 | 1 | 0 | 0 |

**Table 3.6   Dictionary cache statistics in report.txt.**

| NAME | GET_ REQS | GET_ MISS | SCAN_ REQ | SCAN_ MIS | MOD_ REQS | COUNT | CUR_ USAG |
|---|---|---|---|---|---|---|---|
| dc_tablespaces | 72 | 1 | 0 | 0 | 0 | 8 | 4 |
| dc_free_extents | 310 | 67 | 33 | 0 | 165 | 63 | 34 |
| dc_segments | 43 | 4 | 0 | 0 | 35 | 53 | 41 |
| dc_rollback_seg | 56 | 0 | 0 | 0 | 0 | 10 | 8 |
| dc_used_extents | 66 | 33 | 0 | 0 | 66 | 50 | 32 |
| dc_users | 31 | 0 | 0 | 0 | 0 | 21 | 14 |
| dc_user_grants | 20 | 0 | 0 | 0 | 0 | 21 | 14 |

*(continued)*

| NAME | GET_REQS | GET_MISS | SCAN_REQ | SCAN_MIS | MOD_REQS | COUNT | CUR_USAG |
|---|---|---|---|---|---|---|---|
| dc_objects | 33 | 3 | 0 | 0 | 0 | 222 | 214 |
| dc_usernames | 9 | 1 | 0 | 0 | 0 | 20 | 4 |
| dc_object_ids | 14 | 1 | 0 | 0 | 0 | 132 | 130 |
| dc_profiles | 3 | 0 | 0 | 0 | 0 | 3 | 1 |
| dc_histogram_de | 73 | 73 | 0 | 0 | 73 | 77 | 73 |

**Table 3.6 Dictionary cache statistics in report.txt (continued).**

The *buffer cache* is the area in memory where data is stored from tables, indexes, rollback segments, clusters, and sequences. When you have a good buffer cache hit ratio, you can speed execution by reducing reads from disk to satisfy data requests. If the buffer cache hit ratio is less than 80 to 90 percent and the database has been operating with activity for some time, you might need to increase the **DB_BLOCK_BUFFERS** parameter or reevaluate the indexes and SQL in your applications. Table 3.7 shows report.txt statistics that can be used to determine the buffer cache hit ratio.

The formula used to determine the buffer cache hit ratio is

```
Logical reads = db block gets + consistent gets
```

and then this:

```
Buffer cache hit ratio (%) = (( logical reads - physical reads)
                            / logical reads) * 100
```

In this example, the buffer cache hit ratio is 99.39 percent.

> *Note: The V$SYSSTAT view also provides information to determine the buffer cache hit ratio, but the statistics reflected in V$SYSSTAT are from instance startup.*

**Table 3.7 Buffer cache statistics from report.txt.**

| Statistic | Total | Per Transaction | Per Logon | Per Second |
|---|---|---|---|---|
| consistent gets | 2,631,477 | 3,099.5 | 14,867.1 | 768.54 |
| db block gets | 182,024 | 214.4 | 1,028.38 | 53.16 |
| physical reads | 17,181 | 20.24 | 97.07 | 5.02 |

The report.txt file provides information on sorts in memory and on disk. Ideally, you want most of your sorting done in memory. This requires proper configuration of **SORT_AREA_SIZE** and **SORT_AREA_RETAINED_SIZE**. Sorts to disk indicate the number of sorts writing to the temporary tablespace on disk. Sorts to memory indicate the number of sorts performed in the SGA. The **sorts (rows)** statistic in report.txt indicates the number of rows sorted during the monitoring period. Oracle recommends that the ratio of **sorts(disk)** to **sorts(memory)** be less than 5 percent. Table 3.8 lists sort statistics from report.txt.

Another useful set of statistics provided by report.txt is file I/O statistics, which provide information about file read and write statistics. Use this information to determine how well the I/O load is distributed across disk devices on your system and to pinpoint disks where excessive I/O could be a problem. Ideally, the disk I/O should be as even as possible between disks. If you find that the disk I/O is too high on one or more disks, you should consider moving a data file to a disk with lighter activity. Table 3.9 shows a partial listing of report.txt statistics that can be used to determine the file I/O distribution. The total I/O activity for a disk can be determined by summing the **BLKS READ** and **BLKS WRIT** columns.

**Table 3.8    Sort statistics in report.txt.**

| Statistic Per Second | | | Total | Per Transaction | Per Logon |
|---|---|---|---|---|---|
| sorts (disk) | 4 | 0 | | .02 | 0 |
| sorts (memory) | | | 10,468  12.33 | 59.14 | 3.06 |
| sorts (rows) | | | 319,077  375.83 | 182.09 | 93.19 |

**Table 3.9    Disk I/O statistics in report.txt.**

| Tablespace | File_Name | Blks Read | Read Time | Blks Writ | Write Time | Megabytes |
|---|---|---|---|---|---|---|
| ap_data | db01ce/oratst/ad01.dbf | 402 | 163 | 125 | 1,248 | 524 |
| ap_indexes | db02nc/oratst/apx01.dbf | 270 | 159 | 670 | 7,540 | 524 |
| system | db03ce/oratst/system1.dbf | 4,421 | 454 | 253 | 3,290 | 524 |
| temp | db04ce/oratst/temp1.dbf | 0 | 0 | 617 | 9,216 | 524 |

*Latches* protect access to internal structures such as the shared cursors in the library cache or the least recently used (LRU) list for the buffer cache. A process must acquire a latch when making a change to these types of structures. You should aim for a latch hit ratio of at least 0.98. If your hit ratio is below 0.98, this could indicate latch contention problems. Table 3.10 shows a partial listing of latch contention statistics in report.txt.

Another statistic provided by report.txt involves rollback segments. The TRANS_TBL_GETS column indicates the number of rollback segment accesses. The TRANS_TBL_WAITS column indicates the number of times a user process waited on a rollback segment. The ratio of TRANS_TBL_WAITS to TRANS_TBL_GETS should be less than 5 percent. If you have a high number of TRANS_TBL_WAITS, you should add additional rollback segments. Excessive shrinks indicate that the OPTIMAL size for the rollback segment may be too low. Oracle recommends that you set MINEXTENTS to 20 for rollback segments. You should set OPTIMAL at a number that will ensure that rollback segments do not shrink below 20 extents. Rollback segments should be equal in size. The exception might be a large rollback segment that's used for lengthy transactions or batch jobs. Table 3.11 shows rollback statistics in report.txt.

**Table 3.10   Latch contention statistics in report.txt.**

| LATCH_NAME | GETS | MISSES | HIT_RATIO | SLEEPS | SLEEPS/MISSES |
|---|---|---|---|---|---|
| cache buffer handle | 180 | 0 | 1 | 0 | 0 |
| cache buffers chain | 5445625 | 98 | 1 | 13 | .133 |
| cache buffers lru | 20657 | 4 | 1 | 1 | .25 |

**Table 3.11   Rollback segment statistics in report.txt.**

| UNDO SEGMENT | TRANS TBL GETS | TRANS TBL WAITS | UNDO BYTES WRITTEN | SEGMENT SIZE BYTES | XACTS | SHRINKS | WRAPS |
|---|---|---|---|---|---|---|---|
| 0 | 16 | 0 | 0 | 180,224 | 0 | 0 | 0 |
| 1 | 1,009 | 0 | 1,978,858 | 21,295,104 | 1 | 0 | 2 |
| 2 | 685 | 0 | 975,323 | 21,295,104 | 1 | 0 | 1 |
| 3 | 310 | 0 | 296,471 | 21,295,104 | 1 | 0 | 1 |
| 4 | 674 | 0 | 814,744 | 21,295,104 | 0 | 0 | 1 |
| 5 | 903 | 0 | 1,502,274 | 21,295,104 | 0 | 0 | 1 |
| 6 | 32 | 0 | 932,786 | 42,590,208 | 0 | 0 | 0 |

Report.txt includes all database initialization file parameters that are not set to the default value. The date and time of the beginning and ending statistical period are also included in report.txt.

## SQL*Trace

When SQL statements are performing poorly, you can use the SQL*Trace utility to obtain performance statistics for the SQL statements being executed. SQL*Trace writes a trace file that contains statistics on the parse, execute, and fetch stages of statement execution. It reports on the number of logical buffers retrieved (reads from memory) and the number of physical blocks retrieved from disk. In addition, SQL*Trace provides its own rendition of Explain Plan to determine an execution plan, and it also provides the optimizer hint, if one is used during statement execution. The trace file can be formatted using TKPROF. SQL*Trace is detailed in Chapter 4.

## Explain Plan

The Explain Plan tool can be used to determine the access path used by the optimizer without running the actual SQL statement. When you run Explain Plan, you insert rows into a table called **PLAN_TABLE**. The PLAN_TABLE is created using the utlxplan.sql script, which is found in the $ORACLE_HOME/rdbms/admin directory (on Unix), or its equivalent. The rows in **PLAN_TABLE** can then be evaluated to check the efficiency of the access path and determine which indexes are being used during execution of the SQL statement. Chapter 4 covers Explain Plan concepts and usage in detail.

## Trace Files

Trace files assist in the troubleshooting process. There are three categories of trace files: server trace files, background process trace files, and a special trace file called the alert log.

Server processes write internal error data to their associated trace file. Additionally, server processes can write information to help in the tuning process of their associated trace files. In order to write tuning information to the server process trace files, the parameter **SQL_TRACE** must be set to **TRUE**. This can be done on the instance level by setting the initialization parameter **SQL_TRACE** to **TRUE**. **SQL_TRACE** can be set at the session level with the **ALTER SESSION** command in conjunction with the **SQL_TRACE** parameter. For example, the following command enables trace file writing for the session:

```
ALTER SESSION SET SQL_TRACE = TRUE;
```

When an Oracle instance is started, several background processes are started to support the Oracle database system. In Oracle8, you will have a minimum of five background processes on your system:

➤ *SMON*—Responsible for instance recovery

➤ *PMON*—Responsible for recovery from a user process

➤ *DBWn*—Writes from database buffers to database files

➤ *LGWR*—Writes from the redo log buffer to the online redo logs

➤ *CKPT*—Handles the checkpoint process. If set to false, the checkpoint process can be handled by the LGWR process

When you encounter an error in a background process, Oracle will write information about the error to its trace file, which uses the .trc extension. For example, an error in the SMON process might create a trace file named ptw01_smon_3204.trc. The information in these files can assist you in the troubleshooting process. Some of the information in trace files is used only by kernel experts at Oracle WorldWide Support for troubleshooting.

Oracle writes a chronological log of major database events and errors within an instance to an alert log. The alert log file is a special kind of trace file that usually includes the instance name. For example, an instance named **TEST** might have the alert log file name alert_TEST.log on a Unix system. The alert log file includes:

➤ All internal errors, deadlock errors, and block corruption errors.

➤ Administrative commands, such as **CREATE, ALTER,** or **DROP TABLESPACE, DATABASE,** or **ROLLBACK SEGMENT** SQL statements. (There is no **DROP DATABASE** command in Oracle).

➤ Startup, shutdown, and log switch information.

➤ Optionally, all checkpoint start and stop times if **LOG_CHECK-POINTS_TO_ALERT** is set to **TRUE.**

You should periodically check the alert log file and trace files to see whether any errors have been encountered. The **BACKGROUND_DUMP_DEST** parameter in the database initialization file specifies the location of the alert log file and all background trace files.

You can control the maximum size of all trace files (with the exception of the alert log file) using the init.ora parameter **MAX_DUMP_FILE_SIZE.** This parameter specifies, in operating system blocks, the maximum size of each trace file.

All entries in the alert log file are appended to the existing alert log file. This file can easily grow to an unmanageable size if not monitored and maintained regularly. Keep the alert log file to a reasonable size by renaming it periodically. You can do this while the database is closed or open. If Oracle cannot find the expected name for the alert log file for a given instance, it will create a new alert log file with the proper name.

# Tuning For Application Environments

When tuning an Oracle system, it's important to keep in mind the different tuning goals for the various types of applications. The two primary application environments are the online transaction processing (OLTP) system and the decision support system (DSS). A hybrid system is a combination of an OLTP system and a DSS. With the multithreaded server (MTS) architecture, multiple users share a single server process. The MTS configuration helps to maximize server memory utilization and can be used in conjunction with an OLTP, DSS, or hybrid system.

## Online Transaction Processing Systems

An OLTP system is a high-activity system characterized by frequent insert, delete, and update transactions. An example of such a system might be a banking system that's accessed by a high number of concurrent users accessing data that's frequently updated. In an OLTP environment, you need to ensure that the potentially large number of users accessing the system simultaneously does not affect system performance. The goals of an OLTP system are availability, speed, concurrency, and recoverability.

Because OLTP systems store frequently changed data, it's important to make sure that your indexing strategy is as efficient as possible. Indexing is important because most of your requests for data will involve indexed retrievals rather than full-table scans. However, you should avoid excessive indexing, which will affect performance during inserts, updates, and deletes. Indexes might need to be rebuilt regularly because of their frequent modifications.

Oracle recommends that you try to avoid dynamic space allocation in an OLTP system. To do this, you must be familiar with your data and its projected growth activity so that you can explicitly preallocate space to tables, clusters, and indexes. Preallocating extents will allow you to avoid the performance hit encountered when Oracle creates a new extent. In an OLTP system, you should also try to use bind variables whenever possible. By doing so, you can increase the amount of shared code and reduce parse time.

Rollback segments must be configured correctly for an OLTP system. Most transactions in this type of system are likely to be very short. You probably will have enough rollback segment space, but you need to make sure that you have enough rollback segments to prevent contention for rollback segment transaction tables. Oracle recommends that you set **MINEXTENTS** to 20, because the dynamic growth of rollback segments is as much of a performance degradation as dynamic growth of data segments. In an OLTP system, you will probably need more rollback segments that are generally smaller in size than those in other systems.

## Decision Support Systems

A DSS holds large volumes of data (usually historical) and is most frequently used for reporting purposes. Generally, decision support applications perform large queries on data that has been loaded from an OLTP system. Managers and other decision makers typically use this information to make strategic business decisions. The goals of a decision support system are speed, accuracy, and availability.

Oracle's Parallel Query option is best utilized in DSSes in which large, intense queries (full-table scans) are performed. Parallel Query is also useful when a large amount of data is being loaded or indexed, as is the case in most decision support systems.

Oracle recommends that you set **DB_BLOCK_SIZE** to the maximum value that your operating system will support. This is especially true for DSSes because this type of application system performs many full-table scans.

Your usage of indexes should be minimal in a decision support system because most data is accessed using full-table scans. If you do use indexes in this type of system, you should use them selectively on a limited number of tables. Bitmapped indexes are especially useful in a DSS in which the column values are of low cardinality. Chapter 4 explains the usage of bitmapped indexes.

You probably won't need as many rollback segments in a DSS, but the segments will need to be larger to support batch transactions and read consistency.

## Hybrid Systems

A hybrid system is a multipurpose configuration that can combine an OLTP system and a DSS. In most cases, data gathered by the OLTP system is fed into the DSS. In this type of environment, both systems could use the same database, but the conflicting goals of the two systems could result in performance problems. To resolve this issue, Oracle recommends that an image of the OLTP database be copied into a second database to be used by the decision support application. Because the data may be copied to the DSS system only once a day, this configuration could possibly compromise the DSS's goal of accuracy. However, the resolution of performance issues might be worth the tradeoff.

# Multithreaded Server

Oracle provides a multithreaded server (MTS) architecture to allow for environments in which the user load might exceed available memory. MTS allows multiple users to share a single connection process to the database. Generally, Oracle recommends that MTS not be used until the user load exceeds 150 concurrent users. However, many experts agree that MTS can improve performance on systems with limited memory with as few as 50 to 100 concurrent users.

In MTS environments, the DBA must configure the initial number and the maximum number of dispatcher and server processes for the instances. The configuration of MTS is accomplished using the MTS initialization parameters. Table 3.12 describes these parameters.

| Table 3.12 The major MTS initialization parameters. | | |
|---|---|---|
| **Parameter** | **Value** | **Description** |
| mts_dispatchers | "TCP, 10" | Sets up the minimum number of dispatchers for the specified protocol. |
| mts_max_dispatchers | 20 | Sets the maximum number of dispatchers for all protocols. |
| mts_servers | 10 | Sets the minimum number of servers. |
| mts_max_servers | 300 | Sets the maximum number of servers. |
| mts_service | ORCNETP1 | Names service (usually the same as SID). |
| mts_listener_address | "(ADDRESS= (PROTOCOL= TCP) (HOST=90.11. 244.157) (PORT=1521))" | Sets address information for listeners; one address set per protocol is required. |

When using MTS, servers and dispatchers are automatically brought online to their preset maximum counts, as needed, to service the user load. However, if you find that you have underestimated the number of servers or dispatchers that you need, you can use the **ALTER SYSTEM** command to temporarily increase the values of **MTS_MAX_DISPATCHERS** and **MTS_MAX_ SERVERS** until you can reset their values in the initialization file and restart the database. If the values of **MTS_MAX_SERVERS** and **MTS_MAX_ DISPATCHERS** are reset, Oracle will bring new dispatchers or servers online, as needed, to service new user connections. It should be obvious that the basis for determining how many shared servers will be needed on your system depends solely on the expected number of concurrent processes.

Several files must be configured on your system for MTS to work properly. The initialization file parameters have already been discussed, but two other key files must be set up: tnsnames.ora and listener.ora. The tnsnames.ora file must be set up with the proper instance names and address data for your system because MTS uses SQL*Net for access control. The listener.ora file must contain the proper addresses, which must match the entries for the **MTS_LISTENER_ADDRESS** parameters in the initialization file. If the address values in the initialization file for MTS do not match the entries in the listener.ora file, users will receive dedicated rather than shared connections.

One note of caution about MTS. Because it forces some sorting activity to be done in the shared pool area (specifically, the UGA section that's added for MTS systems), you will need to increase the shared pool to accommodate the additional memory requirements for MTS systems.

# Practice Questions

## Question 1

> You have run the UTLBSTAT/UTLESTAT utility, and report.txt shows a latch hit ratio of 0.99. What does this value indicate about latch activity for the database?
>
> ○ a.  Latch contention is high.
>
> ○ b.  Latch contention is at normal levels.
>
> ○ c.  The value is not accurate, and report.txt should be regenerated.

The correct answer is b. The latch hit ratio for this database is 99 percent, which is an acceptable level. Your goal for the latch contention hit ratio should be at least 98 percent. Anything less could indicate potential latch contention problems.

## Question 2

> A mail order system has a DML-intensive order entry system. Which type of system is this?
>
> ○ a.  Data warehouse
>
> ○ b.  DSS
>
> ○ c.  Hybrid
>
> ○ d.  OLTP

The correct answer is d. A characteristic of an OLTP system is that it performs frequent DML operations, such as **INSERT, UPDATE,** and **DELETE.** A data warehouse system does not change very often, hence no DML. Therefore, answer a is incorrect. A DSS stores large volumes of data that's most frequently used for reporting (**SELECT**) purposes. Therefore, answer b is incorrect. A hybrid system is a combination of an OLTP and a DSS system. Therefore, answer c is incorrect.

# Question 3

> To which value should you set the Oracle block size when creating a database?
>
> ○ a.  2K
>
> ○ b.  4K
>
> ○ c.  32K
>
> ○ d.  Maximum value allowed by the operating system

The correct answer is d. Oracle recommends that you set your block size to the maximum value allowed by the operating system. This is especially true for decision support systems (DSSes), which perform frequent full-table scans. Therefore, answers a, b, and c are incorrect.

# Question 4

> Which statistics are obtained when UTLBSTAT.SQL is executed?
>
> ○ a.  Beginning database statistics for that point in time
>
> ○ b.  Ending database statistics for that point in time
>
> ○ c.  Beginning database statistics at startup
>
> ○ d.  Ending database statistics at startup

The correct answer is a. The letter *B* in UTLBSTAT indicates *beginning* statistics. The letter *E* in UTLESTAT indicates *ending* statistics. Therefore, answers b and d are incorrect. UTLBSTAT creates and populates a set of tables with database statistics beginning at the time that UTLBSTAT was submitted. Therefore, answer c is incorrect. Database statistics are continually gathered until UTLESTAT is submitted, at which time the gathering of these statistics is halted and the report.txt file generated.

# Question 5

In which file can you find information about database events?

○ a.  event.log

○ b.  alert.log

○ c.  alert.trc

○ d.  error.log

The correct answer is b. The alert log file stores information about all major database events within the database. It's located in the destination specified in the **BACKGROUND_DUMP_DEST** parameter of the database initialization file. The event.log, alert.trc, and error.log files are not default files within the Oracle system. Therefore, answers a, c, and d are incorrect.

# Question 6

Performance has degraded significantly on your system, and you discover that paging and swapping is occurring. What is a possible cause of this problem?

○ a.  The SGA is too small.

○ b.  The PGA is too large.

○ c.  The SGA is too large.

○ d.  The PGA is too small.

The correct answer is c. If paging and swapping are occurring on the system, the SGA might be too large. This could cause the operating system to temporarily swap all or portions of the SGA out of main memory to satisfy other memory requirements. Answers b and d are incorrect because the PGA's size is fixed and operating-system specific.

# Question 7

Which component of Oracle8 protects access to internal structures?

- ○ a.  Transaction locking
- ○ b.  Latches
- ○ c.  Locks
- ○ d.  Roles
- ○ e.  Privileges

The correct answer is b. Latches protect access to internal structures, such as the library cache, buffer cache, and log buffer. When a process needs to make a change to one of these structures, it must first acquire a latch. Transaction locking refers to locks placed on objects like tables or rows. Therefore, answer a is incorrect. Locks are used for database objects, not internal structures. Therefore, answer c is incorrect. Roles and privileges are used for overall access restriction to database objects. Therefore, answers d and e are incorrect.

# Question 8

Which type of system uses a combination of OLTP and DSS for the same instance?

- ○ a.  OLTP
- ○ b.  DSS
- ○ c.  Client/server
- ○ d.  Hybrid

The correct answer is d. A hybrid system is a combination of an online transaction processing (OLTP) system and a decision support system (DSS), and it might require special configurations to meet the performance needs of both types of systems.

# Question 9

Data is collected by the Oracle Expert in which of the following categories? [Choose three]

- ❑ a. User
- ❑ b. Process
- ❑ c. Instance
- ❑ d. Structure
- ❑ e. Application

The correct answers are c, d, and e. User and process are not data categories collected by Oracle Expert. Therefore, answers a and b are incorrect.

# Question 10

Why would you want to modify a default Oracle Expert rule?

- ○ a. To modify a recommendation
- ○ b. To override a recommendation
- ○ c. To modify an analysis while it's running
- ○ d. To modify an analysis after it's complete

The correct answer is b. In order to generate a new recommendation and its accompanying implementation files, the rule needs to be modified and the analysis rerun. Answer a is incorrect because modifying the recommendation has no effect on the implementation file. Answers c and d are incorrect because these tasks can't be done.

# Question 11

Which information is generated by UTLESTAT.SQL?

○ a. Ending database statistics

○ b. Beginning database statistics

○ c. The difference between starting and ending database statistics

The correct answer is c. This question needs to be read carefully. UTLE-STAT.SQL does generate ending database statistics, but the question asks what *information* is generated by UTLESTAT.SQL. Therefore, answer a is incorrect. UTLBSTAT, not UTLESTAT, generates the beginning database statistics. Therefore, answer b is incorrect.

# Need To Know More?

 Aronoff, Eyal, Kevin Loney, and Noorali Sonawalla. *Oracle8 Advanced Tuning and Administration*. Oracle Press, 1998. ISBN 0-07882-534-2.

 Ault, Michael R. *Oracle8 Black Book*. The Coriolis Group, 1998. ISBN 1-57610-187-8.

 Ault, Michael R. *Oracle8i Administration and Management*. Wiley Computer Publishing, 1999. ISBN 0-471-35453-8.

 Corey, Michael, Michael Abbey, and Daniel J. Dechichio, Jr. *Oracle8 Tuning*. Oracle Press, 1997. ISBN 0-07882-390-0.

 The first place to go for more information is the *Oracle8 Tuning Manual* and the *Oracle8 Server Reference Manual*.

# SQL Tuning

**Terms you'll need to understand:**

√ Explain Plan

√ Autotrace

√ SQL*Trace

√ TKPROF

√ **DBMS_APPLICATION_INFO**

√ Optimizer

√ Hints

**Techniques you'll need to master:**

√ Creating the **PLAN_TABLE** and using Explain Plan

√ Using SQL*Trace and TKPROF

√ Understanding the basics of the **DBMS_APPLICATION_INFO** package

√ Understanding how to use indexes

√ Using the optimizer and hints

Your biggest return in the area of increasing performance is tuning your application code, and tuning your application code means tuning the SQL that's executed from those applications. Before you begin tuning the Oracle database, you should tune your applications. Regardless of how well you tune your database, poorly written SQL statements will result in poor performance. This chapter explains how to use autotrace, Explain Plan, SQL*Trace, and TKPROF for tuning your SQL statements. This will lead to a discussion of how indexes can be used to increase the performance of your SQL as well as how they can result in very poor SQL performance. The chapter concludes with a discussion of using the optimizer and hints to tune your applications further.

# Statement Tuning

Tuning every SQL statement in an application is unrealistic. You need to identify and tune individual SQL statements that are creating problems. Before tuning these statements, you need to understand how Oracle is executing your SQL. Oracle provides several utilities to help you understand the methods it is using to execute your code. Once you know how Oracle is executing your SQL statements, you can look at rewriting the code to improve performance.

The following are some of the most common problems encountered in poorly performing SQL statements:

➤ The optimizer is unable to use an index.

➤ The use of **CONNECT BY** without an index on the **CONNECT BY** and **START WITH** columns.

➤ The **GROUP** functions, especially with the use of the **HAVING** clause.

➤ The use of a complex view.

➤ The use of the **DISTINCT** keyword, which causes sorting.

➤ Queries that are written differently and do not take advantage of bind variables.

The first step to performance tuning the application is to determine the SQL statement or statements that are using the most resources and resulting in the slowest response time. The second step is to obtain information on the execution plan that Oracle is using for the SQL statement and statistical information on the resources used by the SQL statement. Explain Plan is used to obtain the execution plan. SQL*Trace creates a trace file of statistical and performance information that's then formatted with TKPROF.

# Explain Plan

Explain Plan is a command that provides information on how the Oracle database is optimizing and executing your SQL statements. A row for each step in the execution plan is placed into a user-specified table or into the **PLAN_ TABLE**. To use Explain Plan, you must create the **PLAN_TABLE** or a table with the equivalent columns. The **PLAN_TABLE** is created by running the utlxplan.sql script located in the $ORACLE_HOME/rdbms/admin directory (the name of this script can vary, depending on the operating system). Table 4.1 shows the columns in the **PLAN_TABLE**.

| Table 4.1    Description of the PLAN_TABLE. | |
|---|---|
| **Column** | **Definition** |
| statement_id | The identifier assigned at the time the **EXPLAIN PLAN** statement is issued (optional). |
| timestamp | The date and time that the **EXPLAIN PLAN** statement was issued. |
| remarks | Comments that can be added to the explain plan by the user. |
| operation | The actual operation performed at this step. |
| options | Options used for the execution of the statement. |
| object_node | Database link used, if any. |
| object_owner | Owner of the object referenced. |
| object_name | Name of the object referenced. |
| object_instance | Position of the object in the SQL statement. |
| object_type | Description of the type of object referenced. |
| optimizer | The current mode of the optimizer. |
| search_columns | Not currently used but might be in the future. |
| id | The ID number assigned by Oracle to this step in the plan. |
| parent_id | The parent statement for this step of the execution plan. |
| position | The order in which this step was performed. (If the cost-based optimizer (CBO) is being used, this value in the first line of the plan represents the cost assigned to this statement; if the rule-based optimizer is being used, this value will be null in the first line of the plan.) |
| cost | The cost of the execution step. |

*(continued)*

| Table 4.1 Description of the PLAN_TABLE (continued). | |
|---|---|
| **Column** | **Definition** |
| cardinality | The number of rows returned by the current operation (estimated by the CBO). |
| bytes | The number of bytes returned by the current operation. |
| other_tag | Describes the function of the SQL text in the **OTHER** column. Values for **OTHER_TAG** are: |
| | **SERIAL**—The SQL is the text of a locally executed, serial query plan. Currently, SQL is not loaded in **OTHER** for this case. |
| | **SERIAL_FROM_REMOTE**—The SQL text shown in the **OTHER** column will be executed at a remote site. |
| | **PARALLEL_COMBINED_WITH_PARENT**—The parent of this operation is a data flow operator (DFO) that performs both operations in the parallel execution plan. |
| | **PARALLEL_COMBINED_WITH_CHILD**—The child of this operation is a DFO that performs both operations in the parallel execution plan. |
| | **PARALLEL_TO_SERIAL**—The SQL text shown in the **OTHER** column is the top-level of the parallel plan. |
| | **PARALLEL_TO_PARALLEL**—The SQL text shown in the **OTHER** column is executed and output in parallel. |
| | **PARALLEL_FROM_SERIAL**—This operation consumes data from a serial operation and outputs it in parallel. |
| partition_start | The start partition of a range of accessed partitions. |
| partition_stop | The stop partition of a range of accessed partitions. |
| partition_id | The step that has computed the pair of values of the **PARTITION_START** and **PARTITION_STOP** columns. |
| other | Holds SQL text for remote cursors and parallel-execution slaves. |
| distribution | The distribution method. |

To populate the **PLAN_TABLE** with the steps of the execution plan, you must execute the syntax shown in Figure 4.1.

The **SET STATEMENT_ID** specifies the statement ID you want for that execution plan in the **PLAN_TABLE**. The use of a statement ID allows several statements to be placed into the same **PLAN_TABLE**. The **INTO** clause allows you to place the information into a table other than the **PLAN_TABLE**.

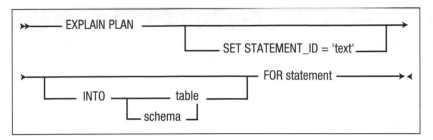

**Figure 4.1**    The syntax for the **EXPLAIN PLAN** command.

If no other table is specified with the **INTO** clause, Oracle will assume that the information should be placed in the **PLAN_TABLE**. The statement following the **FOR** keyword is the statement for which you would like to have Oracle generate an execution plan.

The **EXPLAIN PLAN** command does not actually execute the statement. This is helpful when you want to obtain information on a long-running SQL statement and do not want to wait for the statement to execute. To use Explain Plan, follow these steps:

1. Execute the statement to fill in the **PLAN_TABLE**:

```
EXPLAIN PLAN SET statement_id = 'EMPLOYEE_STATE'
FOR
SELECT last_name, first_name state.name
FROM employee, state
WHERE employee.state_code = state.code
AND state.code = 'VA';
```

2. Execute a query against the **PLAN_TABLE** to obtain the execution plan:

```
SELECT  id, parent_id,
LPAD(' ',2*level)||operation  access_plan
, options, object_name
FROM plan_table WHERE statement_id = 'EMPLOYEE_STATE'
CONNECT BY prior id = parent_id START WITH id = 0;
```

3. Review the optimization plan. Table 4.2 shows the resulting optimization plan.

4. Create an index on the **state_code** column in the employee table:

```
CREATE INDEX employee_state ON employee(state_code);
```

| ID | PARENT_ID | ACCESS_PLAN | Options | OBJECT_NAME |
|----|-----------|-------------|---------|-------------|
| **Table 4.2** | **The initial optimization plan.** | | | |
| 0 | | SELECT STATEMENT | | |
| 1 | 0 | MERGE JOIN | | |
| 2 | 1 | SORT | | JOIN |
| 3 | 2 | TABLE ACCESS | FULL | STATE |
| 4 | 1 | SORT | | JOIN |
| 5 | 4 | TABLE ACCESS | FULL | EMPLOYEE |

5. Truncate the **PLAN_TABLE** or delete the rows related to that access plan:

```
TRUNCATE TABLE PLAN_TABLE;
```

or

```
DELETE FROM PLAN_TABLE WHERE statement_id = 'EMPLOYEE_STATE';
```

*Note: You can also use a different statement ID for the second execution plan.*

6. Execute the statement to fill in the **PLAN_TABLE** with the new execution plan:

```
EXPLAIN PLAN SET statement_id = 'EMPLOYEE_STATE'
FOR
SELECT last_name, first_name, state.name
FROM employee, state
WHERE employee.state_code = state.code
AND state.code = 'VA';
```

7. Execute a query against the **PLAN_TABLE** to obtain the new execution plan:

```
SELECT  id, parent_id,
LPAD(' ',2*level)||operation  access_plan
, options, object_name
FROM plan_table WHERE statement_id = 'EMPLOYEE_STATE'
CONNECT BY prior id = parent_id START WITH id = 0;
```

8. Review the new optimization plan. Table 4.3 shows the new optimization plan.

| ID | PARENT_ID | ACCESS_PLAN | Options | OBJECT_NAME |
|---|---|---|---|---|
| **Table 4.3   New optimization plan.** | | | | |
| 0 | | SELECT STATEMENT | | |
| 1 | 0 | NESTED LOOPS | | |
| 2 | 1 | TABLE ACCESS | FULL | STATE |
| 3 | 1 | TABLE ACCESS | BY ROWID | EMPLOYEE |
| 4 | 3 | INDEX | RANGE SCAN | EMPLOYEE_ STATE |

The **PLAN_TABLE** is always read from the bottom up and inside out. The second execution plan involves performing actions in the following order:

➤ An index range scan using the **employee_state** index

➤ A table access by row ID of the **employee** table

➤ A full-table scan of the **state** table

➤ A nested loop operation

➤ The **SELECT** statement

The two different Explain Plans demonstrate the results of adding an index on a column that's used to join two tables (a foreign key column). The initial query included two full-table scans and a sort/merge join. After the index is added, a range scan on the index allowed row ID access on the employee table, reduced the full-table scans to one, and used a nested loop access instead of a sort/merge join. Nested loops are much faster than sort/merge joins. In addition, if the **employee** table is very large, a full-table scan should be avoided. The changes in the access path should improve performance for this SQL statement.

## Autotrace

Another way to obtain and display information on the execution plan generated for SQL statements is to use **SET AUTOTRACE ON** within SQL*Plus. Autotrace will place information on the execution plan steps into the **PLAN_TABLE** after execution of each statement. After each SQL statement is executed, information from the **PLAN_TABLE** is displayed along with statistical information on the statement executed. The information in the **PLAN_TABLE** is then deleted.

The advantages to using autotrace are:

➤ The **PLAN_TABLE** is cleaned up after the information is displayed.

➤ The information is displayed automatically.

The disadvantage to using autotrace is that it will execute each statement before displaying the information. Listing 4.1 provides an example of using the autotrace utility. After you've completed your performance tuning and use of the autotrace utility, you can turn autotrace off with **SET AUTOTRACE OFF**. If you fail to turn autotrace off, it will remain in effect until you exit and end your session.

### Listing 4.1 An example of using autotrace.

```
SET AUTOTRACE ON;

SELECT last_name, first_name state.name   state
FROM scott.employee, scott.state
WHERE employee.state_code = state.code
AND state.code = 'VA';


last_name               first_name            state
-------------------     -------------------   --------------------
CANE                    JOHN                  Virginia
ROLLAND                 BILL                  Virginia
CLINTON                 JAKE                  Virginia
ANDERSON                WAYNE                 Virginia


Execution Plan
----------------------------------------------------------------
0       SELECT STATEMENT Optimizer=CHOOSE (Cost=2 Card=2 Bytes=84)
1    0    NESTED LOOPS (Cost=2 Card=2 Bytes=84)
2    1      TABLE ACCESS (FULL) OF 'STATE' (Cost=1 Card=1 Bytes=15)
3    1      TABLE ACCESS (BY ROWID) OF 'EMPLOYEE'
4    3        INDEX (RANGE SCAN) OF 'EMPLOYEE_STATE' (NON-UNIQUE)

Statistics
----------------------------------------------------------------
        0   recursive calls
        2   db block gets
        7   consistent gets
        0   physical reads
        0   redo size
      347   bytes sent via SQL*Net to client
      406   bytes received via SQL*Net from client
        3   SQL*Net roundtrips to/from client
```

```
0  sorts (memory)
0  sorts (disk)
4  rows processed
```

```
SET AUTOTRACE OFF;
```

# SQL*Trace

SQL*Trace is used to generate statistics into a trace file, which is then formatted using TKPROF. SQL*Trace can be used to identify SQL statements that are consuming the most resources, that are consuming the most resources per row, and that are executing the most often. To use SQL*Trace, you must first set **TIMED_STATISTICS=TRUE** in your database initialization parameter file and restart the database to enable SQL tracing. The default for **TIMED_STATISTICS** is FALSE. This parameter can be changed dynamically with an **ALTER SYSTEM SET TIMED_STATISTICS=TRUE** statement. Statistics will be timed to 1/100th of a second. SQL*Trace will use the **MAX_DUMP_FILE_SIZE** (default 500 blocks) and the **USER_DUMP_DEST** parameters from the database parameter file. These parameters set the maximum size and the location of the trace file, respectively.

SQL*Trace can be performed for an instance or for a session. Because tracing will affect performance, you should set tracing at the session level. To perform SQL*Trace for an instance, you must set **SQL_TRACE=TRUE** in the database initialization parameter file. Setting **SQL_TRACE** at the instance level enables tracing for all users. To enable tracing for a session, you can execute the **DBMS_SESSION.SET_SQL_TRACE** package or use the **ALTER SESSION** command.

You can use either of the following commands to enable session-level tracing:

```
ALTER SESSION SET SQL_TRACE=TRUE;
```

or

```
EXECUTE SYS.DBMS_SESSION.SET_SQL_TRACE(TRUE);
```

You can disable tracing for a session by exiting SQL*Trace, or you can use either of the following commands:

```
ALTER SESSION SET SQL_TRACE=FALSE;
```

or

```
EXECUTE SYS.DBMS_SESSION.SET_SQL_TRACE(FALSE);
```

You can use **DBMS_SYSTEM.SET_SQL_TRACE_IN_SESSION** to start tracing for another user's session. This requires the session ID (the value of the **SID** column in the **V$SESSION** table), the serial ID (the **SERIAL#** column in the **V$SESSION** table), and either **TRUE** or **FALSE**. The following is an example of the code that can be used to obtain information on another user's session:

```
BEGIN
      SYS.DBMS_SYSTEM.SET_SQL_TRACE_IN_SESSION(10,2345,TRUE);
END;
```

After the user has completed executing the SQL statements, you should set **SQL_TRACE** to **FALSE** for that user. The following example shows how to turn off SQL*Trace for another user:

```
BEGIN
      SYS.DBMS_SYSTEM.SET_SQL_TRACE_IN_SESSION(10,2345,FALSE);
END;
```

# TKPROF

TKPROF is used to generate a readable report on the basis of the statistical information gathered with SQL*Trace.

The following process is used to obtain performance data using SQL*Trace and TKPROF:

1. Set the **TIMED_STATISTICS** initialization parameter to **TRUE**.

2. Turn on SQL*Trace.

3. Execute the application SQL statements.

4. Turn off SQL*Trace.

5. Execute TKPROF to format the trace information.

6. Review the results.

The statistical information provided by the TKPROF report is listed in Table 4.4. Statistical information is provided for the following stages:

➤ Parse

➤ Execute

➤ Fetch

| Column | Definition |
|--------|------------|
| **Table 4.4** | **Statistical information provided by TKPROF.** |
| **count** | Number of times the statement was parsed or executed; the number of fetch calls issued. |
| **CPU** | Total CPU used in seconds; if this is found in the shared pool, it's 0. |
| **elapsed** | Total seconds in elapsed time. |
| **disk** | Total physical data blocks read from database files; if the blocks are buffered, this will be very low. |
| **query** | Total number of logical buffers retrieved in consistent mode; usually used for **SELECT** statements. |
| **current** | Total number of logical buffers retrieved in current mode; usually used for Data Manipulation Language (DML) statements. |
| **rows** | Total number of rows processed, excluding rows processed by a subquery. This is in the fetch phase for **SELECT** statements and in the execute phase for DML statements. |

The **tkprof** command is executed at the command line, not within SQL*Plus. Here's the syntax for this command:

```
tkprof   infile=filename   outfile=filename
  [sort=option (, option)] [print=integer] [explain=user/password]
  [table=schema.tablename] [sys=NO] [record=filename]
  [insert=filename]
```

**INFILE** is the name of the trace file on which the TKPROF utility will be executed. **OUTFILE** is the name of the file into which the report will be placed. The **SORT** option allows the information to be sorted by the options specified by the user before being placed into **OUTFILE**. Table 4.5 lists the options that can be used for sorting the SQL Trace file. The **PRINT** option allows the user to limit the number of SQL statements to include in the file. If the **PRINT** option is omitted, all SQL statements are included. The **EXPLAIN** option executes an Explain Plan for statements issued by the specified user. The **TABLE** option allows you to specify a table for use by TKPROF. If you specify **TABLE** but do not use **EXPLAIN**, TKPROF will ignore this option. **SYS=NO** will ignore recursive SQL statements executed as **SYS**. The **RECORD** option will record nonrecursive statements into the trace file for use later in replaying the recorded events. The **INSERT** option creates an SQL script that can be executed to create a table and insert statistics into that table for each SQL statement traced.

| Table 4.5 | Sort options for TKPROF. |
|-----------|--------------------------|
| **Option** | **Definition** |
| PRSCNT | Number of times parsed |
| PRSCPU | CPU time spent parsing |
| PRSELA | Elapsed time spent parsing |
| PRSDSK | Number of physical reads from disk during parse |
| PRSQRY | Number of consistent mode block reads during parse |
| PRSCU | Number of current mode block reads during parse |
| PRSMIS | Number of library cache misses during parse |
| EXECNT | Number of executes |
| EXECPU | CPU time spent executing |
| EXEELA | Elapsed time spent executing |
| EXEDSK | Number of physical reads from disk during execute |
| EXEQRY | Number of consistent mode block reads during execute |
| EXECU | Number of current mode block reads during execute |
| EXEROW | Number of rows processed during execute |
| EXEMIS | Number of library cache misses during execute |
| FCHCNT | Number of fetches |
| FCHCPU | CPU time spent fetching |
| FCHELA | Elapsed time spent fetching |
| FCHDSK | Number of physical reads from disk during fetch |
| FCHQRY | Number of consistent mode block reads during fetch |
| FCHCU | Number of current mode block reads during fetch |
| FCHROW | Number of rows fetched |

Listing 4.2 shows sample output from TKPROF using the following command:

```
tkprof ifile=ora_100334.trc outfile=tkprof_rpt explain=scott/tiger
```

Note that this command does not include **SYS=NO**, which would ignore the recursive SQL statements. In addition, no table was given for use in obtaining the optimizer plan. When no table is specified, TKPROF will create a table named **PROF$PLAN_TABLE**, use this table for the optimizer plan information, and then drop the table. You should also remember that the Explain

Plan results are obtained when the TKPROF utility is executed. If any changes have been made to the objects, such as adding an index, the optimizer access plan might use the new index and might not reflect the plan that was used during the SQL*Trace. Therefore, if you want to include the optimizer plan, you should execute the TKPROF utility immediately after you've finished gathering your SQL*Trace statistics.

## Listing 4.2    An example of output from a TKPROF report.

```
TKPROF: Release 8.0.5.0.0 - Production on Sun Feb 20 8:31:27 2000
(c) Copyright 1998 Oracle Corporation.  All rights reserved.
Trace file: ora_100334.trc
Sort options: default
********************************************************************
count     = number of times OCI procedure was executed
cpu       = cpu time in seconds executing
elapsed   = elapsed time in seconds executing
disk      = number of physical reads of buffers from disk
query     = number of buffers gotten for consistent read
current   = number of buffers gotten in current mode (usually
                                                      for update)
rows      = number of rows processed by the fetch or execute call
********************************************************************
alter session set sql_trace=true
```

| call | count | cpu | elapsed | disk | query | current | rows |
|------|-------|------|---------|------|-------|---------|------|
| Parse | 0 | 0.00 | 0.00 | 0 | 0 | 0 | 0 |
| Execute | 1 | 0.02 | 0.06 | 0 | 0 | 0 | 0 |
| Fetch | 0 | 0.00 | 0.00 | 0 | 0 | 0 | 0 |
| total | 1 | 0.02 | 0.06 | 0 | 0 | 0 | 0 |

```
Misses in library cache during parse: 0
Misses in library cache during execute: 1
Optimizer goal: CHOOSE
Parsing user id: 48  (SCOTT)
********************************************************************
SELECT LAST_NAME, FIRST_NAME, STATE.NAME
FROM EMPLOYEE, STATE
WHERE EMPLOYEE.STATE_CODE = STATE.CODE
AND STATE.CODE = 'VA'
```

| call | count | cpu | elapsed | disk | query | current | rows |
|------|-------|------|---------|------|-------|---------|------|
| Parse | 7 | 0.02 | 0.06 | 0 | 0 | 0 | 0 |
| Execute | 7 | 0.00 | 0.00 | 0 | 0 | 0 | 0 |
| Fetch | 7 | 0.00 | 0.00 | 0 | 49 | 14 | 28 |
| total | 21 | 0.02 | 0.06 | 0 | 49 | 14 | 28 |

```
Misses in library cache during parse: 1
Optimizer goal: CHOOSE
Parsing user id: 48  (SCOTT)
Rows    Execution Plan
------  -------------------------------------------------------
    0   SELECT STATEMENT   GOAL: CHOOSE
    4    NESTED LOOPS
   51     TABLE ACCESS   GOAL: ANALYZED (FULL) OF 'STATE'
    4     TABLE ACCESS   GOAL: ANALYZED (BY ROWID) OF 'EMPLOYEE'
    5      INDEX   GOAL: ANALYZED (RANGE SCAN) OF 'EMPLOYEE_STATE'
              (NON-UNIQUE)
```

```
********************************************************************
select  *  from  state
call      count    cpu   elapsed   disk   query   current   rows
Parse        1    0.00    0.00      0       0        0        0
Execute      1    0.00    0.00      0       0        0        0
Fetch        4    0.01    0.01      0       4        2       51
------------------------------------------------------------------
total        6    0.01    0.01      0       4        2       51
```
```
Misses in library cache during parse: 1
Optimizer goal: CHOOSE
Parsing user id: 48  (SCOTT)
Rows    Execution Plan
------  -------------------------------------------------------
    0   SELECT STATEMENT   GOAL: CHOOSE
   51    TABLE ACCESS   GOAL: ANALYZED (FULL) OF 'STATE'
```
```
********************************************************************
alter session set sql_trace=false
call      count    cpu   elapsed   disk   query   current   rows
Parse        1    0.00    0.00      0       0        0        0
Execute      1    0.00    0.00      0       0        0        0
Fetch        0    0.00    0.00      0       0        0        0
------------------------------------------------------------------
total        2    0.00    0.00      0       0        0        0
```
```
Misses in library cache during parse: 1
Optimizer goal: CHOOSE
Parsing user id: 48  (SCOTT)
********************************************************************
OVERALL TOTALS FOR ALL NON-RECURSIVE STATEMENTS
call      count    cpu   elapsed   disk   query   current   rows
Parse       13    0.03    0.08      0       0        0        0
Execute     14    0.02    0.06      0       0        0        0
Fetch       15    0.02    0.02      0      63       20       91
------------------------------------------------------------------
total       42    0.07    0.16      0      63       20       91
```

```
Misses in library cache during parse: 4
Misses in library cache during execute: 1
OVERALL TOTALS FOR ALL RECURSIVE STATEMENTS
call      count    cpu    elapsed    disk    query    current    rows
Parse        0     0.00     0.00       0        0          0        0
Execute      0     0.00     0.00       0        0          0        0
Fetch        0     0.00     0.00       0        0          0        0
---------------------------------------------------------------
total        0     0.00     0.00       0        0          0        0
Misses in library cache during parse: 0
   14   user  SQL statements in session.
    0   internal SQL statements in session.
   14   SQL statements in session.
3   statements explained in this session.
*********************************************************************
Trace file: ora_100334.trc
Trace file compatibility: 7.03.02
Sort options: default
        1   session in trace file.
       14   user  SQL statements in trace file.
        0   internal SQL statements in trace file.
       14   SQL statements in trace file.
        7   unique SQL statements in trace file.
3   SQL statements explained using schema:
            SCOTT.prof$PLAN_TABLE
              Default table was used.
              Table was created.
              Table was dropped.
      183   lines in trace file.
```

# The DBMS_APPLICATION_INFO Package

You can track performance and resource usage for application modules with the **DBMS_APPLICATION_INFO** package. To use this package, you need to execute the dmbsapin.sql and prvtapin.plb scripts. These scripts are called by the catproc.sql script, which is usually executed when the database is created. The application module that's to be tracked must register with the database, after which the performance and use of resources can be tracked.

**DBMS_APPLICATION_INFO** contains the following procedures:

➤ **SET_MODULE** (module and action)

➤ **SET_ACTION** (action)

➤ **SET_CLIENT_INFO** (client)

➤ READ_MODULE (module and action)

➤ READ_CLIENT_INFO (action)

The **SET_MODULE** procedure is used to set the name of the module and to store this information in the **V$SQLAREA** table. The **SET_MODULE** procedure can also be used to set the action instead of using the **SET_ACTION** procedure. You should call this procedure when the module starts.

The **SET_ACTION** procedure should be called before each new transaction to set the name of the current action to be traced and to store this information in **V$SQLAREA**. After the procedure executes, **SET_ACTION** should be set to null.

The **SET_CLIENT_INFO** procedure sets the client information. This additional information is stored in **V$SESSION**.

The **READ_MODULE** and **READ_CLIENT_INFO** procedures read information from **V$SESSION** and **V$SQLAREA**. The **READ_MODULE** procedure reads the **SET_ACTION** and **SET_MODULE** information. The **READ_CLIENT_INFO** procedure is used to read the last client information for the session.

 Although the exam section covered in this chapter focuses on the SQL statement itself, you need to have an understanding of the packages and structures used for SQL tuning, as well as the scripts used to create them. In addition to the **DBMS_ APPLICATION_INFO** package and its script, make sure you are familiar with the explain table.

# Indexes

The use of indexes can either improve performance or drastically increase the time necessary for an SQL statement to execute. The correct use of indexes will allow the optimizer to choose an efficient path and avoid unnecessary full-table scans. An index scan will retrieve data on the basis of the value in one or more indexed columns. The index stores the value of the column or columns specified for the index and the row ID for a row in the table. A full-table scan will search every row of the table.

A *composite index* is one that consists of more than one column. The order of the columns in the index is very important. If a column in the **WHERE** clause references the first column in the index, it will be able to use that index. If a column in the **WHERE** clause references only the column in the second position in the index, that index cannot be used. If the **WHERE** clause references columns at the beginning of the index, it is said to reference the leading edge of the index. Composite indexes should be considered when two or more columns are frequently used together in the **WHERE** clause. The first column in the composite index should be the column most frequently referenced in the **WHERE** clause. If all the columns are equally used, consider ordering the columns from the most selective to the least selective.

# Index Usage

The type of work that end users are performing is a key element in determining when to create an index. For applications that are insert, update, and delete intensive, indexes add additional overhead by requiring values to be added and/or changed in the index as well as the table. For applications that are highly query intensive, more indexes are usually required. Many data warehouses are very query intensive during the day and updated with large batch jobs at night. In this hybrid situation, it might be advisable to drop the indexes before executing the batch job and to re-create the indexes after the batch job completes.

When there's no index on a table, Oracle must read every row of the table to determine which rows meet the requirements of the SQL statement. In some cases, a full-table scan is the best way to access a table. A full-table scan is preferable in the following situations:

➤ When tables are small and have very few values.

➤ When SQL statements will change or fetch a large portion of the rows.

An index scan is preferable in the following situations:

➤ When selected rows are uniformly located throughout the blocks associated with the table and the number of rows to be selected is less than 4 percent of the data in the table.

➤ When selected rows are randomly located throughout the blocks associated with the table and the number of rows to be selected is less than 25 percent of the table.

Even if an index is created on a column or columns, the optimizer might not use it. This might be because of the way the SQL statement is written or because the optimizer has determined that the index should not be used. The following conditions will cause the index to be ignored:

➤ The **IS NULL** or **IS NOT NULL** qualifier is used in the **WHERE** clause.

➤ The **NOT IN** or != qualifier is used in the **WHERE** clause.

➤ The **LIKE** qualifier is used in the **WHERE** clause with a pattern match for the initial character (for example, '%pattern').

➤ The **NOT EXISTS** subquery is used.

➤ The index column is modified in some way by a function in the **WHERE** clause.

➤ The **WHERE** clause is based on a nonindexed column or a column that's not the leading edge of an index.

When trying to decide which columns should be indexed, you should consider how the columns are used. Columns used within queries in the following ways are good candidates for indexing:

➤ Columns used in a **WHERE** clause (especially equality queries)

➤ Columns often used to join tables

➤ Columns not frequently modified

## Types Of Indexes

Several types of indexes can be created on columns and tables. The types of indexes are:

➤ Unique

➤ Nonunique

➤ Bitmapped

➤ Hashkey

When you create a unique or primary key constraint on a column or columns, a *unique index* is generated to ensure uniqueness. There is no need to create a separate unique index for columns already used in a unique or a primary key constraint. If you have already created a unique index and later alter the table to add a unique or primary key constraint, the unique index will be used by the unique or primary key constraint if an exact match exists. The referenced columns must be the same and must be in the same order. Rather than creating unique indexes, you should consider creating unique or primary constraints for the indexed column or columns.

A *nonunique index* is an index created on a column or columns that can have multiple rows with the same values.

Both unique and nonunique indexes are usually stored using a B-tree index. Over time, the addition and deletion of data can fragment the B-tree index. The index will grow in width, and SQL code using the index will degrade in performance. Dropping and re-creating or rebuilding the index will resolve this problem.

*Bitmapped indexes* are often used for a decision support system (DSS) environment or for data warehouses. They work best on large tables with values of low cardinality for the bitmapped columns. When bitmapped indexes are used properly, they result in excellent performance and an indexing scheme that requires much less storage space than the traditional B-tree index structure. A bitmap is created for each value with an entry for each row. Bitmapped indexes are especially useful when used in conjunction with other bitmapped indexes. Bitmapped indexes do not work well for columns in which additional values can be used or the values are updated often. The following provides an example of using a bitmapped index. The possible entries and the column values are listed in Table 4.6.

Given the columns and values shown in Table 4.6, the following **SELECT** statement

```
SELECT * FROM employee WHERE email = 'Y' AND gender = 'F';
```

will have the following result set:

```
Result set:<110000100100>
```

Hashkey indexes can be used for a single table or for clustering two tables. In order to use a hashkey index, a column or columns in the table must be designated as the key value. A hash function is applied to the specified key value to determine the hash value. The hash value is then used to determine the location of the row in the table.

| Table 4.6  The columns in a sample bitmapped index. | | |
|---|---|---|
| **Column Name** | **Possible Entries** | **Column Values** |
| email | Y=Has an email address | Y:<111000111100> |
| | N=Does not have an email address | N:<000111000011> |
| gender | F=Female | F:<110011100111> |
| | M=Male | M:<001100011000> |

# Turning Off Index Usage

In some cases, an individual query will execute faster if the index is not used. You can turn the use of the index off for that individual query in several ways. The **WHERE** clause can be altered to invalidate the use of the index by changing the indexed column referenced in the **WHERE** clause. You can concatenate a null string (two single quotes) to a varchar column, add zero to a number column, use a function on the column, or use a hint (discussed later in this chapter). When you're tuning your database for performance, you need to recognize that the index has been invalidated. You should ask yourself whether that was really what the user intended. Here are some examples of how to invalidate the use of an index:

➤ An index will be used, if available:

```
SELECT * FROM department WHERE code = 'ABC';
```

➤ The index will be ignored:

```
SELECT * FROM department WHERE code||''= 'ABC';
```

➤ An index will be used, if available:

```
SELECT * FROM class WHERE number = 30;
```

➤ The index will be ignored:

```
SELECT * FROM class WHERE number+0 = 30;
```

# Optimizer Tuning

Currently, Oracle supports two methods of optimization: rule-based optimizer (RBO) and cost-based optimizer (CBO). Oracle originally started with only an RBO. The CBO was introduced with Oracle7. Eventually, the RBO will no longer be supported by Oracle and only the CBO will be available.

The optimizer mode can be set at the instance, session, and statement levels. To set the optimizer at the instance level, the **OPTIMIZER_MODE** parameter is set to either **CHOOSE** or **RULE** in the database initialization parameter file; the default is **CHOOSE**. The **CHOOSE** option will default to **RULE** unless statistics are found for an object. If statistics are found, the default will change to **COST**. If the **OPTIMIZER_MODE** parameter is set to **RULE**, any statistics will be ignored and rule-based optimization will be performed.

Setting **ALTER SESSION SET OPTIMIZER_GOAL = RULE** or **ALTER SESSION SET OPTIMIZER_GOAL = CHOOSE** will change the optimizer mode used until it's changed again or the user session ends. **ALTER SESSION SET OPTIMIZER_GOAL** can also be set to either **ALL_ROWS** or **FIRST_ROWS**. Setting the optimizer goal to **ALL_ROWS** will optimize the query for the fastest total throughput, returning the entire data set in the fastest time. Setting the optimizer goal to **FIRST_ROWS** will result in a faster return of the initial records. The first record will be returned to the user before the entire data set is returned. These options will use the CBO.

To change the optimizer at the statement level, you can use hints (covered later in this chapter).

Rule-based optimization determines the fastest access path on the basis of the **WHERE** clause. Rule-based optimization has a set of rules, and each rule is assigned a rank. The lowest rank is the fastest method. The RBO ignores the order of the statements in the **WHERE** clause. If an index can be used, the RBO will always use the index, even if a full-table scan would be faster. If your applications are developed under the RBO by developers who understand the use of the optimizer rules, you'll probably find that these applications will perform better using the RBO. Table 4.7 lists some of the general access paths used by the RBO from the lowest rank (fastest) to the highest rank (slowest).

**Table 4.7  Access paths used by the RBO (from fastest to slowest).**

| Access Method | Description |
| --- | --- |
| ROWID | Rows are selected on the basis of the row ID. |
| UNIQUE | All columns for a unique or primary key index are specified in the **WHERE** clause using the equals (=) operator. |
| COMPOSITE KEY | All the columns of a composite index are specified in the **WHERE** clause using the equals (=) operator. |
| NONUNIQUE | The **WHERE** clause includes one or more single-table indexes using the equals (=) operator. |
| RANGE SCAN | The **WHERE** clause includes the column indexed in a single-column index or the leading edge column of a composite index. |
| SORT/MERGE | A sort/merge is used for a join operation. |
| SPECIAL CONDITIONS | The **WHERE** clause uses **MAX** or **MIN**, the statement includes an **ORDER BY** clause, and there's a single-column index, or the leading edge of a composite index can be used (special restrictions might apply). |
| FULL TABLE SCAN | A full-table scan. |

The CBO uses statistics on the tables, indexes, and columns to determine the fastest access path. This information is generated using the **ANALYZE** command. The CBO computes the cost of each possible access path and chooses the access path with the lowest cost. It also takes into consideration the estimated resources (especially the number of logical reads), CPU utilization, and memory requirements for each access path considered. Even if an index is available, the CBO might determine that it would be faster to perform a full-table scan, the actual cost of which depends on the number of multiblock reads required to scan the entire table. The number of blocks that can be read simultaneously is determined by the database initialization parameter file entry for **DB_FILE_MULTIBLOCK_READ_COUNT**.

The CBO relies on statistics obtained using the **ANALYZE** command or the **DBMS_UTILITY.ANALYZE_SCHEMA** package. This package requires that the schema and the method (**COMPUTE** or **ESTIMATE**) be supplied. This package will analyze all the objects owned by the specified schema.

The **ANALYZE** command supports two methods to obtain the statistics: **ESTIMATE** and **COMPUTE**. The **ESTIMATE** method uses a sample of the data to determine the statistical information. The **ESTIMATE** option allows you to specify the amount of data to be analyzed (**SAMPLE**). **SAMPLE** can be either the number of rows to be analyzed or the percent of the object to be analyzed. The **COMPUTE** method provides exact statistics on the object analyzed. The **COMPUTE** option uses all the data of the object being analyzed and requires more system resources to complete. The process of analyzing an index uses much fewer system resources than does the process of analyzing a table.

It is very important that statistics be updated regularly and after large batch loads; otherwise, the CBO will not have the correct statistics and might choose incorrect access paths that negatively affect performance. In addition, the CBO assumes that the operating system has a very low buffer cache hit rate. If you have a single-user system with a large buffer cache, the CBO will perform differently even if the objects have been analyzed.

When a table, index, or cluster is analyzed, information is placed in the data dictionary. You can view this information using the **DBA** views (or the **USER_** equivalents) listed in Table 4.8. Users can access table, column, index, and cluster information for objects they own. In addition, the **ALL_TABLES, ALL_TAB_ COLUMNS**, and **ALL_INDEXES** views provide information on objects that are accessible to the users.

| Table 4.8 Data dictionary views with statistical information. | |
|---|---|
| **Column** | **Definition** |
| **DBA_TABLES** | |
| owner | Table owner. |
| table_name | Table name. |
| tablespace_name | Name of the tablespace containing the table; null for partitioned tables. |
| cluster_name | Name of the cluster, if any, to which the table belongs. |
| iot_name | Name of the index organized table, if any, to which the overflow entry belongs. |
| pct_free | Minimum percentage of free space in a block; null for partitioned tables. |
| pct_used | Minimum percentage of used space in a block; null for partitioned tables. |
| ini_trans | Initial number of transactions; null for partitioned tables. |
| max_trans | Maximum number of transactions; null for partitioned tables. |
| initial_extent | Size of the initial extent in bytes; null for partitioned tables. |
| next_extent | Size of secondary extents in bytes; null for partitioned tables. |
| min_extents | Minimum number of extents allowed in the segment; null for partitioned tables. |
| max_extents | Maximum number of extents allowed in the segment; null for partitioned tables. |
| pct_increase | Percentage increase in extent size; null for partitioned tables. |
| freelists | Number of process free lists allocated to this segment; null for partitioned tables. |
| freelist_groups | Number of free list groups allocated to this segment; null for partitioned tables. |
| logging | Indicates whether logging is enabled (yes or no); null for partitioned tables. |
| backed_up | Specifies whether the table has been backed up since the last modification. |
| num_rows | Number of rows returned by the **ANALYZE** command. |

*(continued)*

**Table 4.8 Data dictionary views with statistical information (continued).**

| Column | Definition |
|---|---|
| **DBA_TABLES** | |
| blocks | The number of blocks below the high-water mark. |
| empty_blocks | The number of empty (never used) data blocks in the table. |
| avg_space | The average available free space in the table. |
| chain_cnt | The number of chained rows in the table. |
| avg_row_len | The average row length, including row overhead. |
| avg_space_ freelist_blocks | The average free space of all blocks on a free list. |
| num_freelist_blocks | The number of blocks on the free list. |
| degree | Number of query servers used for a full-table scan. |
| instances | The number of instances across which the table is to be scanned. |
| cache | Indicates whether the table is to be cached in the buffer cache. |
| table_lock | Indicates whether table locking is enabled or disabled. |
| sample_size | Sample size used in analyzing this table. |
| last_analyzed | Date of the most recent time this table was analyzed. |
| partitioned | Indicates whether this table is partitioned. It's set to yes if the table is partitioned. |
| iot_type | If this is an index-organized table, **iot_type** is **iot** or **iot_overflow**. If this is not an index-organized table, **iot_type** is null. |
| temporary | Indicates whether the table is temporary (**y** or **n**). |
| nested | Indicates if the table is a nested table. |
| buffer_pool | Pool name of the default buffer pool for the appropriate object; null for partitioned tables. |
| row_movement | Indicates whether partitioned row movement is enabled or disabled. |
| global_stats | Indicates whether the statistics are calculated without merging underlying partitions. |
| user_stats | Indicates whether the statistics were entered by the user. |

*(continued)*

| Table 4.8 | Data dictionary views with statistical information (continued). |
|---|---|
| **Column** | **Definition** |
| **DBA_TABLES** | |
| duration | If the object is a temporary table, then the value of **duration** is **SYS$SESSION** or **SYS$TRANSACTION**; otherwise, it's null. |
| skip_corrupt | Indicates whether skip corrupt blocks is enabled or disabled. |
| **DBA_TAB_COLUMNS** | |
| owner | Owner of the table, view, or cluster. |
| table_name | Table, view, or cluster name. |
| column_name | Column name. |
| data_type | Data type of the column. |
| data_type_mod | Data type modifier of the column. |
| data_type_owner | Owner of the data type of the column. |
| data_length | Length of the column in bytes. |
| data_precision | Decimal precision for number data type; binary precision for float data type; null for all other data types. |
| data_scale | Digits to the right of the decimal point in a number. |
| nullable | Does the column allow null values? |
| column_Id | Sequence number of the column as created. |
| default_length | Length of the default value for the column. |
| data_default | Default value for the column. |
| num_distinct, low_value, high_value, density, num_nulls | These columns remain for backward compatibility with Oracle7. This information is now in the **{tabl\|part}_col_statistics** views. |
| num_buckets | The number of buckets in the histogram for the column. |
| last_analyzed | The date of the most recent time this column was analyzed. |
| sample_size | The sample size used in analyzing this column. |
| character_set_name | The name of the character set: **char_cs** or **nchar_cs**. |
| char_col_decl_length | Declaration length of the character type column. |

*(continued)*

## Table 4.8   Data dictionary views with statistical information (continued).

| Column | Definition |
| --- | --- |
| **DBA_TAB_COLUMNS** | |
| global_stats | Indicates whether the statistics were calculated without merging the underlying partitions. |
| user_stats | Indicates whether the statistics were entered by the user. |
| avg_col_len | Average column length in bytes. |
| **DBA_CLUSTERS** | |
| owner | Owner of the cluster. |
| cluster_name | Name of the cluster containing the cluster. |
| tablespace_name | Name of the tablespace containing the cluster. |
| pct_free | Minimum percentage of free space in a block. |
| pct_used | Minimum percentage of used space in a block. |
| key_size | Estimated size of the cluster key plus associated rows. |
| ini_trans | Initial number of transactions. |
| initial_extent | Size of the initial extent in bytes. |
| next_extent | Size of secondary extents in bytes. |
| min_extents | Minimum number of extents allowed in the segment. |
| max_extents | Maximum number of extents allowed in the segment. |
| pct_increase | Percentage increase in extent size. |
| freelist_groups | Number of free list groups allocated to this segment. |
| avg_blocks_per_key | Average number of blocks containing rows with a given cluster key. |
| cluster_type | Type of cluster: B-tree index or hash. |
| function | If a hash cluster, the value is the hash function. |
| hashkeys | If a hash cluster, the value is the number of hash keys (hash buckets). |
| degree | The number of threads per instance for scanning the table. |
| instances | The number of instances across which the table is to be scanned. |
| cache | Whether the table is to be cached in the buffer cache. |

*(continued)*

| Table 4.8 | Data dictionary views with statistical information (continued). |
|---|---|
| **Column** | **Definition** |
| **DBA_CLUSTERS** | |
| **buffer_pool** | Name of the default buffer pool for the appropriate object. |
| **single_table** | This is **y** if the cluster is single table; **n** if not. |
| **max_trans** | Maximum number of transactions. |

# Hint Usage

The application developer and end users know more about the data and how it is used than the optimizer does. Oracle provides a method known as *hints* to enable you to tell the optimizer the method to use for the SQL statement. Oracle recommends that hints not be used as the main method of controlling the optimization for SQL statements. Instead, the SQL statement should be appropriately rewritten for better performance.

An SQL statement can have only one comment containing hints. The hint must be placed after the **SELECT, UPDATE,** or **DELETE** command in the SQL statement. It should be preceded by /*+ and followed by */. An alternate approach is to precede the hint with --+. If multiple hints are used, they must be separated by spaces. Figure 4.2 shows the syntax for a hint.

If hints are incorrectly specified, Oracle will treat the hints as comments and will ignore them during SQL statement optimization. You will not receive an error message. If multiple hints exist, Oracle will ignore those with syntax errors but will use those that are correctly included in the statement. If any of the hints provide conflicting optimization requests, Oracle will not choose between them, and conflicting hints will be ignored.

Hints are categorized as follows:

➤ Optimization mode and goals

➤ Access methods

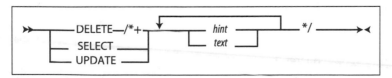

**Figure 4.2**  Syntax diagram for hints.

➤ Join operations

➤ Parallel query execution

The four types of hints for optimization mode and goals are:

➤ **CHOOSE**

➤ **RULE**

➤ **ALL_ROWS**

➤ **FIRST_ROWS**

The **CHOOSE** and **RULE** hints specify whether the CBO or the RBO should be used. Correctly specified hints will override the optimizer mode specified. If an optimization approach is specified, that approach will be used regardless of the initialization parameter setting for **OPTIMIZER_MODE** or the session setting for **OPTIMIZER_GOAL**. If statistics are present for even one table and the hint specifies **CHOOSE**, the optimizer will use the CBO. If no statistics are available, the optimizer will use the RBO. The use of the **RULE** hint will cause the optimizer to ignore any other hints specified.

Both the **ALL_ROWS** and the **FIRST_ROWS** hints use the CBO. If no statistics are available, the optimizer will use whatever storage information is available. The **ANALYZE** command should be used to provide statistics before using either the **ALL_ROWS** or the **FIRST_ROWS** hint. If a hint specifying an access path or join operation is also specified, it will be given precedence over the **ALL_ROWS** and **FIRST_ROWS** hints.

The **ALL_ROWS** hint concentrates on the best throughput with the minimum total resource consumption. **FIRST_ROWS** optimizes with the goal of the best response time and the minimum resource usage necessary to return the first row. The **FIRST_ROWS** hint will be ignored for **DELETE** and **UPDATE** statements. Because the statements in the following list require that all rows be accessed before any results are returned, the **FIRST_ROWS** hint will be ignored if the SQL statement contains:

➤ Set operators (**UNION, UNION ALL, INTERSECT**, and **MINUS**)

➤ The **GROUP BY** clause

➤ The **FOR UPDATE** clause

➤ Group functions

➤ The **DISTINCT** operator

If the described access method requires an index that does not exist, the hint will be ignored. The table must be specified in the hint the same as it is in the SQL statement. If an alias is used for the table, the table specified in the hint must use the table alias instead of the table name. You cannot use the schema name for the table, even if the table is fully qualified with the schema name in the **FROM** clause. Table 4.9 lists the hints that can be used for specification of the access method.

The syntax for the **FULL** hint is:

FULL(*table*)

The syntax for the **ROWID** hint is:

ROWID(*table*)

The syntax for the **CLUSTER** hint is:

CLUSTER(*table*)

The syntax for the **HASH** hint is:

HASH(*table*)

| Table 4.9 | Table access method hints. |
|-----------|---------------------------|
| **Hint** | **Description** |
| **FULL** | Full-table scan. |
| **ROWID** | Full-table scan using row ID. |
| **CLUSTER** | Cluster scan. |
| **HASH** | Hash scan. |
| **INDEX** | Specifies the index to be used. |
| **INDEX ASC** | Specifies the index to be used. If applicable, it will perform range scan of the specified index in ascending order; this is equivalent to the **INDEX** hint (at this time). |
| **INDEX_DESC** | Specifies the index to be used. If applicable, it will perform a range scan of the specified index in descending order; useful only for single-table SQL statements. |
| **AND_EQUAL** | Merges the scans on several single-column indexes. |
| **USE_CONCAT** | Changes the **OR** conditions in a **WHERE** clause into **UNION ALL** operations. |

The syntax for the **INDEX** hint is shown in Figure 4.3.

If the **INDEX** hint specifies more than one index, the optimizer will use one or all of the specified indexes and will ignore any other indexes. If this hint does not include a specific index, the optimizer will choose which index to use.

The syntax for the **INDEX_ASC** hint is shown in Figure 4.4, the syntax for the **INDEX_DESC** hint is shown in Figure 4.5, and the syntax for the **AND_EQUAL** hint is shown in Figure 4.6.

Hints can be used to specify the order in which join operations are performed. Table 4.10 describes the join hints.

The syntax for the **USE_NL** hint is shown in Figure 4.7, the syntax for the **USE_HASH** hint is shown in Figure 4.8, and the syntax for the **USE_MERGE** hint is shown in Figure 4.9.

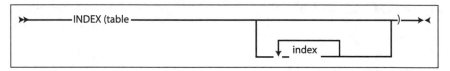

**Figure 4.3**   The syntax for the **INDEX** hint.

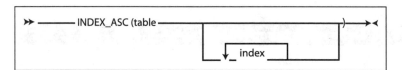

**Figure 4.4**   The syntax for the **INDEX_ASC** hint.

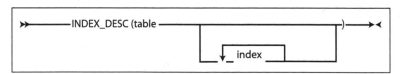

**Figure 4.5**   The syntax for the **INDEX_DESC** hint.

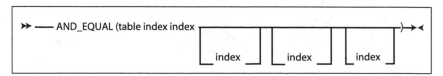

**Figure 4.6**   The syntax for the **AND_EQUAL** hint.

**Figure 4.7**   The syntax for the **USE_NL** hint.

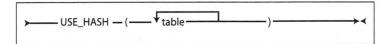

**Figure 4.8**   The syntax for the **USE_HASH** hint.

**Figure 4.9**   The syntax for the **USE_MERGE** hint.

| Table 4.10   Join hints. | |
|---|---|
| **Hint** | **Description** |
| **ORDERED** | Joins tables in the order specified in the **FROM** clause. |
| **USE_NL** | Specifies the use of nested loops. This hint requires that the **ORDERED** hint and the specification of the table be used for the inner table. |
| **USE_HASH** | Specifies the use of a hash join. |
| **USE_MERGE** | Specifies the use of a **sort_merge** join. This hint requires the **ORDERED** hint. |

Table 4.11 describes the hints available for parallel query execution optimization.

The syntax for the **PARALLEL** hint is shown in Figure 4.10.

The first value in the syntax for the **PARALLEL** hint specifies the degree of parallelism for the specified table; the second value is used for a Parallel Server to specify the split between the two servers.

The syntax for the **NOPARALLEL** hint is:

```
NOPARALLEL(table)
```

The **NOPARALLEL** hint can also be specified by using the **PARALLEL** hint and setting the degree of parallelism to 1.

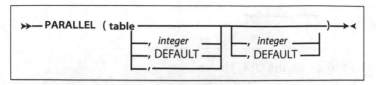

**Figure 4.10** The syntax for the **PARALLEL** hint.

| Table 4.11 | Hints available for parallel query execution optimization. |
|---|---|
| **Hint** | **Description** |
| **PARALLEL** | Specifies the number of parallel query servers to be used. |
| **NOPARALLEL** | Disables parallel scanning. This hint overrides the degree of parallelism specified when the table was created. |
| **CACHE** | Places the blocks for the table at the most recently used end of the LRU (Least Recently Used). |
| **NOCACHE** | Places the blocks for the table at the least recently used end of the LRU. |
| **PUSH_SUBQ** | Evaluates subqueries at the first opportunity instead of as the last step. This hint will be ignored for remote tables and merge join operations. |

The syntax for the **CACHE** hint is:

```
CACHE(table)
```

The syntax for the **NOCACHE** hint is:

```
NOCACHE(table)
```

# Practice Questions

## Question 1

Which facility within Oracle8 is used to format the output of an SQL*Trace session?

○ a. The **ANALYZE** command

○ b. TKPROF

○ c. Explain Plan

○ d. Server Manager

The correct answer is b. The TKPROF utility is used at the operating system command line to format information obtained using SQL*Trace. The ANALYZE command is used to create statistics for the cost-based optimizer. Therefore, answer a is incorrect. Explain Plan is used to obtain information on the execution plan for the SQL statement. Therefore, answer c is incorrect. The Server Manager is the utility for performing database maintenance and recovery functions. Therefore, answer d is incorrect.

## Question 2

Which script must be executed to create the **PLAN_TABLE**?

○ a. utlexcpt.sql

○ b. utlmontr.sql

○ c. utlxplan.sql

○ d. utlsidsx.sql

The correct answer is c. The utlxplan.sql script is used to create the **PLAN_TABLE**, which is used by the **EXPLAIN PLAN** command. Oracle usually makes the script name self-explanatory. An exception to this is the dbmsutil.sql script, which creates several utility packages.

## Question 3

If SQL statements are not performing well, what can sometimes be done to improve performance?

○ a.  Create larger redo log files.

○ b.  Resize the shared pool to a smaller value.

○ c.  Create indexes where appropriate.

The correct answer is c. Creating indexes can improve performance provided that they're created on the appropriate columns. Improperly sized redo logs affect the database as a whole, not just specific SQL statements. Therefore, answer a is incorrect. Resizing the shared pool to a smaller value usually has a negative effect on performance. Therefore, answer b is incorrect.

## Question 4

Which Oracle8 facility can you use to identify SQL areas that might be causing performance problems?

○ a.  UTLESTAT.SQL

○ b.  TKPROF

○ c.  Explain Plan

○ d.  SQL*Trace

The correct answer is d. SQL*Trace is the Oracle8 facility that actually traces the SQL statement execution performance, including the access plan and statistical information. The UTLESTAT.SQL script is used to obtain statistics on database activity for the instance. Therefore, answer a is incorrect. TKPROF is used to generate a report on the information obtained using SQL*Trace. Therefore, answer b is incorrect. Explain Plan provides information on the access plan for the query. Therefore, answer c is incorrect.

# Question 5

> You run the SQL*Trace utility to trace a user session. What will the formatted output contain?
>
> ○ a.  All user process information for the specified period
>
> ○ b.  User process information for the specified user
>
> ○ c.  Database activity information for the specified period
>
> ○ d.  SQL activity for all user processes

The correct answer is b. The SQL*Trace utility can be used at both the instance and the session level. When used at the session level, it will trace the processes for the user until that user turns off SQL*Trace or ends the session. The SQL*Trace command does not have a parameter to set a time period. Therefore, answers a and c are incorrect. Because the question specifies a user session, you can eliminate the answers that include "all user" processes. Therefore, answer d is incorrect.

# Question 6

> What is an important factor when you're examining SQL statements for performance purposes?
>
> ○ a.  Change SQL statements only after users have been notified.
>
> ○ b.  Consider using alternative queries to achieve the same results with less overhead.
>
> ○ c.  Do not change any application code.
>
> ○ d.  Do not change any SQL statements that include DML.

The correct answer is b. The first thing to examine when a performance problem is encountered is the SQL statement. It's important to remember that SQL is very flexible and supports alternative ways to obtain the same information. SQL statements can also be written in alternative ways, thus allowing you to change statements without needing to notify all users. Therefore, answer a is incorrect. SQL statements are embedded in and are a part of the application code. You can't modify SQL without changing the code. Therefore, answer c is incorrect. DML is exactly the type of SQL you will be looking at for performance issues. Therefore, answer d is incorrect.

## Question 7

> You want to run the SQL*Trace facility to gather performance information. How long should you run the process before stopping it and analyzing the output?
>
> ○ a.  Until the database is restarted
>
> ○ b.  Until the user session is completed
>
> ○ c.  Until all user sessions are completed

The correct answer is b. The SQL*Trace parameter can be dynamically changed for the database and does not require that the database be restarted. Therefore, answer a is incorrect. Setting SQL*Trace at the instance level to trace all user sessions will cause excessive overhead. Therefore, answer c is incorrect. So, the answer is to perform a SQL*Trace for a user session, executing the SQL statements that are having performance problems.

## Question 8

> Which TKPROF option would you set to ignore recursive SQL?
>
> ○ a.  **EXPLAIN**
>
> ○ b.  **SORT**
>
> ○ c.  **INSERT**
>
> ○ d.  **SYS**
>
> ○ e.  **RECORD**

The correct answer is d. Recursive SQL involves SQL statements performed by the user SYS. By setting **SYS=NO** when formatting the results of a SQL*Trace, you exclude recursive SQL from the report. The **EXPLAIN** option is used to set the user and password for statements for which an Explain Plan will be generated. Therefore, answer a is incorrect. **SORT** allows sorting by options. Therefore, answer b is incorrect. The **INSERT** option creates an SQL script to store the trace file statistics in the database. Therefore, answer c is incorrect. **RECORD** places a record of the nonrecursive statements into the trace file. Therefore, answer e is incorrect.

# Question 9

Which of the following items can you track using the **DBMS_AP-PLICATION_INFO** package provided by Oracle8? [Choose two]

- ❏ a.  User information
- ❏ b.  Performance
- ❏ c.  Resource usage
- ❏ d.  Network information
- ❏ e.  Database files
- ❏ f.  Error information

The correct answers are b and c. The built-in **DBMS_APPLICATION_INFO** package is provided by Oracle to obtain information specifically on performance and resource consumption and does not provide information for any of the other choices. A variety of tables are provided for user information and database files. Therefore, answers a and e are incorrect. Because **DBMS_APPLICATION_INFO** is an Oracle-stored package, it does not trace network information. Therefore, answer d is incorrect. For error information, the log and trace files are very useful. Therefore, answer f is incorrect.

# Question 10

Which SQL clause can be used with group functions to exclude unwanted rows?

- ○ a.  **GROUP BY**
- ○ b.  **HAVING**
- ○ c.  **WHERE**
- ○ d.  **BETWEEN**

The correct answer is c. The **GROUP BY** clause does just that: It groups values. However, it does nothing to eliminate unwanted rows. Therefore, answer a is incorrect. The **HAVING** clause is used for aggregate functions. Therefore, answer b is incorrect. Answer d is where the trick comes in. **BETWEEN**, just like **WHERE**, can be used to exclude rows, but **BETWEEN** is an operator, not a clause. Therefore, answer d is incorrect.

# Need To Know More?

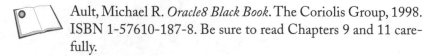

Aronoff, Eyal, Kevin Loney, and Noorali Sonawalla. *Oracle8 Advanced Tuning and Administration*. Oracle Press, 1998. ISBN 0-07882-534-2.

Ault, Michael R. *Oracle8 Black Book*. The Coriolis Group, 1998. ISBN 1-57610-187-8. Be sure to read Chapters 9 and 11 carefully.

Ault, Michael R. *Oracle8i Administration and Management*. Wiley Computer Publishing, 1999. ISBN 0-471-35453-8.

Corey, Michael, Michael Abbey, and Daniel J. Dechichio, Jr. *Oracle8 Tuning*. Oracle Press, 1997. ISBN 0-07882-390-0.

The first places to go for more information are the *Oracle8 Tuning Manual* and the *Oracle8 Server Reference Manual*.

# Tuning The
# Shared Pool

. . . . . . . . . . . . . . . . . . . . . . . . . . . .

### Terms you'll need to understand:

√ Library cache

√ **GETHITRATIO**

√ UTLBSTAT and UTLESTAT

√ Dictionary cache

√ Shared pool

√ Reloads/pins ratio

√ User global area (UGA)

√ Multithreaded server (MTS) option

√ Large pool

### Techniques you'll need to master:

√ Determining the optimal configuration for the primary shared pool

√ Evaluating the additional shared pool requirements when implementing the Oracle multithreaded server (MTS) option

The shared pool is an area of the SGA that contains two main memory structures:

➤ Library cache

➤ Dictionary cache

The efficiency of the shared pool is determined mainly by its hit ratios. These are the *get hit ratio* and the *pin hit ratio*. The hit ratios reveal how often the SQL or PL/SQL statement or data dictionary information required by a process was already located in the shared pool, without requiring physical reads from disk.

The library cache and the dictionary cache cannot be independently sized. Oracle determines the size of the library cache and dictionary cache based on the size of the shared pool, which is determined by the **SHARED_POOL_SIZE** initialization file parameter. Because all requests in Oracle must access the dictionary cache, Oracle gives preference to this area. Therefore, if the library cache is optimally tuned, the dictionary cache will also be functioning optimally.

The default size of the shared pool is 3,500,000 bytes; this size is generally inadequate for most systems. The size of the shared pool should be large enough to achieve a good hit ratio on the library cache and dictionary cache. However, it should not be so large that it wastes memory or causes paging and swapping to occur because of memory constraints that cannot accommodate such a large shared pool size.

If the database is using the MTS architecture, additional memory considerations are required for proper sizing of the shared pool or large pool areas. This is because some user information that is stored in the shared pool with an MTS configuration is moved to the large pool if the large pool is configured. These requirements are covered later in this chapter.

This chapter explains how to tune the shared pool. This discussion includes, in order of importance, the proper sizing of the following items:

➤ The library cache

➤ The data dictionary cache

➤ The reserved space from the shared pool

# Tuning The Library Cache

The library cache is the most tunable component of the shared pool. It stores SQL statements and PL/SQL blocks, including procedures, packages, and triggers issued in the database. These statements are parsed and ready for execution.

SQL entries in the library cache are managed by a least recently used (LRU) algorithm. When memory is insufficient to store a new SQL statement, the LRU algorithm ages the least recently used SQL statements out of the library cache first. Proper sizing of the library cache will help to prevent shared SQL statements from being prematurely aged out of memory.

Each SQL statement in the library cache has an entry in the shared SQL area and an entry in the private SQL area.

The shared SQL area of the library cache contains a parse tree and an execution plan for each SQL statement. A primary goal of tuning the library cache is to keep parsing to a minimum by reusing SQL statements in the shared SQL area. When an SQL statement is issued, Oracle searches the shared SQL area for the identical SQL code before loading that statement into the library cache. To identify the exact statement, the SQL is translated to the numeric value of the ASCII text, and a hash function is used to locate the statement. If the statement is found from a previous request, Oracle will discard the new SQL statement and reuse the parsed and executable SQL statement already in the shared SQL area. A statement must be an exact match for Oracle to use the same shared SQL area. For example, the following statements are not considered identical by Oracle:

```
SELECT * FROM dept;

SELECT    * FROM dept;

SELECT * FROM Dept;

SELECT * FROM DEPT;
```

Whenever possible, SQL statements should use bind variables rather than constants to maximize the reusable database code. Packages are also recommended to increase the efficiency of the library cache because they always use generic code and are loaded into the shared SQL area when any section of them is accessed. In environments in which many packages or stored procedures are used, the shared SQL area of the library cache can consume a significant amount of memory. The method for determining the amount of sharable memory utilized by existing objects in the library cache is covered later in this chapter.

For each SQL statement, each user must have a separate entry in the private SQL area of the library cache. A private SQL area is the part of the library cache that contains data such as runtime buffers and bind information. Multiple private SQL areas can be associated with one shared SQL area. A private SQL area consists of two memory components:

➤ Persistent area

➤ Runtime area

The persistent area uses memory in the library cache for the span of an open cursor. This portion of the private SQL area continues to exist until the corresponding cursor is closed. If a statement is reused frequently, it might be more efficient to leave the cursor open, provided you can afford the additional memory in your shared pool. However, if cursors are left open unnecessarily after SQL processing for the cursor has completed, the private SQL area could result in inefficient memory usage.

The runtime area contains information that's required while an SQL statement is executing. The size of the runtime area depends on the complexity of the SQL statement and the size of the rows that are processed by that statement. The runtime memory area is released immediately after an **INSERT**, **UPDATE**, or **DELETE** statement has completed execution. For **SELECT** statements, runtime area memory is released only after all rows have been fetched or the query is canceled.

The number of private SQL areas that a user can allocate is limited by the **OPEN_CURSORS** initialization file parameter. The value for this parameter indicates the maximum number of cursors that a user process can have open at any one time. The default value for **OPEN_CURSORS** is 50. Trying to open a cursor beyond the maximum will result in the error message "ORA-01000 Maximum open cursors exceeded." The solution for this error is to modify the program to use fewer open cursors or to increase the value of **OPEN_ CURSORS** in the initialization file and then restart the instance.

# Views

Several V$ views provide statistics about the library cache. These views can be used to provide detailed information about the library cache area of the shared pool and can help identify the SQL being executed and its frequency, the database objects cached, and the hit ratio of the library cache objects since instance startup. To select from these views, you must have the **SELECT ANY TABLE** system privilege. The dynamic views of the library cache include:

➤ **V$LIBRARYCACHE**

➤ **V$SQLAREA**

➤ **V$SQLTEXT**

➤ **V$DB_OBJECT_CACHE**

➤ **V$SGASTAT**

# V$LIBRARYCACHE

The **V$LIBRARYCACHE** view, described in Table 5.1, reflects statistics about the library cache activity since instance startup. This view is used to determine the overall performance of the library cache. The **PINS** column indicates the

| **Table 5.1 The V$LIBRARYCACHE view.** | |
|---|---|
| **Column** | **Description** |
| NAMESPACE | Library cache namespace: **SQL AREA, TABLE/ PROCEDURE, BODY, TRIGGER, INDEX, CLUSTER, OBJECT**, and **PIPE**. |
| GETS | Number of times a lock was requested for the namespace objects. |
| GETHITS | Number of times the object's handles are already allocated in the cache. |
| GETHITRATIO | Number of **GETHITS** divided by **GETS**; values close to 1 indicate that most of the handles that the system has attempted to acquire are cached. |
| PINS | Number of times a pin was requested for the namespace objects. |
| PINHITS | Number of times all the metadata pieces of the library object were already allocated and initialized in the cache. |
| PINHITRATIO | Number of **PINHITS** divided by number of **PINS**. |
| RELOADS | Number of times library objects must be reinitialized and reloaded with data because they have been aged out or invalidated. |
| INVALIDATIONS | Number of times objects in the namespace were marked invalid because of the modification of a dependent object. |
| DLM_LOCK_REQUESTS | Number of **GET** lock instance locks; DLM indicates the distributed lock manager, which is used for Parallel Server. |
| DLM_PIN_REQUESTS | Number of PIN-distributed lock manager locks. |
| DLM_PIN_RELEASES | Number of releases on a pin by the distributed lock manager. |
| DLM_INVALIDATION_ REQUESTS | Number of distributed lock manager requests for invalidation instance locks. |
| DLM_INVALIDATIONS | Number of invalidation pings received from other instances. |

number of times the system issued a pin request for objects in the cache in order to access them. The **RELOADS** column reveals whether parsed statements have been aged out of the shared SQL area, essentially becoming unavailable to other requests without reparsing the statement. Ideally, the **RELOADS** column should be zero, but it should never be more than 1 percent of the value of the **PINS** column.

The **V$LIBRARYCACHE** view is also useful in identifying the percentage of parse calls that found a cursor to share in the library cache. Table 5.2 provides an example of the query results from the following **V$LIBRARYCACHE** view:

```
SELECT namespace, gethitratio
    FROM V$LIBRARYCACHE
    WHERE namespace = 'SQL AREA';
```

The **GETHITRATIO** for the namespace **SQL AREA** in the library cache should be in the high 90s. If sufficient space is allocated to the shared pool and the hit ratio is not in this range, the application code should be evaluated for efficiency. An additional consideration might be that the statistics reflected in the **V$LIBRARYCACHE** view are from instance startup to the current time. If you want library cache statistics for a specific time period, remember to run UTLBSTAT/UTLESTAT after the instance has been up and running with activity for a period of time sufficient to populate the SGA. This will discount expected misses in the library cache immediately after instance startup.

### V$SQLAREA

The **V$SQLAREA** view gives full statistics on the shared cursor cache. Each row stores statistics on one shared cursor. This view lists the first 80 characters of the SQL statement. **V$SQLAREA** is useful for determining the most frequently used SQL statements and the number of times that an SQL statement has been executed since instance startup. It also lists the number of users currently executing an SQL statement from the **USERS_EXECUTING** column of the view. Table 5.3 describes the **V$SQLAREA** view.

| Table 5.2  Sample results of a query on V$LIBRARYCACHE. | |
|---|---|
| NAMESPACE | GETHITRATIO |
| SQL AREA | .965208231 |

| Table 5.3 | The V$SQLAREA view. |
| --- | --- |
| **Column** | **Description** |
| SQL_TEXT | The first 80 characters of the SQL statement for the current cursor. |
| SHARABLE_MEM | The amount of memory in bytes that's sharable between users. |
| PERSISTENT_MEM | The amount of memory in bytes that persists for the life of the cursor. |
| RUNTIME_MEM | The amount of memory in bytes that's needed only during execution. |
| SORTS | The number of sorts performed by the SQL statement. |
| VERSION_COUNT | The number of different versions of this cursor; the same SQL text might be used by different users, each on his or her own version of a table. |
| LOADED_VERSIONS | The versions of the cursor that are currently fully loaded with no parts aged out. |
| OPEN_VERSIONS | The number of versions on which some user has an open cursor. |
| USERS_OPENING | The number of users who currently have this SQL statement parsed in an open cursor. |
| EXECUTIONS | The total number of times this SQL statement has been executed. |
| USERS_EXECUTING | The number of users currently executing this cursor. |
| LOADS | The number of times the object was loaded or reloaded. |
| FIRST_LOAD_TIME | The timestamp when the object was first loaded into the SGA. |
| INVALIDATIONS | The sum of invalidations. |
| PARSE_CALLS | The number of times users executed a parse call for this cursor. |
| DISK_READS | The number of disk reads by this cursor. |
| BUFFER_GETS | The number of buffer **GETS** by this cursor and all cursors caused to be executed by this cursor. |
| ROWS_PROCESSED | The total number of rows returned by the statement. |
| COMMAND_TYPE | Oracle command-type definition. |
| OPTIMIZER_MODE | The optimizer mode: RULE, CHOOSE, FIRST_ROWS, or ALL_ROWS. |

*(continued)*

## Table 5.3    The V$SQLAREA view (continued).

| Column | Description |
| --- | --- |
| PARSING_USER_ID | The user who parsed the statement the first time the statement was run. |
| PARSING_SCHEMA_ID | The schema ID that was used for the initial parse. |
| KEPT_VERSIONS | The number of child versions that have been pinned in the library cache using the **DBMS_SHARED_POOL** package. |
| ADDRESS | Used with **HASH_VALUE** to select the full text of the SQL statement from **V$SQLTEXT**. |
| HASH_VALUE | Used with **ADDRESS** to select the full text of the SQL statement from **V$SQLTEXT**. |
| MODULE | Contains the name of the module that was executing at the time that the SQL statement was first parsed by calling **DBMS_APPLICATION_INFO.SET_MODULE**. |
| MODULE_HASH | The hash value of the module that's named in the **MODULE** column. |
| ACTION | Contains the name of the action that was executing at the time the SQL statement was first parsed by calling **DBMS_APPLICATION_INFO.SET_ACTION**. |
| ACTION_HASH | The hash value of the action that's named in the **ACTION** column. |
| SERIALIZABLE_ABORTS | The number of times the transaction fails to serialize, producing ORA-8177 errors, per cursor. |

## V$SQLTEXT

The **V$SQLTEXT** view lists the full SQL statement, without truncation, of each SQL cursor in the shared SQL area of the SGA. Multiple rows can exist in this view for one SQL statement, if necessary. This view is useful if you need to obtain the full SQL statement for input to an **EXPLAIN PLAN** execution. Table 5.4 describes the **V$SQLTEXT** view.

## V$DB_OBJECT_CACHE

The **V$DB_OBJECT_CACHE** view lists the database objects in the library cache. These objects include tables, indexes, clusters, synonym definitions, PL/SQL procedures, packages, and triggers. Columns of particular importance in this view are the **LOADS** and **EXECUTIONS** columns. An object that's frequently executed and must be reloaded often might indicate that **SHARED_POOL_SIZE** is too small. Objects might also benefit from being pinned in the library cache using the **DBMS_SHARED_POOL.KEEP**

### Table 5.4   The V$SQLTEXT view.

| Column | Description |
| --- | --- |
| ADDRESS | Used with **HASH_VALUE** to identify a uniquely cached cursor. |
| HASH_VALUE | Used with **ADDRESS** to identify a uniquely cached cursor. |
| PIECE | The number used to order the pieces of SQL text. |
| COMMAND_<br>TYPE | The code for the type of SQL statement (for example, **SELECT** or **INSERT**). |
| SQL_TEXT | This column contains one piece of the SQL text. |

procedure. The **DBMS_SHARED_POOL** package is created using the dbmspool.sql and prvtpool.plb scripts located in the $ORACLE_HOME/rdbms/admin directory on Unix. This package is not created by the catproc.sql script during the database build. The **KEPT** column has a value of **YES** if the object has been pinned in the library cache. Table 5.5 describes the **V$DB_OBJECT_CACHE** view.

### Table 5.5   The V$DB_OBJECT_CACHE view.

| Column | Description |
| --- | --- |
| OWNER | The owner of the object. |
| NAME | The name of the object. |
| DB_LINK | The database link name, if any. |
| NAMESPACE | The library cache namespace of the object: **TABLE/<br>PROCEDURE, BODY, TRIGGER, INDEX, CLUSTER, OBJECT**. |
| TYPE | The type of object: **INDEX, TABLE, CLUSTER, VIEW, SET,<br>SYNONYM, SEQUENCE, PROCEDURE, FUNCTION,<br>PACKAGE, PACKAGE BODY, TRIGGER, CLASS, OBJECT,<br>USER, DBLINK**. |
| SHARABLE_<br>MEM | The amount of sharable memory in the shared pool consumed by the object. |
| LOADS | The number of times the object has been loaded; this count also increases when an object has been invalidated. |
| EXECUTIONS | The total number of times this object has been executed. |
| LOCKS | The number of users currently locking this object. |
| PINS | The number of users currently pinning this object. |
| KEPT | Has a value of **YES** if the object has been pinned in the shared pool using **DBMS_SHARED_POOL.KEEP** or **NO** if the object is not pinned. |

| Table 5.6   The **V$SGASTAT** view. | |
|---|---|
| Column | Description |
| NAME | The SGA component name |
| BYTES | The size of the memory area in bytes |

## V$SGASTAT

The **V$SGASTAT** view lists sizes of all structures within the SGA. Table 5.6 describes the **V$SGASTAT** view.

# Determining The Size Of The Library Cache For An Existing Application

To calculate the size required for the library cache on an existing application, Oracle recommends that you start by setting the shared pool to a very large size. This might be at the expense of other structures if additional memory is limited. Run the application at a time that provides the best representation of normal to high application usage. Be sure to allow sufficient time after the application is started for the library cache to be loaded with shared SQL statements and for multiple requests to be issued for those statements. A series of database queries is then submitted to determine the optimal size for the library cache for that particular application. The collective sum of the query results will provide a good estimate of the optimal size of the library cache. If dynamic SQL is used in the database, additional memory will be required for the library cache to accommodate those statements. The following list shows examples of the queries required to estimate the size of the library cache:

➤ Determine the sharable memory that's currently used for cached objects such as packages and views:

```
SELECT SUM(sharable_mem)
   FROM V$DB_OBJECT_CACHE;
```

Here is a sample result of the query:

```
SUM(sharable_mem)
        489400
```

➤ Determine the amount of sharable memory that's currently used for shared SQL statements that have been executed more than five times since instance startup:

```
SELECT SUM(sharable_mem)
       FROM V$SQLAREA
       WHERE executions > 5;
```

Here is a sample result of the query:

```
SUM(sharable_mem)
          392707
```

➤ Determine the amount of sharable memory required for the user's open cursors; 250 bytes of memory for each open cursor is recommended:

```
SELECT SUM(250 * users_opening)
    FROM V$SQLAREA;
```

Here is a sample result of the query:

```
SUM(250 * users_opening)
               66750
```

These examples indicate that the existing application will require a minimum of 948,857 bytes in the library cache to sufficiently support the application.

> *Note: The library cache size calculation does include any dynamic SQL. In some environments, especially in a decision support system (DSS), dynamic SQL can consume a significant amount of the library cache memory. If the application is operating in an environment that also generates dynamic SQL, the library cache size requirements will be greater.*

The library cache is indirectly sized by the **SHARED_POOL_SIZE** database initialization file parameter. It's important to note that this single parameter specifies the total memory allocation for the library cache and the dictionary cache. In addition, if you're using the MTS architecture, you must allocate additional memory in the shared pool to accommodate some user session information, unless the large pool is also configured. The maximum value for SHARED_POOL_SIZE is operating-system dependent.

# The DBMS_SHARED_POOL Package

The **DBMS_SHARED_POOL** package is provided by Oracle and allows PL/SQL objects to be pinned (or *kept*) in the shared SQL area. Once an object is pinned in the library cache, it will remain in shared memory and not be aged out. Packages, procedures, triggers, and cursors can be pinned in the library cache area of the shared pool. An object that's pinned can never be flushed out of memory until it's explicitly unpinned or the database is shut down. The performance advantage of a pinned object is realized when the object is accessed by multiple processes. The object will always be found in memory.

The dbmspool.sql and prvtpool.plb scripts are executed to create the package specification and package body for the **DBMS_SHARED_POOL** package. These scripts are not called by the catproc.sql script, so the database administrator must run these scripts manually before executing the **DBMS_SHARED_POOL** package. To pin an object in memory, the user account that owns the **DBMS_SHARED_POOL** package must have the **EXECUTE** privilege; normally, this user is SYS. This privilege is required because packages and procedures are executed with the privileges of the user who created the object, not the person executing the package or procedure.

The **DBMS_SHARED_POOL.KEEP** procedure is used to pin an object in the shared pool. The following statement illustrates an example of pinning a package into the library cache area of the shared pool:

```
EXECUTE DBMS_SHARED_POOL.KEEP ('scott.GL_package');
```

As stated earlier, a pinned object will remain in the shared pool until the database is shut down or the object is unpinned from the shared pool (usually a single pool flush will not remove pinned objects, but multiple sequential flushes will). The following statement illustrates how to unpin a package from the shared pool:

```
EXECUTE DBMS_SHARED_POOL.UNKEEP ('scott.GL_package');
```

The following steps outline the procedure for pinning a PL/SQL area using the **DBMS_SHARED_POOL** package:

1. Determine which objects are to be pinned in memory.

2. Start the database.

3. Reference the object to cause it to be loaded into the library cache. You cannot reference a package or procedure without executing it. However, when any part of a package is executed, the entire package is loaded into the library cache. To pin a package in the library cache after instance startup, include a dummy variable definition in every package that can be referenced without making any undesired changes to the database. This will result in the entire package being loaded into the library cache. To reference a trigger, issue a statement that causes the trigger to fire, if it's possible to do so without making undesired changes to the database.

4. Execute **DBMS_SHARED_POOL.KEEP** to pin the object.

The following large Oracle packages should be pinned in the SGA at instance startup. This will increase the likelihood that contiguous memory will be available to store these packages. Ensure that your database is using these packages before pinning them in the SGA:

➤ SYS.STANDARD

➤ SYS.DBMS_STANDARD

➤ SYS.DBMS_DESCRIBE

➤ SYS.DBMS_UTILITY

➤ SYS.DBMS_LOCK

➤ SYS.DBMS_PIPE

➤ SYS.DBMS_OUTPUT

 Many DBAs include scripts for loading these packages in their database startup routines.

The **V$DB_OBJECT_CACHE** view is useful for identifying the objects loaded in the library cache. These objects include tables, clusters, indexes, PL/SQL procedures, packages, and triggers. If the value of the **KEPT** column is **YES**, the object is pinned in the library cache. Table 5.7 provides an example of partial query results for the **V$DB_OBJECT_CACHE** view. Issue the following query to identify objects that are loaded in the library cache, the sharable

**Table 5.7 Sample query results for the V$DB_OBJECT_CACHE view.**

| owner | name | type | sharable_mem | kept |
|-------|------|------|--------------|------|
| SCOTT | MB_REQUISITION_PKG4 | PACKAGE BODY | 11,394 | YES |
| SCOTT | IB_NOTIFICATIONS_SR23 | PACKAGE BODY | 20,713 | YES |
| SCOTT | KO_CUST | PACKAGE BODY | 5,392 | YES |
| SCOTT | EB_CUSTOM_WITH_PKG | PACKAGE | 10,930 | YES |

*(continued)*

**Table 5.7   Sample query results for the VSDB_OBJECT_CACHE view (continued).**

| owner | name | type | sharable_mem | kept |
|---|---|---|---|---|
| SCOTT | BB_ASL_ATTRIBUTES_THS | PACKAGE | 14,978 | YES |
| SCOTT | EINBR_DISC | PACKAGE BODY | 5,221 | YES |
| SCOTT | RB_NOTIFICATIONS_SR244 | PACKAGE BODY | 8,849 | YES |
| SCOTT | AB_MESSAGES_PKG | PACKAGE BODY | 6,677 | YES |
| SCOTT | RO_ONLINE_REPORT | PACKAGE | 12,401 | YES |
| SCOTT | DB_REQUISITION_DESC_PKG6 | PACKAGE BODY | 11,230 | YES |
| SCOTT | IB_AUTOMATIC_CLEAR_PKG | PACKAGE BODY | 14,990 | YES |
| SCOTT | LB_FUNDS_CONTRL_PKG8 | PACKAGE BODY | 60,421 | YES |
| SCOTT | OB_FLEX_MASTER | PACKAGE | 15,673 | YES |
| SCOTT | VF_PRICE_LIST | SYNONYM | 467 | NO |
| SCOTT | EVEN_LINE_DETAIL | SYNONYM | 478 | NO |
| SYSTEM | YEAR_PROFILE | TABLE | 470 | NO |
| SCOTT | OET_PRIMARY_SS | TABLE | 220 | NO |
| SCOTT | USER_CHECKS | VIEW | 854 | NO |
| ARPR | AXA_TERMS | TABLE | 587 | NO |
| ABREF | DEPT_FOLDER | TABLE | 474 | NO |
| SCOTT | RBC_PENDING_ITEM | VIEW | 228 | NO |
| SCOTT | IBC_TRANSACTIONS_INT | TABLE | 231 | NO |
| SCOTT | ABC_UNITS_OF_MEASURE | SYNONYM | 473 | NO |
| SCOTT | NO_ORDER_TYPES | VIEW | 1,155 | NO |
| PO | BO_REFR_VENDORS | TABLE | 217 | NO |
| SCOTT | RBC_ATTCH_BLK_ENTITIES | SYNONYM | 480 | NO |
| SCOTT | OFR_OPTX_VALIDATION_ | SYNONYM | 235 | NO |
| SCOTT | WFR_TRANS_VLD | SYNONYM | 479 | NO |

*(continued)*

| Table 5.7 | Sample query results for the **V$DB_OBJECT_ CACHE** view (continued). | | | | |
|-----------|------|------|--------------|------|
| **owner** | **name** | **type** | **sharable_mem** | **kept** |
| SCOTT | NXCG_REPORTS | TABLE | 215 | NO |
| SCOTT | TTLXP_PLANNERS | TABLE | 217 | NO |
| AR | HO_VENDOR_ CONTACTS | TABLE | 597 | NO |
| AR | AA_CUST_TRX_TYPES | TABLE | 472 | NO |
| OE | NO_REPORT_ PARAMETERS | TABLE | 471 | NO |
| AR | KA_DEPT_TRANS | TABLE | 370 | NO |
| OE | SECTIONS | TABLE | 422 | NO |

memory consumed by each object, and whether the object has been pinned with **DBMS_SHARED_POOL.KEEP**:

```
SELECT owner, name, type, sharable_mem, kept
   FROM V$DB_OBJECT_CACHE;
   ORDER BY kept DESC;
```

# Initialization File Parameters For The Library Cache

Several important database initialization file parameters affect the library cache. Properly configuring these parameters is vital to optimizing the performance of the library cache:

➤ SHARED_POOL_SIZE

➤ SHARED_POOL_RESERVED_SIZE

➤ SHARED_POOL_RESERVED_MIN_ALLOC

➤ CURSOR_SPACE_FOR_TIME

The **SHARED_POOL_SIZE** parameter indicates the size, in bytes, of the shared pool buffer in the SGA. This pool stores shared SQL and PL/SQL blocks, packages, procedures, functions, triggers, the data dictionary cache, and user session information when the MTS option is used.

The **SHARED_POOL_RESERVED_SIZE** parameter specifies the shared pool space that's reserved for large objects. This memory area is referred to as the *reserve list.* The minimum size that defines a large object is specified by the **SHARED_POOL_RESERVED_MIN_ALLOC** parameter. This parameter can be used to help reduce fragmentation in the shared pool because smaller objects are not stored in this area, thus reducing the possibility of fragmentation in the reserve list. The default value for this parameter is 0 bytes. **SHARED_POOL_RESERVED_SIZE** must be greater than **SHARED_POOL_RESERVED_MIN_ALLOC** for a reserved list to be created. **SHARED_POOL_RESERVED_SIZE** can be specified by a numerical value or a number followed by the suffix *K* or *M*. (If neither K nor M is used, the default value will be in bytes.)

The **SHARED_POOL_RESERVED_MIN_ALLOC** parameter indicates the minimum size of a large object that can occupy space in the reserve list. The larger the size of this parameter, the more restrictive it is in allowing objects into this memory area. The default value for this parameter is 5,000 bytes. The **SHARED_POOL_RESERVED_MIN_ALLOC** parameter can be specified by a numerical value or a number followed by the suffix *K* or *M*. (If neither K nor M is used, the default value will be in bytes.)

The **CURSOR_SPACE_FOR_TIME** is a Boolean parameter that indicates when shared SQL areas are aged out of the library cache. The default value for this parameter is **FALSE**. If this parameter is set to **TRUE**, shared SQL areas are kept pinned in the shared pool and private SQL areas are not deallocated until all cursors referencing them are closed. If this parameter is set to **FALSE**, Oracle must verify whether the SQL statement is located in the shared SQL area of the library cache. This parameter should not be changed from the default value unless the value of **RELOADS** in the **V$LIBRARYCACHE** view is consistently zero. If any dynamic SQL is used in the database, this parameter should not be changed from the default value (**FALSE**).

# Dictionary Cache

The data dictionary is a collection of tables and views that contain extensive information about the Oracle database. This information includes the names and detailed information of all objects in the database, including user information and privileges. The data dictionary must be referenced each time a user issues a request for data.

The data dictionary cache, or simply dictionary cache, is an area of the shared pool that contains data dictionary information in memory. When Oracle allocates memory to the various components of the shared pool, it gives precedence to the dictionary cache. Therefore, if the library cache is tuned for optimum performance, the dictionary cache will most likely perform well also. The dictionary cache is sized only indirectly by the **SHARED_POOL_SIZE** database initialization file parameter. The objective for the data dictionary cache is to keep as much of the information regarding the database structures and objects in memory, thus reducing the frequency of disk reads as much as possible. As with the library cache, the performance of the dictionary cache is gauged by its hit ratio. However, it is sometimes easier to see a problem using the inverse of the hit ratio—the miss ratio.

The following query determines the hit ratio of the dictionary cache. You should not expect the **GETMISSES** value to be zero. Oracle must load the object definition into the cache when an initial request is issued after instance startup. The ratio of the collective sum of **GETMISSES** to the collective sum of **GETS** should be less than 15 percent. Table 5.8 provides an example of the results of the query on **V$ROWCACHE**. Here's the query:

| Table 5.8   Sample results of a query on V$ROWCACHE. | | | |
|---|---|---|---|
| PARAMETER | GETS | GETMISSES | Miss Percent |
| dc_free_extents | 9,841 | 829 | 8.4239407 |
| dc_used_extents | 606 | 305 | 50.330033 |
| dc_segments | 177,014 | 10,988 | 6.2074186 |
| dc_tablespaces | 17,020 | 16 | .09400705 |
| dc_tablespaces_quotas | 338 | 6 | 1.7751479 |
| dc_users | 49,391 | 70 | .14172623 |
| dc_rollback_segments | 2,257 | 7 | .31014621 |
| dc_objects | 90,209 | 6,496 | 7.2010553 |
| dc_object_ids | 150,692 | 5,032 | 3.3392615 |
| dc_tables | 327,423 | 3,697 | 1.1291204 |
| dc_synonyms | 31,885 | 1,212 | 3.8011604 |
| dc_sequences | 4,374 | 87 | 1.9890261 |
| dc_usernames | 108,592 | 42 | .03867688 |
| dc_histogram_defs | 733 | 263 | 35.879945 |
| dc_users | 1,716 | 12 | .6993007 |
| dc_columns | 5,992,323 | 120,263 | 2.0069512 |
| dc_table_grants | 326,371 | 13,382 | 4.1002417 |
| dc_indexes | 144,702 | 7,137 | 4.9322055 |
| dc_constraint_defs | 19,673 | 2,445 | 12.428201 |
| dc_sequence_grants | 3,865 | 131 | 3.389392 |
| dc_user_grants | 34,255 | 27 | .07882061 |

```
SELECT parameter,
       gets,
       getmisses,
       (getmisses / gets * 100) "Miss Percent"
  FROM v$rowcache
  WHERE gets > 100
  AND getmisses > 0;
```

Each row in the **V$ROWCACHE** view contains statistics for a single param-
eter of the dictionary cache since instance startup. The **PARAMETER** column
specifies the particular data dictionary item. The **GETS** column specifies the
total number of requests for that dictionary item. The **GETMISSES** column
specifies the number of requests that resulted in a cache miss.

# Tuning Reserved Space From
# The Shared Pool

If Oracle has difficulty in finding contiguous memory, the shared pool can
become fragmented, thus resulting in performance degradation.

The **SHARED_POOL_RESERVED_SIZE** initialization parameter can be
used to reserve memory in the shared pool for large memory allocations for
operations such as PL/SQL and trigger compilation. The value of **SHARED_
POOL_RESERVED_SIZE** should be about 10 percent of **SHARED_POOL_
SIZE**. The **SHARED_POOL_RESERVED_MIN_ALLOC** initialization
parameter is used to set a minimum threshold for the size of the code that can be
placed in the shared pool reserved area. If the size of the code is less than the
threshold, the code is placed in the unreserved area of the shared pool. This helps
keep contiguous areas in the shared pool reserved area available for larger programs. When the memory allocated from the shared pool reserved area is freed,
it returns to the reserved list.

The **V$SHARED_POOL_RESERVED** view can be used to help you accu-
rately tune the **SHARED_POOL_RESERVED_SIZE**. Use the following
SQL to determine the activity in the shared pool reserved area:

```
SELECT
   FREE_MEMORY.
   REQUEST_MISSES,
   REQUEST_FAILURES
FROM
   V$SHARED_POOL_RESERVED;
```

Ideally, **REQUEST_MISSES** = 0 is the goal to shoot for, but realistically, most systems do not have enough memory to achieve this. Because this is rarely possible, try for **REQUEST_FAILURES** = 0, or at least prevent it from increasing.

If the value of **REQUEST_FAILURES** is more than zero and increasing, **SHARED_POOL_RESERVED_SIZE** is too small. This can be resolved by increasing the value of **SHARED_POOL_RESERVED_SIZE** and **SHARED_POOL_SIZE** accordingly. This increases the amount of available memory for the reserved list without impacting users not using the reserved memory.

If **REQUEST_MISS** equals zero, or is not increasing, and **FREE_MEMORY** is greater than or equal to **SHARED_POOL_RESERVED_SIZE**, then **SHARED_POOL_RESERVED_SIZE** is too large and should be reduced in size.

# MTS And The Shared Pool

In an MTS environment, some user session information is stored in the shared pool (or, if it is configured, the large pool) rather than in the memory area of the user processes. The information stored in the SGA under the MTS architecture includes private SQL areas, cursor state information, and sort areas. Because server processes are shared in an MTS environment, this user information must be stored in an area where any server can access any user's information at any time. This area of the SGA is called the *user global area (UGA)*. The **SHARED_POOL_SIZE** parameter value must be configured to accommodate the additional shared pool memory requirements of the UGA when using the MTS architecture if the large pool is not configured using the **LARGE_POOL** parameter.

The **V$SESSTAT** and **V$STATNAME** views can be queried to calculate the additional space required by the UGA. Issue the following query at a time of high activity to determine how much UGA memory is currently in use:

```
SELECT SUM(value)||' bytes ' "Total Session Memory"
   FROM v$sesstat a, v$statname b
   WHERE name = 'session uga memory'
   AND a.statistic# = b.statistic#;
```

The result of this query provides a good estimate of how much larger you'll need to make the shared pool or what size to configure the large pool if you use the MTS architecture.

# The Large Pool

In Oracle8, a new memory structure, the *large pool*, can be used to store MTS session information. The **LARGE_POOL_SIZE** initialization parameter is used to set the size of the large pool. If the initialization parameter is not set, Oracle will allocate memory for the MTS session information from the shared pool area. Using the large pool instead of the shared pool also decreases SGA fragmentation.

 For the section of the exam covered by this chapter, the reader should pay particular attention to the optimal recommended ratios for the various buffers. Pay particular attention to the get hit/get miss ratios as well as the pins/reload ratio. Be sure to read the questions carefully; the value for a pins to reloads ratio is not the same as for the reloads to pins ratio.

# Practice Questions

## Question 1

> The ratio of **RELOADS** to **PINS** in the **V$LIBRARYCACHE** should always be what value?
>
> ○ a.  Less then 10 percent
>
> ○ b.  Less the 1 percent
>
> ○ c.  Greater the 10 percent
>
> ○ d.  Greater the 1 percent

The correct answer is b. If the **RELOADS** to **PINS** ratio is greater then 1 percent, the **SHARED_POOL_SIZE** parameter in the init.ora file should be increased.

## Question 2

> Which situation would cause an object definition to be aged out of the library cache?
>
> ○ a.  The user process was terminated.
>
> ○ b.  The process timed out.
>
> ○ c.  New objects definitions that needed more space were loaded.
>
> ○ d.  The object definitions were invalid.

The correct answer is c. Objects are aged out of the library cache using a least recently used (LRU) algorithm. When memory is insufficient to store a new SQL statement, the LRU algorithm ages the least recently used SQL out of the library cache to make room for the new statement. Answers a and b are incorrect because a process does not have to be active for the SQL it initiated to remain in the library cache. Answer d is incorrect because invalidating an object does just that—it is marked as invalid but not flushed (aged) out of the library cache.

# Question 3

In which part of the shared pool are shared SQL and PL/SQL stored?

- O a. Dictionary cache
- O b. Database buffer cache
- O c. Library cache
- O d. User global area (UGA)

The correct answer is c. The library cache is the area of the shared pool that stores all cached SQL and PL/SQL objects. The dictionary cache stores a collection of database tables and views containing reference information about the database, its structures, and its users. Therefore, answer a is incorrect. The database buffer cache is the portion of the SGA that holds copies of data blocks read from data files. Therefore, answer b is incorrect. The UGA is where user session information is stored. Therefore, answer d is incorrect.

# Question 4

The UTLBSTAT and UTLESTAT statistics indicate a high **GET_MISS** to **GET_REQ** ratio for a number of items. What should you do to reduce this value?

- O a. Increase the shared pool size
- O b. Decrease the shared pool size
- O c. Increase the reserved pool area
- O d. Increase the size of the data dictionary

The correct answer is a. The data dictionary size can be increased *indirectly* by increasing the size of the shared pool. Obviously, if answer a is correct, answer b is incorrect. Increasing the reserved pool without also increasing the shared pool can cause performance problems. Therefore, answer c is incorrect. Although it's the data dictionary that needs to be increased, a *direct* adjustment of the data dictionary is no longer possible. Therefore, answer d is incorrect.

# Question 5

> What information does the **PINS** column of the **V$LIBRARYCACHE** view represent?
>
> ○ a.  The number of times a reload has occurred
>
> ○ b.  The number of executions of SQL statements or procedures in the library cache
>
> ○ c.  The number of object definitions aged out of the library cache for this object
>
> ○ d.  The size of the SQL statements of PL/SQL blocks currently pinned in the library cache

The correct answer is b. The value represents the number of executions or reads of objects in the library cache.

# Question 6

> Where does Oracle8 store user session and cursor state information in a multithreaded server (MTS) environment?
>
> ○ a.  User global area (UGA)
>
> ○ b.  Program global area (PGA)
>
> ○ c.  System global area (SGA)

The correct answer is a. The UGA is an area of the shared pool that stores user session information when the MTS option is used. The shared pool does not have a UGA in a non-MTS environment. The PGA is not used to store this information in an MTS environment. Therefore, answer b is incorrect. The SGA contains structures such as the data buffers, redo logs, and shared pool. Therefore, answer c is incorrect.

## Question 7

Which Oracle package can you use to pin large PL/SQL packages in the library cache?

○ a. **DBMS_STANDARD**

○ b. **DBMS_SHARED_POOL**

○ c. **STANDARD**

○ d. **DIUTIL**

The correct answer is b. **DBMS_SHARED_POOL.KEEP** is used to pin a package in the shared pool. **DBMS_SHARED_POOL.UNKEEP** is used to *unpin* a package from the shared pool.

## Question 8

A user issues an SQL statement, and Oracle8 places it into the library cache. Another user issues the same SQL statement. How does Oracle handle the statement issued by the second user?

○ a. Oracle8 removes the first statement and uses the second statement because it is more recent.

○ b. Oracle8 uses the cached version and doesn't need to process the second request.

○ c. Oracle8 cannot process both statements at the same time, so the second statement waits for the first statement to complete.

○ d. Oracle8 caches the second statement into the library cache and processes each statement separately.

The correct answer is b. If Oracle finds an identical SQL statement from a previous request, the new statement will be discarded, and Oracle will use the parsed and executable version of the SQL statement already in the library cache.

# Question 9

Which objects can you pin into the library cache using the **DBMS_SHARED_ POOL** package? [Check all that apply]

❑ a.  Triggers

❑ b.  Procedures

❑ c.  SQL statements

❑ d.  PL/SQL packages

❑ e.  Cursors

❑ f.  Data blocks

The correct answers are a, b, d, and e. Triggers, procedures, PL/SQL packages, and cursors can be pinned in the shared pool. Remember, the *pinning* of an object refers to the library cache, not the buffer cache. SQL statements and data blocks cannot be pinned. Therefore, answers c and f are incorrect.

# Question 10

What does Oracle use to manage the SQL and PL/SQL in the library cache?

○ a.  Program global area (PGA)

○ b.  User global area (UGA)

○ c.  Clusters

○ d.  Database buffer cache

○ e.  LRU algorithm

The correct answer is e. Oracle uses a least recently used (LRU) algorithm to manage the library cache. An LRU algorithm is also used to manage the buffer cache. The PGA, UGA, clusters, and database buffer cache have no bearing on the library cache. Therefore, answers a, b, c, and d are incorrect.

# Question 11

Your application has large PL/SQL packages, and you want to accommodate these in the library cache. Which parameter can you set to accomplish this task?

○ a. **SHARED_POOL_SIZE**

○ b. **SHARED_AREA_SIZE**

○ c. **SHARED_POOL_RESERVED_SIZE**

○ d. **CURSOR_SPACE_FOR_TIME**

The correct answer is c. **SHARED_POOL_RESERVED_SIZE** indicates the bytes in the shared pool that you want to reserve solely for large objects. Smaller objects will not be allowed to occupy this area of the library cache. **SHARED_POOL_RESERVED_MIN_ALLOC** defines the size of "large" in bytes. **SHARED_POOL_RESERVED_SIZE** must be greater than **SHARED_POOL_RESERVED_MIN_ALLOC** for a reserved list to be created. **SHARED_POOL_SIZE** refers to the overall size of the shared pool, but has no bearing on the size of the objects. Therefore, answer a is incorrect. **SHARED_AREA_SIZE** is a nonexistent parameter name. Therefore, answer b is incorrect. **CURSOR_SPACE_FOR_TIME** controls the duration of cursors in memory and has nothing to do with the size of the objects. Therefore, answer d is incorrect.

# Question 12

Which view can you query to check the amount of sharable memory used by a cached PL/SQL object?

○ a. **V$DB_OBJECT_CACHE**

○ b. **V$ROWCACHE**

○ c. **V$SQLAREA**

○ d. **V$LIBRARYCACHE**

The correct answer is a. **V$DB_OBJECT_CACHE** lists objects that are cached in the library cache. These objects include tables, clusters, indexes, PL/SQL procedures, packages, and triggers.

# Question 13

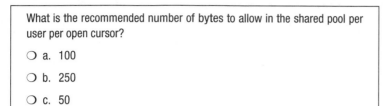

What is the recommended number of bytes to allow in the shared pool per user per open cursor?

○ a.  100

○ b.  250

○ c.  50

○ d.  10

The correct answer is b. When you're calculating the size of the library cache, Oracle recommends that you allocate 250 bytes per user per open cursor.

# Need To Know More?

 Aronoff, Eyal, Kevin Loney, and Noorali Sonawalla. *Advanced Oracle Tuning and Administration*. Oracle Press, 1997. ISBN 0-07-882241-6. (Pay close attention to Chapters 3 and 6.)

 Ault, Michael R. *Oracle8 Black Book*. The Coriolis Group, 1998. ISBN 1-57610-187-8. (Be sure to read Chapters 9 and 11 carefully.)

 Corey, Michael, Michael Abbey, and Daniel J. Dechichio, Jr. *Tuning Oracle*. Oracle Press, 1995. ISBN 0-07-881181-3.

 The first place to go for more information is the *Oracle8 Tuning Manual* and the *Oracle8 Server Reference Manual*.

 RevealNet Corporation provides Oracle Administration, a superior software reference tool for Oracle database administration. RevealNet's Web address is **www.revealnet.com**.

# Tuning The Data Buffer Cache

**6**

### Terms you'll need to understand:

√ System global area (SGA)

√ Database buffer cache

√ Cache hit ratio

√ Multiple buffer pools

√ Keep buffer pool

√ Recycle buffer pool

√ Default buffer pool

### Techniques you'll need to master:

√ Determining the optimal configuration for the database buffer cache

√ Configuring multiple buffer caches

An Oracle instance consists of the background processes (for example, SMON, PMON, DBWn, and LGWR) and the system global area (SGA). Both the background processes and the SGA are allocated when the instance is started and deallocated when the instance is shut down. The SGA is a highly tunable shared memory area that stores information for a particular instance. Several initialization file parameters determine the size of the SGA at instance startup. Access to information in memory is always faster than disk access. Therefore, the ideal scenario is to use the cached information in the SGA to satisfy multiple requests for shared data, performing as few physical reads as possible. Proper sizing and allocation of the SGA is vital to achieving this goal.

The SGA consists of three memory structures:

➤ Database buffers

➤ Shared pool

➤ Redo log buffer

# Tuning The Buffer Cache

The database buffer cache is an area of the SGA that stores copies of Oracle database blocks in memory. The database blocks are read into the data buffer cache by server processes to satisfy user requests. These blocks are available to be shared by all users and contain data from tables, clusters, indexes, rollback segments, and sequences. There can be several copies of a database block in the buffer cache at any given time. One current copy of the block will always exist, and Oracle might keep one or more read-consistent copies of the block using rollback segment data.

When the server receives a request for a particular block, it first checks the buffer cache to determine whether the block is already in memory. Oracle uses a hash function to make this determination, much like the process that's used to locate a statement in the library cache. If the block is not found in the buffer cache, the server process must perform a physical read from disk to retrieve the block from the appropriate data file.

The performance of the buffer cache is generally gauged by its *hit ratio*. The hit ratio represents the amount of data available to processes in the buffer cache. As with other structures of the SGA, the objective of the buffer cache is to keep as much of the requested data blocks in memory as possible, thus reducing the frequency of cache misses. Oracle recommends that the hit ratio on the buffer cache be 80 to 90 percent depending on the type of system—Data Warehousing or OLTP.

Obtaining a good buffer cache hit ratio is more important in online transaction processing (OLTP) environments than it is in historical environments, such as decision support systems (DSS) or data warehouse systems. DSS and data warehouse applications typically perform many full-table scans, increasing the amount of physical reads and reducing the probability of a high buffer cache hit ratio. With these types of application environments, it's vital that you concentrate your tuning efforts on minimizing I/O.

Three system statistics are used to measure the hit ratio of the database buffer cache:

➤ **DB BLOCK GETS**

➤ **CONSISTENT GETS**

➤ **PHYSICAL READS**

The **DB BLOCK GETS** value indicates the access to current copies of the data blocks. The **CONSISTENT GETS** value indicates the access to the read-consistent copies of the blocks, built from the rollback segments. The sum of the **DB BLOCK GETS** and **CONSISTENT GETS** statistics will provide the total number of logical reads. The **PHYSICAL READS** value indicates the total number of physical reads from disk. The following code shows two queries that can be issued against **V$SYSSTAT** to determine the buffer cache hit ratio since instance startup.

The first query is more complex and will calculate the cache hit ratio:

```
SELECT (1-(phy.value / (cur.value + con.value))) * 100
"Buffer Cache Hit Ratio"
  FROM V$SYSSTAT cur,
       V$SYSSTAT con,
       V$SYSSTAT phy
         WHERE cur.name = 'db block gets'
  AND con.name = 'consistent gets'
  AND phy.name = 'physical reads';
```

Here is a sample result of the query:

```
Buffer Cache Hit Ratio
           96.115
```

The second query is easier to remember and provides the database statistics needed to calculate the buffer cache hit ratio manually.

```
SELECT name,
       value
  FROM V$SYSSTAT
  WHERE name IN
        ('db block gets', 'consistent gets', 'physical reads');
```

Here's a sample result of the query:

```
NAME                VALUE
db block gets       142924
consistent gets     124556
physical reads       10394
```

Use the following calculation to calculate the buffer cache hit ratio manually:

```
Hit Ratio=1-(physical reads/(db block gets + consistent gets))
```

The calculation on these statistics results in a .96 (96 percent) buffer cache hit ratio.

 The report.txt file also provides information that you can use to determine the buffer cache hit ratio. The statistics provided are from the time that UTLBSTAT was submitted until the time that UTLESTAT was submitted. These statistics can present a truer picture of the buffer cache hit ratio than **V$SYSSTAT** because you can control the monitoring time period, thus bypassing the time period when the buffer cache is initially being populated with the initial buffer cache load after instance startup.

The size of the buffer cache is determined by two database initialization file parameters:

➤ DB_BLOCK_SIZE

➤ DB_BLOCK_BUFFERS

The **DB_BLOCK_SIZE** initialization parameter determines the size of each block and is a multiple of the physical data block size of the underlying system. The **DB_BLOCK_BUFFERS** initialization parameter sets the number of data block buffers for the Oracle instance. The **DB_BLOCK_SIZE** parameter multiplied by the **DB_BLOCK_BUFFERS** parameter will determine the size of the buffer cache in bytes. **DB_BLOCK_SIZE** is specified at database creation and cannot be altered unless the database is re-created. Therefore, unless the database is re-created, the only parameter that can be modified to alter the size of the buffer cache is **DB_BLOCK_BUFFERS**.

When an index access is used, Oracle always reads only one block of data at a time into the buffer cache. When a full-table scan access is used, multiple blocks are read into the cache at one time. The number of blocks read during full-table scans is determined by the **DB_FILE_MULTIBLOCK_READ_COUNT** database initialization file parameter.

The buffer cache is managed by the DBWn background process using two lists: the dirty list and the least recently used (LRU) list. The *dirty list* contains dirty buffers that have been modified in memory but have not yet been written to disk. The LRU list keeps the most recently used blocks in memory. When any process accesses a database buffer, the buffer is moved to the most recently used end of the LRU list. Blocks that are not frequently referenced are moved to the least recently used end of the LRU list and are eventually aged out of the buffer cache. The LRU list contains free buffers, pinned buffers, and dirty buffers that have not yet been moved to the dirty list. It's the responsibility of the DBWn background process to write dirty buffers to disk, working from the least recently used end of the LRU list. This process helps ensure that free buffers are found in the buffer cache for current and subsequent user processes. If a server process cannot find a free block in the LRU list, the server process will signal the DBWn background process to flush the dirty blocks to disk.

Generally, when full-table scans are performed, the batch of blocks retrieved are placed on the least recently used end of the LRU list. This process tends to age full-table scan blocks out of the buffer cache earlier than blocks retrieved by index access. The logic behind this approach is that multiple blocks are retrieved from a full-table scan, and these blocks potentially can consume a substantial amount of memory in the buffer cache. It is also unlikely that the full set of blocks will be requested again by another process. Full-table scan blocks are moved out of the buffer cache as soon as possible to free the cache for more frequently used blocks.

If full-table scans are frequently performed on static tables, you might want to alter the default behavior and place those blocks on the most recently used end of the LRU list so that the scanned blocks are not aged out as quickly. You can do this on a table-by-table basis by using the **CACHE** clause when creating or altering a table or cluster. You can also code a **CACHE** hint clause in the **SELECT** statement to obtain the same results. Although the **CACHE** hint is useful in some situations, care should be taken in its use. Overuse of the **CACHE** hint will result in overloading of the buffer cache. This means that less memory is available for other data, thus resulting in a decline in the cache hit ratio. The

CACHE_SIZE_THRESHOLD initialization file parameter specifies the maximum number of cached blocks for each table. If a table or cluster exceeds the number of blocks specified in this parameter, the number of blocks cached in the buffer will be limited to the quantity specified in **CACHE_SIZE_ THRESHOLD**.

Access to the buffer cache is managed by LRU chain latches. *Latches* are internal locks used to protect access to shared data structures, such as the buffer cache. Single-processor computers have only one LRU latch. However, if you have a symmetric multiprocessor (SMP) computer, you have the ability to set the number of LRU latches for the buffer cache with the **DB_BLOCK_LRU_ LATCHES** database initialization file parameter. The default for this parameter is half the number of CPUs for the computer. The maximum setting for this parameter is twice the number of CPUs. It's recommended that you reset this parameter only in a system with high activity. Each latch must have a minimum of 50 buffers to its set. The number of data buffer LRU latches is set with the initialization parameter **DB_BLOCK_LRU_LATCHES**.

## Determining The Impact Of Increasing The Buffer Cache

If your buffer cache hit ratio is low, Oracle can collect statistics that will estimate the hit ratio if you were to increase the size of the buffer cache. This test will allow you to determine the likelihood of additional cache hits if the **DB_BLOCK_BUFFERS** parameter were increased by $x$ number of buffers.

The statistics gathered to determine the effect of increasing the number of buffers are placed in the SYS-owned dynamic performance view **V$RECENT_ BUCKET**. Each row in this view shows the relative performance gain of adding one buffer to the buffer cache. Here are the columns included in the **V$RECENT_BUCKET** view:

➤ ROWNUM

➤ COUNT

The value of the **ROWNUM** column is one less than the number of proposed buffers to be added to the buffer cache. The value of the **COUNT** column is the number of additional cache hits that would be achieved if you were to add the **ROWNUM**+1 buffers to the cache. For example, the value of **ROWNUM** in the first row of **V$RECENT_BUCKET** is zero, and the value of **COUNT** is the number of additional cache hits gained by adding one buffer to the cache.

To perform the test of a larger cache size, you must set the **DB_BLOCK_LRU_ EXTENDED_STATISTICS** database initialization file parameter to the number of rows you want to collect in the **V$RECENT_BUCKET** view. For example, if you set the value of this parameter to 200, 200 rows of statistics will be collected in **V$RECENT_BUCKET**. Each row will reflect the addition of one buffer, up to 200 rows. The default value for **DB_BLOCK_LRU_ EXTENDED_STATISTICS** is zero. The database must be stopped and re-started for a new value of this parameter to take effect.

To determine the additional buffer cache hits that would occur by adding 50 buffers to the cache, issue the following query:

```
SELECT SUM(count) ACH
    FROM sys.V$RECENT_BUCKET
    WHERE ROWNUM < 50;
```

You can then determine how those additional hits would affect the cache hit ratio by hard-coding the value of **ACH** (additional cache hits) into the following database query on **V$SYSSTAT**:

```
SELECT (1-(( phy.value - ACH) / ((cur.value +
    con.value))) * 100 "Buffer Cache Hit Ratio"
    FROM V$SYSSTAT cur,
         V$SYSSTAT con,
         V$SYSSTAT phy
    WHERE cur.name = 'db block gets'
    AND   con.name = 'consistent gets'
    AND   phy.name = 'physical reads';
```

If you use the **DB BLOCK GETS, CONSISTENT GETS,** and **PHYSI-CAL READS** statistics from report.txt, use the following formula to estimate the buffer cache hit ratio with the increased buffer size:

```
Hit Ratio=1-(physical reads-ACH/(db block gets+consistent gets))
```

Another way to evaluate the statistics in **V$RECENT_BUCKET** is to separate the additional buffers into groups. Table 6.1 shows an example of the results from the following query:

```
SELECT 100*TRUNC(ROWNUM/100)+1||' to '||100*(TRUNC(ROWNUM/100)+1)
    "Interval",
    SUM(count) "Buffer Cache Hits"
        FROM sys.V$RECENT_BUCKET
        GROUP BY TRUNC(ROWNUM/100);
```

On the basis of the results of the query on **V$RECENT_BUCKET**, shown in Table 6.1, adding 100 buffers to the cache would result in 14,500 additional cache hits. Adding 100 additional buffers, for a total of 200 buffers, would

| Table 6.1 | Sample results of a query on the V$RECENT_BUCKET view. |
| --- | --- |
| Interval | Buffer Cache Hits |
| 1 to 100 | 14,500 |
| 101 to 200 | 10,221 |
| 201 to 300 | 540 |
| 301 to 400 | 9,215 |

increase the buffer cache hits by 24,721 (14,500 + 10,221). The increase from 200 to 300 buffers would result in only 540 additional cache buffer hits. You can use these statistics to determine how many buffers to add to the cache to obtain the most performance gain for the memory resources allocated. To make the buffer cache larger, increase the value of the **DB_BLOCK_BUFFERS** database initialization file parameter by the number of buffers you want to add to the cache and then restart the instance.

## Determining The Impact Of Decreasing The Buffer Cache

If your buffer cache hit ratio is consistently high, Oracle offers the ability to collect statistics on the effect of reducing the size of the buffer cache. This will allow you to determine whether the desired cache hit ratio can be maintained if you reduce the cache by a specific number of buffers. The statistics collected will help you identify over-allocated memory to the buffer cache that might be applied more efficiently to other Oracle memory structures.

The statistics gathered to determine the effect of decreasing the number of buffers in the cache are placed in the SYS-owned dynamic performance view **V$CURRENT_BUCKET**. These statistics estimate the performance effect of a smaller buffer cache. Here are the columns included in the **V$CURRENT_BUCKET** view:

➤ ROWNUM

➤ COUNT

The value of the **ROWNUM** column is the potential number of buffers in the cache. The value of the **COUNT** column is the number of cache hits that can be credited to the buffer number **ROWNUM**. The total number of rows in the **V$CURRENT_BUCKET** view is equal to the number of buffers in the cache, as specified in the **DB_BLOCK_BUFFERS** parameter. The first row of this table is not used for statistics. The **ROWNUM** value is zero, and the **COUNT** value is the total number of blocks moved into the first buffer cache rather than the number of hits.

To perform the test of a smaller cache size, you must set the **DB_BLOCK_ LRU_STATISTICS** database initialization file parameter to **TRUE**. The default value is **FALSE**. The database must be stopped and restarted for the new value of this parameter to take effect.

You can use the statistics in the **V$CURRENT_BUCKET** view to determine the number of additional cache misses that would occur if you reduced the size of the buffer cache. For example, if you currently have 120 buffers in your cache and you want to find out how many cache misses would occur if you reduced the cache buffers to 100, issue the following query on the **V$CURRENT_BUCKET** view:

```
SELECT SUM(count) ACM
    FROM V$CURRENT_BUCKET
    WHERE ROWNUM >= 100;
```

You can then determine how those additional misses would affect the cache hit ratio by including the value of **ACM** (additional cache misses) in the following formula:

```
Hit Ratio=1-(physical reads+ACM/(db block gets + consistent gets))
```

The statistics for **PHYSICAL READS, DB BLOCK GETS,** and **CONSISTENT GETS** can be determined from **V$SYSSTAT** or a current report.txt file.

Another way to evaluate the statistics in **V$CURRENT_BUCKET** is to separate the additional buffers into groups. Table 6.2 shows an example of the results from the following query:

```
SELECT 50*TRUNC(ROWNUM/50)+1||' to '||
       50*(TRUNC(ROWNUM/50)+1)
       "Interval",
       SUM(count) "Buffer Cache Hits"
    FROM sys.V$CURRENT_BUCKET
    WHERE ROWNUM > 0
    GROUP BY TRUNC(ROWNUM/50);
```

On the basis of the results of the query on **V$CURRENT_BUCKET**, as shown in Table 6.2, the first 50 buffers in the cache contribute 3,600 cache hits. The second 50 buffers in the cache contribute an additional 2,200 cache hits. The third 50 buffers are responsible for an additional 2,400 cache hits. The fourth 50 buffers are responsible for only 120 additional cache buffer hits. On the basis of these statistics, if memory is limited on your system, you might want to decrease

| Table 6.2 | Sample results of a query on the V$CURRENT_ BUCKET view. |
|---|---|
| Interval | Buffer Cache Hits |
| 1 to 50 | 3,600 |
| 51 to 100 | 2,200 |
| 101 to 150 | 2,400 |
| 151 to 200 | 120 |

the buffer cache by 50 buffers and allocate the memory more efficiently to other Oracle structures. To make the buffer cache smaller, decrease the value of the **DB_BLOCK_BUFFERS** database initialization file parameter by the number of buffers you want to eliminate from the cache and then restart the instance. The collection of statistics for the buffer cache decrease should be activated only when you're tuning the buffer cache and should be disabled once the statistical collection is completed to reduce performance overhead.

# Tuning Multiple Buffer Pools

The activity in the buffer cache will vary for each object loaded into the buffer cache. When very large segments are read into the buffer cache, even items that have been recently accessed may be flushed from the buffer to make room for the large segment read. Multiple buffer pools have been created in Oracle8 to address this issue. The three buffer pools that make up the multiple buffer pool are the *keep pool*, the *recycle pool*, and the *default pool*. Schema objects can be placed into the different buffer pools depending on the usage of the object.

As its name implies, the keep buffer pool is used to keep schema objects in the database buffer cache for longer periods of time. Schema objects that need to be kept in the buffer cache can be put into this buffer pool.

> *Note: This buffer cache works just like the rest of the caches, using an LRU algorithm to determine what is flushed when space is needed. It's still up to the database administrator to properly size the keep pool to prevent a low cache hit ratio.*

The objects placed in the recycle pool are expected to be flushed at a faster rate than the data in the keep or default pool. The recycle pool is the area in which you would place large table scans or any very large segment reads. The advantage to using the recycle pool for large amounts of data is that the other pools—the keep and the default pools—are not affected by the activity in the recycle pool. Because of the recycle pool's nature, a lower cache hit ratio is to be expected.

Any data not specifically placed into the keep or recycle pools will by default be placed in the default buffer pool.

# Enabling Multiple Buffer Pools

Enabling either the keep or recycle pool is optional, and one or both can be enabled independently of the other. If neither is enabled, the default buffer pool will act the same as the single buffer pool in Oracle7.

The initialization parameters (listed in Table 6.3) for the multiple buffer pools are in the form of **BUFFER_POOL_***NAME*, where *NAME* is either **KEEP** or **RECYCLE**. The default buffer pool always exists. The number of blocks for the default buffer pool is not assigned specifically. Rather, the number of blocks for the default pool is the difference between the total number of blocks allocated to the database buffer cache with the **DB_BLOCK_BUFFERS** initialization parameter minus the number of blocks specifically assigned to the keep and recycle pools.

Here are two examples for defining the keep and recycle pools:

```
BUFFER_POOL_KEEP=(buffers:400, lru_latches:3)
BUFFER_POOL_RECYCLE=(buffers:50, lru_latches:1)
```

| Table 6.3 Initialization parameters used to define buffer pools. | |
|---|---|
| **Initialization Parameter** | **Function** |
| **BUFFER_POOL_KEEP** | Defines the size of the keep buffer pool and the number of LRU latches assigned to it. |
| **BUFFER_POOL_RECYCLE** | Defines the size of the recycle buffer pool and the number of LRU latches assigned to it. |
| **DB_BLOCK_BUFFERS** | Defines the number of buffers for the database instance. Each individual buffer pool is created from this total amount with the remainder allocated to the default buffer pool. |
| **DB_BLOCK_LRU_LATCHES** | Defines the number of LRU latches for the entire database instance. Each buffer pool defined takes from this total in a fashion similar to **DB_BLOCK_BUFFERS**. |

The size allocated to the keep and recycle buffer pools is subtracted from the value defined for the **DB_BLOCK_BUFFERS** initialization parameter. Therefore, the sum of the **KEEP** and **RECYCLE** buffer pool buffers parameter cannot exceed the value of the **DB_BLOCK_BUFFERS** initialization parameter. If the value of the **KEEP** and **RECYCLE** buffer pool buffers parameter does exceed the value of **DB_BLOCK_BUFFERS**, the database cannot be mounted.

When allocating buffers to the keep and recycle buffer pools, remember that there needs to be (or rather, should be) buffer caches available to the default database buffers, which is the difference between the sum of the keep and recycle buffer pools and the value of the **DB_BLOCK_BUFFERS** initialization parameter. The **DB_BLOCK_LRU_LATCHES** parameter behaves in the same manner—that is, the LRU latches for the keep and recycle buffers are subtracted from the total number of LRU latches allocated for the **DB_BLOCK_LRU_LATCHES** parameter. The minimum number of buffers that must be allocated for each pool is 50 times the number of LRU latches allocated for each pool.

## Using The Buffer Pools

Objects are assigned to specific buffer pools with the **BUFFER_POOL** clause. The syntax for the buffer clause is:

```
BUFFER_POOL { KEEP | RECYCLE | DEFAULT }
```

This clause is valid in the **CREATE** and **ALTER table, cluster,** and **index** statements. If an object is not specifically put into a buffer pool using the **BUFFER_POOL** clause, it's placed in the default buffer pool. The partitions of a partitioned table or index can be individually assigned to specific buffer pools. If the partitions are not specifically assigned, they will inherit the buffer pool assignment of the underlying table or index definition.

 There is a heavy focus on the setup and use of the multiple buffer cache in the Oracle8 exam, so be sure to study and understand the preceding discussion. More information can be found in the *Oracle8i Concepts Manual* and the *Oracle8i Tuning Manual*.

Information on objects in the buffer pools is available in tables with **BUFFER_POOL** columns. These tables are listed in Table 6.4.

**Table 6.4    Tables with BUFFER_POOL columns.**

| USER_ Tables | ALL_ Tables | DBA_ Tables |
|---|---|---|
| USER_CLUSTERS | ALL_CLUSTERS | DBA_CLUSTERS |
| USER_INDEXES | ALL_INDEXES | DBA_INDEXES |
| USER_SEGMENTS | ALL_TABLES | DBA_SEGMENTS |
| USER_OBJECT_TABLES | ALL_OBJECT_TABLES | DBA_TABLES |
| USER_TABLES | ALL_ALL_TABLES | DBA_OBJECT_TABLES |
| USER_ALL_TABLES | ALL_PART_TABLES | DBA_ALL_TABLES |
| USER_PART_TABLES | ALL_PART_INDEXES | DBA_PART_TABLES |
| USER_PART_INDEXES | ALL_TAB_PARTITIONS | DBA_PART_INDEXES |
| USER_TAB_PARTITIONS | ALL_IND_PARTITIONS | DBA_TAB_PARTITIONS |
| USER_IND_PARTITIONS | | DBA_IND_PARTITIONS |

Information on the statistics of the buffer pools is given by the dynamic performance views **V$BUFFER_POOL_STATISTICS** and **GV$BUFFER_POOL_STATISTICS**. The **V$BUFFER_POOL_STATISTICS** dynamic performance view details the buffer pools allocated for the local instance, and the **GV$BUFFER_POOL_STATISTICS** dynamic performance view details the buffer pools allocated for the entire database. Running the CATPERF.SQL file creates the previous dynamic performance views. Table 6.5 details the structure of the **V$BUFFER_POOL_STATISTICS** view.

**Table 6.5    The structure of the V$BUFFER_POOL_STATISTICS view.**

| Column | Data Type | Description |
|---|---|---|
| ID | NUMBER | Buffer pool ID number |
| NAME | VARCHAR2(20) | Buffer pool name |
| SET_MSIZE | NUMBER | Buffer pool maximum set size |
| CNUM_REPL | NUMBER | Number of buffers on replacement list |
| CNUM_WRITE | NUMBER | Number of buffers on write list |
| CNUM_SET | NUMBER | Number of buffers in set |

*(continued)*

**Table 6.5    The structure of the V$BUFFER_POOL_STATISTICS view (continued).**

| Column | Data Type | Description |
| --- | --- | --- |
| BUF_GOT | NUMBER | Number of buffers gotten by the set |
| SUM_WRITE | NUMBER | Number of buffers written by the set |
| SUM_SCAN | NUMBER | Number of buffers scanned in the set |
| FREE_BUFFER_WAIT | NUMBER | Free buffer wait statistic |
| WRITE_COMPLETE_WAIT | NUMBER | Write complete wait statistic |
| BUFFER_BUSY_WAIT | NUMBER | Buffer busy wait statistic |
| FREE_BUFFER_INSPECTED | NUMBER | Free buffer inspected statistic |
| DIRTY_BUFFERS_INSPECTED | NUMBER | Dirty buffers inspected statistic |
| DB_BLOCK_CHANGE | NUMBER | Database blocks changed statistic |
| DB_BLOCK_GETS | NUMBER | Database blocks gotten statistic |
| CONSISTENT_GETS | NUMBER | Consistent gets statistic |
| PHYSICAL_READS | NUMBER | Physical reads statistic |
| PHYSICAL_WRITES | NUMBER | Physical writes statistic |

The "sets" referred to in the table pertain to the number of LRU latch sets. As you can see, the V$BUFFER_POOL_STATISTICS view has a lot of useful information to help in determining the activity in the buffer pools.

In a Parallel Server environment, the GV$ views retrieve information from the V$ views. The GV$ views possess an additional column named INST_ID of type INTEGER. The INST_ID column contains the instance number from which the associated V$ view information was obtained.

# Practice Questions

## Question 1

Which component of the SGA stores copies of data blocks that can be shared by all users?

○ a.  Shared pool

○ b.  Data dictionary cache

○ c.  Library cache

○ d.  Database buffer cache

The correct answer is d. The database buffer cache is an area of the SGA that stores data from tables, indexes, clusters, rollback segments, and sequences. This database information can be shared by all users requesting the same data as long as it remains in the buffer cache. The shared pool is an area of the SGA that stores the data dictionary cache and the library cache, at a minimum. Therefore, answer a is incorrect. The data dictionary cache stores data dictionary information in the shared pool. Therefore, answer b is incorrect. The library cache stores SQL and PL/SQL objects in the shared pool. Therefore, answer c is incorrect.

## Question 2

If the number of LRU latches allocated to your instance is 5, what is the least number of database cache buffers you can have in the instance?

○ a.  5

○ b.  50

○ c.  250

○ d.  500

The correct answer is c. There must be at least 50 database buffers allocated for each allocated LRU latch.

# Question 3

What factors govern the sizing of the multiple buffer pools? [Choose two]

- ❑ a. The size of each buffer pool should be equal to **DB_BLOCK_ BUFFERS**.
- ❑ b. The number of LRU latches for the buffers.
- ❑ c. The number of buffers defined for each pool cannot exceed the value of **DB_BLOCK_BUFFERS**.
- ❑ d. The total number of buffers defined for all pools cannot exceed the value of **DB_BLOCK_BUFFERS**.
- ❑ e. The size of each buffer must be the same.

The correct answers are b and d. The number of LRU latches influences the minimum number of buffers that need to be defined (a minimum of 50 buffers for each LRU). Also, the buffer pool sizes are subtracted from the total number of buffer caches (**DB_BLOCK_BUFFERS**), and the sum of the buffer pools cannot exceed this value. If the value is exceeded, the database will not mount. Therefore, answers a, c, and e are incorrect.

# Question 4

You review your company's current system and believe that the database buffer cache is inadequately sized. How can this condition affect applications?

- ○ a. Applications might not load properly.
- ○ b. Applications might generate errors.
- ○ c. Applications might run slowly.
- ○ d. Applications might halt during certain processing.

The correct answer is c. Inadequate sizing of the database buffer cache causes an insufficient number of database blocks to be cached into memory. The buffer cache has nothing to do with loading the application. Therefore, answer a is incorrect Although this constraint negatively affects the performance of the application, it will not halt or generate errors—the application will simply run slowly. Therefore, answers b and d are incorrect.

# Question 5

Which parameter can you reset to increase the size of the database buffer cache?

- ○ a. **DB_BLOCK_SIZE**
- ○ b. **DB_FILES**
- ○ c. **DB_BLOCK_CHECKPOINT_BATCH**
- ○ d. **DB_BLOCK_BUFFERS**

The correct answer is d. The size of the database buffer cache is determined by multiplying **DB_BLOCK_SIZE** by **DB_BLOCK_BUFFERS**. Both of these parameters determine the size of the buffer cache. However, the **DB_BLOCK_SIZE** parameter should never be altered or reset after database creation unless the database is re-created. Read the question carefully. It asks which parameter can be reset to increase the size of the buffer cache. The only parameter that can be reset to change the size of the buffer cache (without re-creation of the database) is **DB_BLOCK_BUFFERS**. Therefore, all other answers (a, b, and c) are incorrect.

# Question 6

Which statistic indicates the availability of data in the database buffers?

- ○ a. Buffer busy waits
- ○ b. Latch contention
- ○ c. LRU latch wait
- ○ d. Cache hit ratio

The correct answer is d. The cache hit ratio is the ratio of the number of blocks found in memory to the number of blocks physically accessed. Answers a and c are incorrect because they involve waits for a resource and do not refer to the availability of the data in the buffer cache. Answer b is incorrect because it is not a statistic.

# Question 7

Which parameter is used to determine the number of blocks for multiple buffer pools?

○ a.  **DB_BUFFER_CACHE**

○ b.  **DB_BLOCK_SIZE**

○ c.  **DB_BLOCK_BUFFERS**

○ d.  **BUFFER_POOL_KEEP**

○ e.  **BUFFER_POOL_RECYCLE**

The correct answer is c. **DB_BLOCK_BUFFERS** is used to determine the number of blocks for multiple buffer pools. Although not exactly a trick question, this question is somewhat fuzzy. **DB_BUFFER_CACHE** is not a parameter. Therefore, answer a is incorrect. Again, it's **DB_BLOCK_SIZE** that's set at database creation and cannot be changed. Therefore, answer b is incorrect. Both **BUFFER_POOL_KEEP** and **BUFFER_POOL_RE-CYCLE** are used to size parts of the multiple buffer cache, but the **DB_BLOCK_BUFFERS** parameter is the one that defines the number of blocks for the entire buffer cache. Therefore, answers d and e are incorrect.

# Question 8

Where is the first place a server process looks for data?

○ a.  Data file

○ b.  Rollback segment

○ c.  Buffer cache

○ d.  Redo log

The correct answer is c. The whole purpose of the buffer cache is to make data available to server applications and prevent them having to read from disk. Answer a is incorrect because data files are located on disks. Answer b is incorrect because it looks in the buffer cache first. Answer d is incorrect because the redo logs are only used in database recovery.

# Question 9

Which process manages the data buffer cache?

○ a. DBWn

○ b. PMON

○ c. SMON

○ d. Enterprise Manager

○ e. ARCH

○ f. LGWR

The correct answer is a. The DBWn process uses the LRU list to determine what to write to disk (flush from the pool). Answer b is incorrect because it monitors processes. Answer c is incorrect because it monitors the system. Answer d is incorrect because it is used to manage the database and is external to the database. Answers e and f are incorrect because they manage the processes associated with database recovery.

# Question 10

What should be the value for the buffer hit ratio during normal data process activities?

○ a. At least 10 percent

○ b. At least 90 percent

○ c. Less the 10 percent

○ d. Less the 90 percent

The correct answer is b. The ratio reflects the number of blocks found in memory to the number of blocks accessed. The higher the ratio, the better the performance of the database.

# Question 11

Which occurrence places blocks in the database buffer cache?

○ a. System startup

○ b. The LGWR process reading blocks into the buffer

○ c. The DBWn process reading blocks into the buffer

○ d. The server process reading blocks into the buffers for users

The correct answer is d. The server process places blocks in the database buffer cache. System startup writes data into the dictionary cache but not the buffer cache. Therefore, answer a is incorrect. The LGWR writes data into the redo log files. Therefore, answer b is incorrect. Your first inclination might be to choose the DBWn background process. DBWn writes data from the buffer cache but does not read data into the cache. Therefore, answer c is incorrect.

# Need To Know More?

 Ault, Michael R. *Oracle8 Black Book.* The Coriolis Group, 1998. ISBN 1-57610-187-8. (Be sure to read Chapters 9 and 11 carefully.)

 Ault, Michael R. *Oracle8i Administration and Management.* Wiley Computer Publishing, 1999. ISBN 0-471-35453-8.

 The first places to go for more information are the *Oracle8 Tuning Manual* and the *Oracle8 Server Reference Manual.*

 RevealNet Corporation provides Oracle Administration, a superior software reference tool for Oracle database administration. RevealNet's Web address is **www.revealnet.com**.

# Tuning Rollback Segments And Redo Logs

## Terms you'll need to understand:

√ Redo

√ Undo

√ Rollback

√ Contention

√ Redo allocation latch

√ Redo copy latch

√ Gets

√ Misses

√ Sleeps

√ Hit ratio

√ Checkpoint

√ Mirroring

√ Public rollback segments

√ Private rollback segments

## Techniques you'll need to master:

√ Sizing rollback segments

√ Tuning rollback segments

√ Monitoring rollback segments

√ Monitoring contention

√ Monitoring redo logs

√ Sizing redo logs

√ Tuning redo logs

One of Oracle's strengths is its recoverability, which it owes to the built-in redo log and rollback segment technology. Redo logs act as transaction journals that record all data-changing transactions that occur in the database. Rollback (or *undo*) segments act as before-image journals that keep copies of all data before it's altered. Redo logs allow for roll forward during recovery operations by recovering committed and uncommitted transactions up to the time the database crashes. Rollback logs allow for the rollback (or the undo) of uncommitted transactions.

Delayed transaction rollback was introduced in Oracle7.3 to speed instance recovery after instance-type failures. Delayed transaction rollback means that rather than perform a roll forward (application or redo logs and archived redo logs) and then a rollback at instance startup or recovery (removing uncommitted transaction changes), rollback is not performed until the data that needs rollback is accessed by a transaction.

Redo logs and rollback segments require a great deal of planning and tuning in a well-constructed database. Significant performance gains for large transactions are realized from properly sized, placed, and tuned redo and rollback processes. Questions concerning the redo logs and rollback segments are extensively covered in both Exam 3: "Oracle8: Backup and Recovery" and Exam 4: "Oracle8 Performance Tuning." This book will focus on the redo logs and rollback segments from a tuning aspect, covering topics related to numbers of redo logs and rollback segments, as well as their sizing and monitoring.

> *Note: The* Oracle8 DBA: Backup and Recovery Exam Cram *(1-57610-623-3) focuses on the redo logs and rollback segments from a backup and recovery aspect, covering topics related to functional use and interaction with processes.*

# Rollback Segments

Rollback segments act as before-image journals and are critical for rollback operations during normal operations and during instance and database recovery. Rollback segments are also used to provide read consistency for queries started before the changed data has been committed. Rollback segments are internal structures, meaning that they are stored in tablespaces. They can be either private (recommended) or public. Private rollback segments must be specified in the initialization file (using the initialization parameter **ROLLBACK_SEGMENTS**) to be brought automatically online at startup. Public rollback segments remain offline until the calculation

```
TRANSACTIONS/TRANSACTIONS_PER_ROLLBACK_SEGMENT
```

tells the Oracle server to bring another segment online.

Rollback segments are usually stored in their own tablespace (other than the single **SYSTEM** rollback segment, which is in the **SYSTEM** tablespace) for two reasons. First, a tablespace cannot be taken offline if it contains even a single online rollback segment. Second, rollback segments grow and shrink as needed (assuming that the **OPTIMAL** setting is used, which is discussed shortly), and, with dynamic tablespace extension, this could result in severe tablespace fragmentation.

Rollback segments allow for the rollback of cancelled transactions, for the rollback of uncommitted changes during recovery operations, and read consistency for transactions (read-consistent images of data being altered are maintained in the rollback segment).

## Sizing Rollback Segments

Rollback segments are created using the **CREATE ROLLBACK SEGMENT** command. This command has an optional **STORAGE** clause. If this clause is not specified in the **CREATE ROLLBACK SEGMENT** command, the default storage for the rollback segment tablespace is used instead. The parameters specified in the **STORAGE** clause for a **CREATE ROLLBACK SEGMENT** are:

➤ INITIAL—Sets the size of the initial extents.

➤ NEXT—Sets the size of subsequent extents.

➤ MINEXTENTS—Sets the number of initial extents (must be set to a minimum of 2).

➤ MAXEXTENTS—Sets the maximum number of extents allowed for the rollback segment.

➤ PCTINCREASE—Starting with version 7.3 and continuing through version 8i, this value can't be set, and it defaults to 0.

➤ OPTIMAL—Sets the size to which the rollback segment will shrink if it grows beyond **OPTIMAL** in size. **OPTIMAL** should be set to at least **MINEXTENTS * DB_BLOCK_SIZE**; otherwise, it will be ignored.

The sizing of rollback segments depends on many factors, such as the number of concurrent users, the size of the average transaction, the size of the largest expected transaction, and the available space. Let's examine how each of the **STORAGE** clause parameters should be derived. A critical dynamic performance view for rollback segments, the **V$ROLLSTAT** view, contains dynamic data about actual rollback segment statistics. The **V$ROLLSTAT** view has the following columns used to size rollback segments:

➤ **HWMSIZE**—The largest transaction.

➤ **SHRINKS**—The cumulative number of times that this rollback segment grew beyond **OPTIMAL** and was forced to shrink.

➤ **WRAPS**—The cumulative number of times a transaction continues writing from one extent in a rollback segment to another existing extent.

➤ **EXTENDS**—The cumulative number of times a new extent is allocated for a rollback segment. (The value of this column would be affected by the use of the **OPTIMAL** parameter.)

➤ **AVESHRINK**—The average amount that this rollback segment has shrunk.

➤ **AVEACTIVE**—The average transaction size of this rollback segment.

## Determining The Size Of The **INITIAL** Storage Parameter
The **INITIAL** storage parameter sets the size of the initial extent for the rollback segment. The value of the **INITIAL** parameter should be set to the size of the average transaction. Usually, the **INITIAL** value will need to be reset by dropping and re-creating the first-try rollback segment after operational experience is gained during system testing.

For **INITIAL**, the critical value in the **V$ROLLSTAT** table is **AVEACTIVE**, averaged over the online rollback segments. Set **INITIAL** equal to the average **AVEACTIVE** value.

## Determining The Size Of The **NEXT** Storage Parameter
**NEXT** is probably the easiest of the parameters to set. The **NEXT** storage parameter should always be equal to the **INITIAL** storage parameter for rollback segments.

## Determining The Size Of The **MINEXTENTS** Storage Parameter
The **MINEXTENTS** storage parameter is determined on the basis of the number of expected concurrent Data Manipulation Language (DML) transactions balanced against the number of desired rollback segments. For example,

if you have a potential for 200 concurrent DML transactions and want to have 10 online rollback segments, set **MINEXTENTS** to 20. Each DML transaction will use one extent in a rollback segment, and multiple transactions can use a single rollback segment simultaneously.

## Determining The Size Of The **MAXEXTENTS** Storage Parameter

The **MAXEXTENTS** storage parameter is set to the result of the calculation

```
MAXEXTENTS = CEILING(Largest HWMSIZE / INITIAL) + 1
```

which takes the largest high-water mark (that is, largest recorded transaction for any of the online rollback segments), divides it by the size of your initial extent (be sure to convert the **INITIAL** size to bytes), and adds 1 to the result to allow for growth. The **CEILING** statement indicates that the calculation rounds up to the nearest integer. Be sure that the rollback segment tablespace is sized appropriately for expected transactions. Large transactions fail mainly because they run out of space in the rollback segment tablespace. They also fail when the **MAXEXTENTS** parameter for the table being updated or inserted into is reached.

## Determining The Size Of The **OPTIMAL** Storage Parameter

Sizing the **OPTIMAL** storage parameter can be problematic. The best method we have found is to set it to **INITIAL** × **USERS_PER_ROLLBACK_SEGMENT** (be sure to monitor the values for wraps and shrinks and adjust as needed). Essentially, you want to increase it until wraps and shrinks are minimized. You should reach a setting at which wraps stay at or near zero and you get only a few shrinks that coincide with large transactions. Remember that **OPTIMAL** should be a multiple of the **INITIAL** parameter. An important consideration in sizing the **OPTIMAL** storage parameter is transaction activity during normal processing loads. The **OPTIMAL** storage parameter should be set to accommodate all transactions during this period.

## Determining The Size Of The **PCTINCREASE** Parameter

Oracle recommends having all rollback segments and their extents sized the same. Therefore, starting in Oracle7.3 and continuing to Oracle8i, the **PCTINCREASE** parameter for extents is not valid for use with rollback segments, and it defaults to 0.

# Using Multiple Rollback Segments Of Different Sizes

In some environments, you might periodically need extremely large rollback segments. If the size of the rollback segments needed for a large transaction exceeds the maximum **MAXEXTENTS** value on the basis of extent sizes sized for your average transaction, you must resort to having several larger rollback segments. When you find yourself in a situation such as using an online transaction processing (OLTP) system during the day and a large batch load operation at night, you can benefit by having two sets of rollback segments.

The first set of rollback segments is normally online for OLTP work and sized as discussed previously, using concurrent DML transaction count and sizing statistics. The second set of rollback segments is normally brought online for the batch loads and sized strictly to take into account the large transaction requirements. Remember that on some systems (such as Sun), a rollback segment larger than 2GB can cause errors even when spread across several discrete data files. Using the **ALTER ROLLBACK SEGMENT** command allows you to toggle the online and offline rollback segments as required.

A large transaction, such as a large batch load of data, can be forced to use a specific rollback segment through the **SET TRANSACTION USE ROLLBACK SEGMENT seg_name;** command. Remember to commit just before using the **SET TRANSACTION** command; any commits will force reuse of the **SET TRANSACTION** command to reassign the rollback segment to the transaction. Generally, large rollback segments are more useful for large batch jobs than for a large SQL query.

You can avoid many problems with rollback segments if you counsel your users to use frequent commits and avoid overly long transactions whenever possible. A major problem with rollback segments involves the "snapshot too old" error, which occurs when a rollback segment wraps and writes over data needed for a read-consistent image. Generally, such errors can be greatly reduced by either making rollback segment extents larger or adding more rollback segments.

# Tuning Rollback Segments

Rollback segments are tuned through proper sizing and file placement. You can monitor several items to determine whether your rollback segments meet the following criteria:

➤ Proper number of rollback segments

➤ Proper number of rollback segment extents

➤ Proper rollback segment size

➤ Proper rollback segment placement

## Monitoring The Proper Number Of Rollback Segments

To monitor the proper number of rollback segments, you need to monitor for rollback segment header contention (the **UNDO** header). This is accomplished by monitoring the **V$WAITSTAT** table using a **SELECT** command similar to the following:

```
SELECT
      class,
      SUM(count) total_waits,
      SUM(time) total_time
FROM v$waitstat
GROUP BY
      Class;
```

The results should be similar to those shown in Table 7.1. You can see that 14 waits occurred for undo headers. This indicates contention (although not at a very serious level) for rollback segments. If the waits become significant, you'll need more rollback segments because transactions are contending for the existing rollback segments. Another source of information on too few rollback segments involves the nonzero values in the **WAITS** column of the

**Table 7.1 Sample output from a "waits" select.**

| Class | Total Waits | Total Time |
| --- | --- | --- |
| Data block | 27 | 23 |
| Free list | 0 | 0 |
| Save undo block | 0 | 0 |
| Save undo header | 0 | 0 |
| Segment header | 0 | 0 |
| Sort block | 0 | 0 |
| System undo block | 0 | 0 |
| System undo header | 0 | 0 |
| Undo block | 0 | 0 |
| Undo header | 14 | 4 |

**V$ROLLSTAT** view. The undo (or rollback) header holds the rollback segment transaction table; if this table becomes full, contention occurs.

A common way to monitor is to combine results from the **V$ROLLSTAT**, **V$ROLLNAME**, and **DBA_ROLLBACK_SEGS** views into a set of two views. One view groups size-related data, whereas the other view groups rollback statistics.

 You need to be familiar with all three views: **V$ROLLSTAT**, **V$WAITSTAT**, and **DBA_ROLLBACK_SEGS**. Spend some time querying and familiarizing yourself with these views and the data they contain, and you'll find the rollback questions easier to answer.

## Monitoring The Proper Number Of Rollback Segment Extents

Values of zero in the **V$ROLLSTAT** view for the **WAITS** column show that the rollback segments have the proper number of extents. The proper balance between the number of rollback segments and the number of rollback segment extents is usually reached (according to Oracle sources) at a maximum of 20 allocated extents per rollback segment. Don't confuse allocated extents with **MAXEXTENTS**; allocated extents will usually be a fraction of the total allowed number of extents as expressed by the **MAXEXTENTS** storage clause value. **MAXEXTENTS** is usually set by determining the absolute largest transaction size you expect and then setting **MAXEXTENTS** to accommodate this size of transaction.

## Monitoring The Proper Size Of Rollback Segment Extents

As discussed previously, rollback segment extent size should be determined by empirical methods. Some fairly complex methods for setting extent sizes for rollback segments have been put forth by various experts, but perhaps the simplest method is to monitor a test database that's executing representative transactions. The view to monitor is the **V$ROLLSTAT** dynamic performance view. You want to size **INITIAL** and **NEXT** storage clause values for extents on the basis of the average of the **AVEACTIVE** column. By adding a comfort factor (say, 10 percent) to the size, you can allow for most average transactions by setting the storage clause **OPTIMAL** value such that the size will accommodate up to the maximum size of the **HWMSIZE** column. All these should be adjusted to minimize **WRAPS** and **EXTENDS**, as indicated in the **V$ROLLSTAT** view.

Generally, depending on statement complexity, an **INSERT** statement generates the least amount of rollback activity, followed by the **DELETE** and then the **UPDATE** statement.

## Monitoring The Proper Placement Of Rollback Segments

To monitor for proper placement of rollback segments, the UTLBSTAT and UTLESTAT report output report.txt should be examined for the I/O report section. The rollback segment tablespace should be placed in such a way that it doesn't contend with other tablespaces or with the redo logs. System monitors such as vmstat and iostat, as well as sar on Unix, should also be used to monitor I/O contention. Generally, write-intensive areas, such as rollback segments, should not be placed on RAID 5 devices but instead on dedicated RAID 0/1 disks.

Rollback segments should not be placed in tablespaces containing data or indexes, nor should they be placed in the temporary tablespace. Setting storage parameters such that all rollback segments in a single tablespace have the same-size extents eliminates problems with the fragmentation of rollback tablespaces.

# Redo Logs

Redo logs act as transaction journals by providing a detailed log of all transactions that affect data for a database. Redo logs are used for recovery caused by media or instance failure and are used to apply transaction data against the database during the roll-forward portion of recovery. If archive logging is initialized using the **LOG_ARCHIVE_START** initialization parameter, filled redo logs are copied through the ARCH process to the location specified by the **LOG_ARCHIVE_DEST** parameter and are named according to the convention specified by the **LOG_ARCHIVE_FORMAT** parameter. All the redo log parameters are specified in the initialization file (init<*SID*>.ora, or simply referred to as the *init.ora file*).

Periodically, Oracle writes system change number (SCN) and timestamp data to the headers of all data files. This process, called a *checkpoint,* can be tuned to be either more frequent than or simultaneous with log file switches. Normally, you tune for log switches and checkpointing to happen simultaneously. The DBWn process performs the file header updates while LGWR performs the log switch. Using the **CHECKPOINT_PROCESS** initialization parameter allows the CKPT process to relieve DBWn of checkpoint responsibilities. If CKPT is not started, and DBWn is creating a checkpoint in the file that LGWR needs, LGWR must pause until DBWn completes the checkpoint.

Oracle requires a minimum of two redo log groups and a minimum of one member for each group. For archive logging, three groups are suggested (but remember that the minimum requirement is still two). If more than one group member is specified, be sure that the second and subsequent members for a group are on separate disks or sets of disks. It does little good to use multiplexed redo logs (known as *mirroring*) if you place both copies on the same disk or on volume groups that share a disk. Chances are good that the disk shared by a volume group or the disk with two members of the same group will be the one to fail. Having multiplexed redo logs builds in redundancy, which you defeat if the logs are on the same disk or share a common disk in their volume groups.

Oracle writes to all members of a log group. When the log group fills, DBWn issues a checkpoint, and one member is selected to be archived if archive logging is enabled. If the member chosen for archiving is corrupt, Oracle will choose another member of the group and attempt to archive that member. If all members of a redo group are corrupt, the instance will hang.

Redo logs and archive logging are very robust features of Oracle. The worst thing that can happen with redo logs and archive logging (short of all members of a log group being corrupted) is that the archive log location fills up and the database hangs until space is available. Although the database hangs, no data is lost, and operations pick up where they left off before the archive destination filled.

# Sizing And Tuning Redo Logs

The proper sizing and tuning of redo logs is critical to database performance and recoverability. Too large a redo log might cause you to lose unacceptable amounts of data if an active (nonmultiplexed or improperly multiplexed) redo log is lost. Too small a redo log might require you to apply hundreds of thousands of the smaller redo logs to recover a database. To speed instance recovery, use smaller redo logs.

## Sizing Redo Logs

Sizing redo logs is an empirical art. You should size redo logs so that they switch at a frequency at which you don't lose a critical amount of data when you lose the online redo log and, for some reason, the mirror copy as well. However, the smaller the redo log, the more checkpoints that are generated.

Checkpoints are generated at each log switch if the initialization parameter **LOG_CHECKPOINT_INTERVAL** is set to a number larger than the number of blocks in a redo log and the **LOG_CHECKPOINT_TIMEOUT** parameter is set to zero; these are the recommended values. A checkpoint forces DBWn to update all data file headers, preventing DBWn from performing dirty buffer writes. To help DBWn, the CKPT process should be started by setting the initialization parameter **CHECKPOINT_PROCESS** to **TRUE**. If activated, the CKPT process takes over the header-update responsibilities.

Indications that redo logs might be too small include checkpoint errors that show up in the alert log for the instance. If you start seeing frequent waits in the alert log (found in the location specified by the initialization parameter **BACKGROUND_DUMP_DEST**) while the checkpoint process completes, this shows either that your redo logs are too small or that you don't have enough redo log groups. What's shown by wait messages for the checkpoint process to complete is that the redo logs are filling so fast that the database fills the one it just switched to before either CKPT or DBWn can finish updating the data file headers. If you're archiving and the alert log shows wait messages that logs are waiting for archival ("Cannot allocate log, archival required") and this is causing the wait, the logs need to be increased in number of groups or size (or both).

To reduce redo requirements, you can use several options in Oracle that were added in version 7.3. One of these options is direct path loading of data in SQL*Loader, where blocks are prebuilt and fully inserted into the database. However, if the insert fails, the load will need to be completely restarted because no redo is generated. Also, the use of the parallel and unrecoverable modes when creating objects such as tables and indexes reduces redo activity but results in reexecuting the complete build if the process fails. In addition, because the **TRUNCATE** command does not generate any redo activity, it should be used instead of the **DELETE** command when you're removing all data from a table.

Another means of reducing redo activity involves the use of the **NOLOGGING** option in the **CREATE** and **ALTER** Data Definition Language (DDL) commands for tables, indexes, partitions, and tablespaces. Although you can set the **NOLOGGING** attribute for a table, partition, index, or tablespace, the **NOLOGGING** attribute does not apply to all DDL commands for those objects. The following is a list of the operations affected by the **NOLOGGING** attribute:

➤ direct load (SQL*Loader)

➤ direct-load **INSERT**

➤ **CREATE TABLE...AS SELECT**

➤ **CREATE INDEX**

- ➤ ALTER TABLE...MOVE PARTITION

- ➤ ALTER TABLE...SPLIT PARTITION

- ➤ ALTER INDEX...SPLIT PARTITION

- ➤ ALTER INDEX...REBUILD

- ➤ ALTER INDEX...REBUILD PARTITION

- ➤ **INSERT, UPDATE,** and **DELETE** on LOBs (large objects) in **NOCACHE NOLOGGING** mode stored out of line

## Tuning Redo Logs
Redo logs are tuned using the following initialization parameters:

- ➤ **LOG_ARCHIVE_BUFFERS**—Sets the number of archive buffer pools to use for archiving (4 is the usual default).

- ➤ **LOG_ARCHIVE_BUFFER_SIZE**—Sets the size of the archive buffer pools in log file blocks (64 is the usual default).

- ➤ **LOG_BUFFER**—Sets the size of the redo circular log buffer in bytes. The default is operating-system specific, but it's usually around 8K. A larger value will reduce redo log I/O. LGWR reads this buffer to write redo log entries. The actual redo log buffers are contained within the system global area (SGA) for the specific instance.

- ➤ **LOG_CHECKPOINT_INTERVAL**—This is set to the number of redo log blocks written between checkpoints. It's normally set to a value larger than the size of a redo log so that checkpoints occur only at log switches. The blocks used in sizing this parameter are operating system blocks, not Oracle buffer blocks.

- ➤ **LOG_CHECKPOINT_TIMEOUT**—Sets the time in seconds between checkpoints. Usually, this should be set to zero to force checkpoints at log switches only.

- ➤ **LOG_BLOCK_CHECKSUM**—This is set to **TRUE** only if you suspect redo write corruption problems. This forces each redo block to use a checksum to validate consistency. This parameter is very CPU intensive.

- ➤ **LOG_ARCHIVE_START**—This is set to **TRUE** if you want automatic archiving. This parameter is used with setting the database to **ARCHIVELOG** mode either at creation in the **CREATE DATABASE** command or after creation using the **ALTER DATABASE** command to turn on automatic archiving. If the database is set to **ARCHIVELOG** mode and this parameter is set to **FALSE**, you must archive the redo logs manually by using the **ARCHIVE LOG** command; otherwise, the database will halt when the last online redo log is filled. The default is **FALSE**.

➤ **LOG_SMALL_ENTRY_MAX_SIZE**—Sets the size, in bytes, of the largest copy to the redo log buffer that can be made under the redo allocation latch. A larger value than **LOG_SMALL_ENTRY_MAX_SIZE** uses a redo copy latch if available. Redo copy latches are available only if the value of **LOG_SIMULTANEOUS_COPIES** is greater than zero.

➤ **LOG_SIMULTANEOUS_COPIES**—Sets the number of redo copy latches—generally twice the number of CPUs for multiple-CPU machines or zero for single-CPU machines. This parameter should be dynamically set based on the automatically set **CPU_COUNT** parameter.

➤ **LOG_CHECKPOINTS_TO_ALERT**—This parameter, if set to **TRUE**, logs all checkpoint activity to the alert log. If you suspect that checkpoints are not occurring as expected, set this parameter to **TRUE**. Normally, checkpoints will happen whenever there's a log switch, and log switches are automatically logged. This parameter should be set to **FALSE**. This parameter can cause increased I/O to the alert log, so I/O monitoring might be indicated if this parameter is set to **TRUE**.

 Some systems have problems with the automatic setting of **CPU_COUNT**. Always check whether **CPU_COUNT**, and therefore **LOG_SIMULTANEOUS_COPIES**, is set properly. Always verify that **LOG_SIMULTANEOUS_COPIES** is set to twice the number of CPUs and that **CPU_COUNT** is set to the number of CPUs in your system. It's more efficient to have the proper number of redo copy latches as set by **LOG_SIMULTANEOUS_COPIES**.

Redo logs are monitored by keeping a close eye on the alert log and by monitoring the following dynamic performance views:

➤ V$LOG

➤ V$LOGFILE

➤ V$LOG_HISTORY

➤ V$ARCHIVED_LOG

➤ V$SYSTEM_EVENT

➤ V$LOGSTAT

➤ V$LATCH

➤ V$LATCHNAME

➤ V$SYSSTAT

The latches that deal with the redo logs are the redo allocation and redo copy latches, which are monitored using the **V$LATCH** view. Redo statistics are monitored using the **V$SYSSTAT** view with a select against the **NAME** and **VALUE** columns, where the name is something like '%redo%'. Use the previously mentioned **V$LOGFILE** and **V$LOG_HISTORY** views to get information on log switches and log file status.

The **V$LATCH** view is used to detect latch contention. If the values from the **V$LATCH** view for the redo copy or allocation latch for the ratio of misses to total gets exceeds 1 percent, contention is occurring and the parameters for the LGWR need adjusting. One caveat concerning redo copy latch tuning is that it's not possible to tune the redo copy latch on single-CPU machines. The latch statistics are also returned in the UTLESTAT report.txt file. The number of times a process has waited on a latch is indicated by the **SLEEPS** column of the **V$LATCH** view.

Each row of the **V$LATCH** view contains statistics for a different latch. The columns of the view reflect various statistics for the latch. The statistics can be broken into two major categories: **WILLING_TO_WAIT** and **IMMEDIATE** statistics. Here are the columns associated with **WILLING_TO_WAIT** requests:

➤ **GETS**—The value in this column increases by one for each successful request.

➤ **MISSES**—The value in this column increases by one each time the initial request for the latch resulted in waiting.

➤ **SLEEPS**—The value in this column increases by one for each miss.

Here are the columns associated with **IMMEDIATE** requests:

➤ **IMMEDIATE GETS**—This column shows the number of successful immediate requests for each latch.

➤ **IMMEDIATE MISSES**—This column shows the number of unsuc-
cessful immediate requests for each latch.

Latch contention for the redo buffers can be monitored using the following
query:

```
SELECT name, gets, misses, immediate_gets, immediate_misses
   FROM v$latch
   WHERE name IN ('redo allocation', 'redo copy')
```

Whereas the redo allocation latch might use a **WILLING_TO_WAIT** request, a redo copy latch will almost always issue an **IMMEDIATE** request. If
you see a value greater than 1 percent for the ratio of misses to gets for a redo
copy latch, you should increase the number of latches, if possible. On a single-
CPU machine, the redo allocation latch is the only latch used. The redo
allocation latch is released by a process only when the work in the latch is
copied to the buffer.

You only need to worry about a few of the values that will be retrieved from the
**V$SYSSTAT** view: **REDO LOG SPACE WAIT, REDO BUFFER AL-
LOCATION RETRIES**, and **REDO SIZE** (these values are also returned in
the UTLESTAT report.txt file), which are discussed in detail here:

➤ *Redo log space wait* —This statistic indicates the number of times a
process had to wait to get space in a redo log buffer. It should be as close
to zero as possible. Increase the **LOG_BUFFER** parameter to correct
excessive waits.

➤ *Redo buffer allocation retries* —This statistic indicates how many attempts
were made to allocate space in the redo buffer. If this value is high
compared to the **REDO ENTRIES** parameter, your redo logs might be
too small and should be increased. This can also result from redo logs
that are small in comparison to the SGA size.

➤ *Redo size* —This statistic is the total redo utilized since startup of the
instance. Divide this value by the size of your redo logs, in bytes, to get
the number of log switches since startup. If this ratio of redo size to log
file size exceeds 1 every 15 minutes, your redo logs might be sized too
small (remember to adjust for low-use periods). On the other hand, if
the ratio is too low—say, only one or two log switches per day—your logs
might be too large.

The **V$SYSTEM_EVENT** view is queried to determine whether the redo logs are experiencing I/O contention. An example is a query against this view indicating waits for the "log buffer space" event. In this case, a larger setting for the **LOG_BUFFER** parameter is indicated.

As with many other aspects of Oracle, redo log sizing and tuning is very instance and application specific. You must tune each instance according to its usage and transaction cross-section.

# Tuning Archiving

Archiving is dependent on the mode of the database (it's either **ARCHIVE-LOG** or **NOARCHIVELOG**) and the setting of the initialization parameters **LOG_ARCHIVE_START**, **LOG_ARCHIVE_DEST**, and **LOG_AR-CHIVE_FORMAT**. The frequency of archive logging is controlled by the size of the redo logs and the number, size, and frequency of transactions (usually DML, such as **INSERT**, **UPDATE**, and **DELETE**, although long-running **SELECT** statements with sorts can also generate redo activity).

Archive logging can be monitored by using the alert log as well as the **V$LOG_HISTORY** view. Additional data on archive logging can be obtained by setting the **LOG_CHECKPOINTS_TO_ALERT** parameter to **TRUE** and then comparing archive log timing to checkpoint timing. However, most data on archive log problems comes from alert log warning and error messages. For example, an alert log message such as "Checkpoint not complete; unable to allocate log" indicates that LGWR has waited for DBWn or CKPT to complete a checkpoint.

Checkpoints can be reduced by setting the initialization parameters to force checkpoints to occur only when a log switch happens and by making your redo logs relatively large. Previous sections of this chapter discussed how to force checkpoints to occur only at log switches.

Archive logging can be done to disk or tape (on certain systems). If you're archiving to disk, you must monitor disk space usage and periodically back up to tape or remove archive logs to prevent the archive log destination from filling. If the archive log destination fills, archive logging halts and the instance stops until the archive destination is changed or room is cleared on the current destination. If the database mode is set to **ARCHIVELOG**, you must make sure that the initialization parameter **LOG_ARCHIVE_DEST** is set to a proper location or that archiving to tape is enabled.

# Practice Questions

## Question 1

> When building applications, what can the developer do to avoid overextend-
> ing a rollback segment?
>
> O  a.  Use **DELETE** rather than **TRUNCATE** statements
>
> O  b.  Avoid long-running queries
>
> O  c.  Not use nested SQL statements
>
> O  d.  Avoid long transactions when possible

The correct answer is d. Long DML transactions generate large amounts of
rollback. This is especially true of **INSERT, UPDATE,** and **DELETE** statements. Answer a is incorrect because it's actually **DELETE** you want to avoid,
because **TRUNCATE** is a DDL statement that doesn't generate rollback.
Answer b is incorrect because a **SELECT** statement, even a long-running one,
doesn't generate rollback; however, it can cause problems with "snapshot too
old" errors because of its need for a read-consistent image. Answer c is incorrect because, again, even nested SQL statements don't generate that much
rollback.

## Question 2

> The size of the **INITIAL** storage parameter for your rollback segment is 2MB.
> To which value should you set the **NEXT** storage parameter?
>
> O  a.  2MB
>
> O  b.  4MB
>
> O  c.  256K
>
> O  d.  1MB

The correct answer is a. The **INITIAL** storage parameter should be based on
transaction sizes for the average transaction. Because each user who is assigned
a rollback segment gets a single extent, each extent should be the same size as
the **INITIAL** value, so **INITIAL** and **NEXT** should be set the same. Therefore, answers b, c, and d are incorrect.

# Question 3

---

You view the alert_*<SID>*.log file and see this error:

```
'Checkpoint not complete; unable to allocate file'
```

What does this indicate?

○ a.  LGWR has waited for a checkpoint to finish.

○ b.  DBWn has waited for LGWR to finish.

○ c.  LGWR has waited for ARCH to finish.

---

The correct answer is a. The error says it all: "Checkpoint not complete; unable to allocate file." LGWR could be waiting on either DBWn or CKPT to finish, but in either case it's waiting on a checkpoint to finish and can't allocate a new log file. Answer b is incorrect because DBWn would be the problem child if CKPT were not initialized and would be performing the checkpoint causing the wait, so it would not be waiting on LGWR. Answer c is incorrect because you're waiting on a checkpoint, not an archival. The ARCH process has nothing to do with checkpoints.

# Question 4

---

You're evaluating rollback segments on your system. Which criteria should you use to determine the number of rollback segments you'll need?

○ a.  The number of redo log buffers

○ b.  The number of concurrent users

○ c.  The number of concurrent DML transactions

○ d.  The number of data files in the tablespace

---

The correct answer is c. A user is not assigned to a rollback segment until something is done that might need rolling back. Only DML can be rolled back, so the number of concurrent DML transactions determines the needed number of rollback segments. Answer a is incorrect because redo log buffers have nothing to do with rollback segments. Answer b is incorrect because a user is not assigned to a rollback segment until a DML action is performed. Answer d is incorrect because, although the number of data files might determine whether you start a checkpoint process, it has nothing to do with rollback segments.

# Question 5

> Which background process writes the data to the redo log file?
>
> ○ a.  CKPT
>
> ○ b.  LGWR
>
> ○ c.  DBWn
>
> ○ d.  ARCH

The correct answer is b. The log writer process, otherwise known as LGWR, writes data from the log buffer to the redo log. Answer a is incorrect because all the CKPT (checkpoint process) does is write the checkpoint information to the data file headers. Answer c is incorrect because DBWn (database writer process) writes dirty buffers to the disk from the db buffer cache and, if no CKPT process is started, performs checkpoints but never writes data to the log files. Answer d is incorrect because ARCH (archive process) writes filled redo logs to the archive location, and that's its only function.

# Question 6

> How many redo log groups must be created for a database running in **ARCHIVELOG** mode?
>
> ○ a.  Six
>
> ○ b.  Three
>
> ○ c.  Two
>
> ○ d.  One

The correct answer is c. You must read this question carefully. The question asks how many groups *must* be created, not *should* be created. Regardless of whether the database is in **ARCHIVELOG** or **NOARCHIVELOG**, you must have a minimum of two redo log groups. Therefore, although a minimum of three or more groups is suggested in **ARCHIVELOG** mode, only two are required and must be present. Therefore, answers a, b, and d are incorrect.

# Question 7

Which DML statement will generate the least amount of rollback on the database?

○ a. **DELETE**

○ b. **INSERT**

○ c. **UPDATE**

The correct answer is b. An **INSERT** statement has a simple one-place entry in a rollback segment, and its inverse is a **DELETE** statement. Answer a is incorrect because for read consistency, a **DELETE** requires a before-image copy of the changed block. Answer c is incorrect because for an **UPDATE**, a before-image copy of the block is also required for read consistency.

# Question 8

In which situation would it be beneficial for you to use the **SET TRANSAC-TION USE ROLLBACK SEGMENT large_rbs;** command (assuming **large_rbs** is indeed a large rollback segment)?

○ a. When running a large PL/SQL package

○ b. When running a large SQL query

○ c. When running a large batch job

The correct answer is c. A large batch job more than likely involves a large DML transaction, such as a large **INSERT, UPDATE,** or **DELETE,** all of which require a large amount of rollback. Answer a is incorrect because, generally, a large PL/SQL package will have many small procedures and functions that would not be run together but rather would be done piecemeal so that only small amounts of redo would be generated. Answer b is incorrect because SQL queries (**SELECT** statements) do not, as a rule, generate large amounts of rollback.

# Question 9

> For which three items are rollback segments used?
>
> ❑ a.  Data entry
>
> ❑ b.  Rollback
>
> ❑ c.  Performance
>
> ❑ d.  Recovery
>
> ❑ e.  I/O
>
> ❑ f.  Read consistency

The correct answers are b, d, and f. Rollback segments are used for rollback operations, for performing rollback operations during recovery, and for ensuring that a read-consistent image of data being manipulated is readily available to other queries. Answer a is incorrect because rollback segments are not used for data entry. Answer c is incorrect because rollback segment usage decreases performance due to the additional write requirements. Answer e is incorrect because rollback segment usage increases I/O.

# Question 10

> What is the worst problem you are likely to encounter with redo mechanisms?
>
> ○ a.  The archive destination fills, and causes the database to hang.
>
> ○ b.  The archive destination fills, and the PMON process hangs.
>
> ○ c.  The archive destination fills, and the background processes halt.

The correct answer is a. If the archive destination is full, the archive process cannot write out any more archive logs to the destination. This means that once all online logs are filled, the LGWR process cannot switch to a new log and therefore the database hangs. Answer b is incorrect because PMON has nothing to do with redo mechanisms. Answer c is incorrect because the archive destination filling up causes a hang, not a halt.

# Question 11

On which of the following SQL statements can the **NOLOGGING** attribute be used? [Select 2]

❑ a. **CREATE TABLE...AS SELECT**

❑ b. **CREATE TABLESPACE**

❑ c. **CREATE INDEX**

❑ d. **CREATE PARTITION**

❑ e. **CREATE TABLE**

The correct answers are a and c. They are among the operations for which **NOLOGGING** is available. A full list can be found in the *Oracle8i Concepts Manual*, under "SQL Statements That Can Use No-Logging Mode." Answers b, d, and e are incorrect because even though you can set the **NOLOGGING** attribute for a table, partition, index, and tablespace, the **NOLOGGING** attribute does not apply to all DDL commands for those objects.

# Need To Know More?

 Aronoff, Eyal, Kevin Loney, and Noorali Sonawalla. *Oracle8 Advanced Tuning and Administration*. Oracle Press, 1998. ISBN 0-07882-534-2.

 Ault, Michael R. *Oracle8 Black Book*. The Coriolis Group, 1998. ISBN 1-57610-187-8. (Be sure to read Chapters 9 and 11 carefully.)

 Ault, Michael R. *Oracle8i Administration and Management*. Wiley Computer Publishing, 1999. ISBN 0-471-35453-8.

 Corey, Michael, Michael Abbey, and Daniel J. Dechichio, Jr. *Oracle8 Tuning*. Oracle Press, 1997. ISBN 0-07882-390-0.

 The first place to go for more information is the *Oracle8 Tuning Manual* and the *Oracle8 Server Reference Manual*.

# Database
# Configuration

. . . . . . . . . . . . . . . . . . . . . . . . . . . . . . . . . . .

## Terms you'll need to understand:

√ Optimal Flexible Architecture (OFA)

√ Striping

√ RAID

√ Chaining and migration

√ High-water mark

√ **FREELISTS**

√ **PCTUSED** and **PCTFREE**

√ Raw devices

√ Clusters

√ Parallelism

√ Multithreaded server (MTS)

## Techniques you'll need to master:

√ Understanding how to balance I/O

√ Understanding the types of Oracle tablespaces and the appropriate uses of each

√ Understanding the differences between manual and operating system striping

√ Understanding storage parameters and how to use them

Regardless of how well you've tuned your application, I/O will limit its performance, and you will have performance problems if significant disk contention exists. Oracle provides several methods of configuring your database to reduce I/O bottlenecks. This chapter focuses on performance tuning from the I/O perspective.

# Optimal Flexible Architecture

Oracle's Optimal Flexible Architecture (OFA) is a recommended standard for database configuration. It includes recommendations for the following:

➤ Naming standards

➤ Security issues

➤ Raw devices

➤ Managing upgrades

➤ File distribution

The naming standards presented by OFA provide a method of organizing files so that files for each database and the types of files (log, database, or control) can be identified easily. The OFA recommends using operating system profiles and separating Oracle files from user files to address security issues. It also provides an overview of the use of raw devices (addressed in more detail in the "Other Database Configuration Options" section later in this chapter). The OFA makes recommendations on directory structures that support multiple versions of Oracle on a single server, thus making upgrades easier to manage.

The OFA makes several recommendations on file distribution. According to Cary V. Millsap of the Oracle National Technical Response Team (as quoted from RevealNet with the permission of the authors), the OFA is based on the following three rules:

➤ Establish an orderly operating system directory structure in which any database file can be stored on any disk resource.

➤ Separate groups of segments (data objects) with different behavior into different tablespaces.

➤ Maximize database reliability and performance by separating database components across different disk resources.

# File Placement

The placement of files belonging to an Oracle database is very important for performance reasons and for backup and recovery issues. Every server is limited in the number of processes that can simultaneously access any disk. Your goal in file placement should be to have I/O evenly spread across the available disk drives to minimize simultaneous access to each disk. As a starting point, Oracle recommends segregating Oracle files from non-Oracle files by placing them on different physical devices. This will make it easier to determine the I/O characteristics of Oracle objects by eliminating any I/O to non-Oracle files. The **V$FILESTAT** view provides statistical information on physical reads (**PHYRDS**) and writes (**PHYWRTS**) by file number (**FILE#**). The total I/O for a physical disk is the sum of the **PHYRDS** and **PHYWRTS**. The rate of I/O is calculated by dividing the total physical I/O by the time interval during which the statistics were gathered.

You need to consider non-Oracle activity and how your operating system handles cache and I/O. If possible, separate Oracle files and non-Oracle files because this will reduce I/O contention between Oracle and non-Oracle activities. You can use operating system monitoring tools to determine the I/O and memory activity on the server for both Oracle and non-Oracle activities.

Where you place your database files has a major effect on the amount of I/O. When tuning I/O, it's important to review statistics on physical reads and writes to determine which files are very active. Highly active files should be placed on a separate disk or striped across several disks to reduce I/O (striping is addressed in more detail later in this chapter in the section "Striping Tables").

For backup and recovery, it's very important that you have copies of your control file and online redo log files on separate disks (commonly known as mirroring). It's also important that you have sufficient space for archive logs if **ARCHIVELOG** mode is in use. Insufficient space for your archive logs can cause your database to hang.

## Physical Files

An Oracle database consists of five types of physical files:

➤ Database files

➤ Control files

➤ Online redo log files

➤ Offline archived redo log files

➤ Parameter files

*Database files* (or *data files*) are the physical operating system files that make up each tablespace. A data file can belong to only one tablespace. However, a tablespace can contain many data files. Although a table can belong to only one tablespace, that tablespace can have multiple data files on several physical disks.

A *control file* is a small binary file used by Oracle to synchronize all the data files and to keep track of all the files belonging to the database. The control file is updated continuously by Oracle. Oracle recommends having a minimum of two copies that are placed on different physical disk drives.

Every database must have at least two online redo logs. These logs contain all the changes made to data. Redo logs are written to in a circular fashion (redo logs are covered more extensively in Chapter 7).

Offline archive redo log files are created when a database is placed in **ARCHIVELOG** mode. These log files are historical copies of redo logs. When you're planning how to place files on the available disks, it's very important that archive redo log files be placed on a separate disk. As stated earlier, online redo logs are written to in a circular fashion. When **ARCHIVELOG** mode is used, each redo log must be archived before it can be used again. If the file system for the archive logs becomes full, additional archive logs cannot be created and the Archiver will wait until there's sufficient free space in the file system to write the new archive log files. If this space problem is not resolved before the online redo logs fill up, the database will not be able to reuse the redo logs because they're waiting to be archived. By placing the archive logs on a separate disk, you can more easily ensure that sufficient space is always available for creating new archive log files.

 Be aware that there are several questions in the "Database Configuration And I/O Issues" section of the exam on the use of checkpoints and the related initialization parameters **LOG_CHECKPOINT_INTERVAL** and **LOG_CHECKPOINT_TIMEOUT**. Because these issues are covered in Chapter 7, you should review that chapter for these items prior to taking the test.

The parameter file contains information read by Oracle at startup to determine the database initialization settings. If no parameter file is specified when the database is started, the default is to look for an init<*SID*>.ora file. On Unix systems, the default location is the $ORACLE_HOME/dbs directory. This file is referenced only when the database is started, and the name of this file is not stored within the Oracle database.

# Disk Configuration

As a rule of thumb, the more disks you have available, the better you'll be able to spread out the I/O activity. Rather than having all your files on one or two gigabyte-size disks, Oracle recommends that you have a minimum of five disks. The following list shows a minimal five-disk configuration based on recommendations in RevealNet and in Oracle's OFA:

➤ *Disk 1*—Oracle executables, user files, **TEMPORARY** tablespace, one copy of the control file, redo logs, **SYSTEM** tablespace

➤ *Disk 2*—Data, one copy of the control file

➤ *Disk 3*—Indexes, one copy of the control file

➤ *Disk 4*—Rollback segments, export files

➤ *Disk 5*—Archive log files

The configuration for file placement in this list is a minimum configuration for all but the smallest Oracle databases. This configuration does not include a second member for each redo log group. Because redo logs are vital for recovery of your database, it's very important that they be mirrored (that is, two members per group on different disks). Oracle will write to all the redo logs in parallel to reduce the overhead. This minimum configuration does not provide flexibility for placing highly active tables on a separate disk. Additional disks provide more flexibility for balancing I/O.

# Tablespaces

Oracle recommends a minimum configuration of the following six tablespaces:

➤ SYSTEM

➤ TEMPORARY

➤ ROLLBACK

➤ USERS

➤ DATA

➤ INDEX

Each of these tablespaces represents a different type of data, and Oracle benefits in performance if each type of tablespace can be separated onto different physical drives. Even if they cannot be separated physically, the type of data placed into each tablespace is different and should not be mixed.

The **SYSTEM** tablespace should contain only data dictionary tables and objects owned by the SYS and SYSTEM accounts. When you issue the **CREATE DATABASE** statement, Oracle creates these data dictionary tables using the sql.bsq script. You can modify the storage parameters in this file to create the data dictionary tables with sizes more appropriate to your requirements. However, you must not drop, add, or rename any columns or tables. In addition, you should not decrease the storage parameters (with the exception of **PCT-INCREASE**).

Only objects owned by the SYS and SYSTEM accounts should be placed in the **SYSTEM** tablespace. This includes all package definitions, function definitions, triggers, sequences, and so on in the **SYSTEM** tablespace as well. When new users are created and they're not specifically assigned a default or temporary tablespace, the **SYSTEM** tablespace will be used. This can negatively affect performance and result in a highly fragmented **SYSTEM** tablespace, which cannot be defragmented without dropping and re-creating the database. When reviewing statistics, such as the report.txt file obtained from the UTLBSTAT/UTLESTAT utility, look for heavy reads and writes for the **SYSTEM** tablespace. This is an indication that users are defaulting to the **SYSTEM** tablespace for data or sorting, or both.

The **TEMPORARY** tablespace is used for sorting when the sort cannot be performed in memory. Chapter 9 contains in-depth information on turning sorts. Placing the **TEMPORARY** tablespace on a separate disk drive will prevent sorting activities from competing with reads and writes for other Oracle files. User data should never be placed in the **TEMPORARY** tablespace. You can designate a tablespace as being a temporary tablespace only if no permanent objects are in the tablespace.

Rollback segments should be created in a separate **ROLLBACK** tablespace. Rollback segments are used to store "before" images of changed data. You cannot use multiple tablespaces unless you have first created and brought online at least one rollback segment, in addition to the initially created rollback segment in the **SYSTEM** tablespace. Rollback segments are used to roll back transactions (that is, reverse the action of an insert, update, or delete) for recovery and for read consistency. Because of the heavy I/O generated by Data Manipulation Language (DML) activity in an online transaction processing (OLTP) environment, you should try to separate the **ROLLBACK** tablespace on a separate physical disk. You should be aware that you cannot take a tablespace offline if it contains an active rollback segment. Oracle recommends naming the **ROLLBACK** tablespace **RBS**.

In some Oracle environments, end users might need to do more than insert, update, and delete data from application tables. They might need to create tables and other Oracle objects. A **USERS** tablespace should be created and used as the default for end users. Placing user objects in a separate tablespace makes maintenance easier. If possible, place the **USERS** tablespace on a separate physical disk to spread the I/O.

The **DATA** tablespace should be used for objects that contain the data for the application. The **INDEX** tablespace should be used only for indexes. The separate tablespaces created for data and indexes should be placed on different physical drives. If data and indexes are placed on the same disks, much more contention for resources will exist. If you do not have a separate tablespace for indexes (not a good idea), place them in the **USER** tablespace if it's available, assuming that the data files for the **USER** tablespace are located on a different physical device than the data files for the **SYSTEM** and the **DATA** tablespaces. Under no circumstance should you place the indexes in either the **SYSTEM** or the **DATA** tablespace.

A side benefit to placing data files and index files in separate tablespaces is that it gives you the ability to easily compare the activity on the two tablespaces for tuning purposes. If there's high I/O activity on the **DATA** tablespace but relatively little activity in the **INDEX** tablespace, it's a sure indication of poor index usage and full-table scans.

# Striping Tables

*Striping* is a method of spreading data for a single table across several physical disks. Striping can be performed either by the operating system or by hand (the former is easier than the latter). Striping can improve performance for applications that perform many full-table scans and databases using the parallel query option. When determining the size of each stripe, you need to consider both the **DB_BLOCK_SIZE** and **DB_FILE_MULTIBLOCK_READ_COUNT** parameters, as specified in your database initialization parameter file. Oracle can only allocate space by blocks (**DB_BLOCK_SIZE**). The number of blocks that are read at one time for a full-table scan is determined by the **DB_FILE_MULTIBLOCK_READ_COUNT** parameter. By making the size of your database stripes a multiple of **DB_FILE_MULTIBLOCK_READ_COUNT** and **DB_BLOCK_SIZE**, you'll be sizing your stripes to match the amount of database blocks that Oracle will read at one time. This will maximize the effect of striping by reducing I/O for full-table scans.

# Striping With The Operating System

Striping performed by the operating system is accomplished using Redundant Array of Inexpensive Disks (RAID). Special hardware is required for RAID striping. Table 8.1 lists the most-often-used forms of RAID. RAID devices can be very useful in read-intensive systems. The most commonly used versions of RAID are RAID 1 and RAID 5.

RAID 0 is the normal file structure in which no mirroring or operating system striping has been used. All striping on a RAID 0 configuration is performed by hand. RAID 0 configurations can provide excellent performance. Because no mirroring is performed, a disk crash will cause all the data files on that disk to be lost.

RAID 1 provides a mirrored copy of each disk. If a disk is lost, the mirrored copy becomes available automatically. If a file is corrupted by software or end-user error, the mirrored copy of the file is also corrupted. Using RAID 1 requires twice as many disks. One erroneous assumption often made about RAID 1 is that if you're mirroring every file, you do not need multiple members for each redo log group and multiple copies of the control file. Even if RAID 1 mirroring is used, Oracle recommends that you still have a second member in every redo log group. If one of the redo log members is corrupted, the mirror may also be corrupted. In the event that a redo log file can no longer be read by Oracle and there's a second member in the redo log group, Oracle will be able to use that second member. Because of the importance of the control file, you should have at least one additional control file placed on a second physical drive in case of file corruption.

RAID 0+1 uses a combination of data mirroring and disk striping.

RAID 3 uses error-correction codes (ECCs), also called *parity*, for data protection and redundancy. The data is distributed across several disks. RAID 3 stores all the ECCs on one physical disk.

| Table 8.1   Frequently used forms of RAID. | |
| --- | --- |
| **RAID Level** | **Description** |
| 0 | Standard file structure |
| 1 | Disk mirroring |
| 0+1 | Combination of disk striping and mirroring |
| 3 | Striping with one dedicated parity disk |
| 5 | Striping with distributed parity |

RAID 5 is the most common form of operating system striping. It uses ECCs that are stored with the data. Data is distributed across several disks. RAID 5 can provide good performance for read-only applications. However, if an application is write intensive, the constant calculation of ECCs makes write operations much slower. An additional disadvantage of using RAID 5 is that recovery operations are more time consuming. If you need to recover a striped tablespace because of file corruption, all the disks over which the tablespace is striped must be involved in the recovery process.

If you determine that you must stripe your data across multiple drives, operating system striping is much easier to do than striping by hand. The use of a RAID configuration is transparent to Oracle. For randomly accessed files, such as data files and archive logs, a RAID 5 device can improve performance in a read-only application system without additional effort on your part. However, files that must be accessed sequentially, such as redo logs and the **TEMPO-RARY** tablespace, should never be placed on a RAID 5 device.

## Striping By Hand

Striping by hand is performed by creating a tablespace with data files that are located on different physical drives. Striping by hand is very labor intensive and requires an in-depth knowledge of the data and how it's used. Two ways to stripe tables and indexes across the data files are through tablespace storage default and table extent allocation.

With the tablespace storage default method, you create the table or index with multiple extents in which each extent is slightly smaller than the size of each data file. The following code is an example of setting up a striped table with this method:

```
CREATE TABLESPACE employee_ts
DATAFILE '/db01/employee_01.dbf' size 161M,
                '/db02/employee_02.dbf' size 161M,
                '/db03/employee_03.dbf' size 161M
DEFAULT STORAGE (initial 160M next 160M minextents 2)';
CREATE TABLE employee
(first_name          varchar2(20)
, last_name          varchar2(20)
, middle_name        varchar2(20)
, address_line1      varchar2(20)
,address_line2       varchar2(20)
,address_line3       varchar2(20)
,state_code          varchar2(2)
,zip_code            number(5))
TABLESPACE     employee_ts;
```

With the table extent allocation method, you explicitly indicate which data file is to be used for each extent allocated. The following code is an example of using this method:

```
ALTER TABLE employee
ALLOCATE EXTENT (DATAFILE '/db01/employee_02.dbf' SIZE 160M);
```

# Storage Parameters

The smallest unit of I/O in Oracle is a *block*, the size of which is determined by the **DB_BLOCK_SIZE** parameter in the database initialization parameter file at the time the database is created. Although you cannot change the **DB_BLOCK_SIZE** parameter after the database is created, storage parameters can be used to determine how much data is stored in each block. Each extent is made up of blocks, and you can use storage parameters to control the number of extents and the size of each.

The **ANALYZE** command can be used to obtain statistics on space usage for tables and indexes. Table 8.2 lists the columns in the **DBA_TABLES** view that are relevant to analyzing space used for each table. You can also access this information with the associated **USER_TABLES** and **ALL_TABLES** views.

The **EMPTY_BLOCKS** column references the number of blocks that have never been used, not the number of blocks currently empty. If the number of empty blocks is high, you should consider reorganizing the table to release this space for use by other objects.

| Table 8.2 | Data dictionary view columns relevant to the space used by a table. |
| --- | --- |
| **Column** | **Description** |
| num_rows | Number of rows in the table |
| blocks | Number of used blocks (blocks below the high-water mark) |
| empty_blocks | Number of blocks that have never been used (blocks above the high-water mark) |
| avg_space | Average available free space below the high-water mark (in bytes) |
| avg_row_len | Average length of a row (including overhead) |
| chain_cnt | Number of chained and migrated rows |

Oracle provides both tablespace and object parameters that can be used to determine space usage. If an individual table does not include explicit storage parameters, the defaults specified for the tablespace are used. If no default storage parameter is specified for the tablespace, the Oracle tablespace defaults are used.

If you decide to reorganize a table, you can use either the export/import method or the create/rename method. In the export/import method, you will need to export the table, drop the table, re-create the table with more appropriate storage parameters, and import the data with the **IGNORE=Y** option. In the create/rename method, you'll need to create a new table using the **CREATE TABLE...AS** command, drop the old table, and rename the new table to the original name. The second option can be used only if you have sufficient space for two copies of the table.

The parameters set for your tablespaces and objects determine how space is used by Oracle blocks. The storage parameters, along with the block size, can determine how efficient your database reads and writes data. Although resetting some of these parameters might require reorganizing a table or index, all the options discussed in this section can be changed without re-creating the database. Table 8.3 lists the storage parameters and their defaults.

| Table 8.3    Storage parameter defaults. | |
| --- | --- |
| **Parameter** | **Default** |
| **INITIAL EXTENT** | Five Oracle data blocks |
| **NEXT EXTENT** | Five Oracle data blocks |
| **MINEXTENTS** | Two for rollback segments; one for all other objects |
| **MAXEXTENTS** | Varies, depending on the operating system |
| **PCTINCREASE** | 50 percent |
| **FREELISTS** | 1 |
| **FREELIST GROUPS** | 1 |
| **OPTIMAL** | Null (used only for rollback segments) |
| **INITRANS** | For clusters, the default value is 2 or the **INITRANS** value for the cluster's tablespace, whichever is greater. The value of this parameter for a cluster cannot be less than 2 or more than the value of the **MAXTRANS** parameter. For indexes, the default value is 2. For tables, the default value is 1. In general, this value should not be changed. |

*(continued)*

| Parameter | Default |
|-----------|---------|
| **MAXTRANS** | Operating-system dependent |
| **PCTFREE** | 10 percent |
| **PCTUSED** | 40 percent (not applicable for indexes) |

Table 8.3  Storage parameter defaults (continued).

# Chaining And Row Migration

Chaining and row migration cause additional I/O because more than one block must be read to obtain the data for a single row. When a row is too large to fit in a single Oracle block, it must be spread across blocks. Rows spread across two or more blocks are referred to as *chained rows*. Chained rows are inevitable if the **DB_BLOCK_SIZE** parameter is smaller than the largest row. For example, if your **DB_BLOCK_SIZE** parameter is 4096 (4K) and your row is equal to 5120 (5K), the row will need to be spread across two blocks. The **AVG_ROW_LEN** column in the **DBA_TABLES, ALL_TABLES,** or **USER_TABLES** table will provide you with information on the average length of a row in the table. If the number of bytes in the **AVG_ROW_LEN** parameter is larger than your **DB_BLOCK_SIZE** parameter, you'll have a problem with row chaining. The only way to resolve this is to re-create the database with a larger block size.

A more manageable problem is row migration. If a row that has been inserted into a block is updated to a size that will no longer fit into that block, the row must be moved to another block that will hold the entire row. When rows are moved from one block to another, they're referred to as *migrated rows*. Oracle sets a pointer at the block that originally contained the row to indicate the new block location for the row. This increases I/O when an index goes to the block to retrieve the specified row and then must go to another block to actually obtain the row. Rows can be migrated more than once. For example, suppose that a row is initially inserted in a block. That row is later updated and can no longer fit into the block. The row is moved to a new block that has sufficient free space for the entire row, and an indicator is left to point to the new location for the row. If the row is updated again in the new location and can no longer fit into that block, an indicator is placed in the second block and the row is moved to another block. With each move of the row, additional I/O is needed to locate the row.

Row migration can be detected, resolved, and prevented. To obtain information on chained and migrated rows, you can execute the **ANALYZE** command. When a table is analyzed, information on the number of chained rows is provided. You can view the **CHAIN_CNT** column in the **DBA_TABLES,**

**ALL_TABLES,** or **USER_TABLES** table to see the number of chained and migrated rows. You can also use the **ANALYZE** command to obtain specific information on which rows are chained or migrated. The following code is an example of using the **ANALYZE** command to obtain information on specific chained and migrated rows:

```
ANALYZE TABLE sandy.employee LIST CHAINED ROWS;
```

By default, the results are placed in the **CHAINED_ROWS** table. You can specify another table to hold the results. If you prefer to use another table, it must match the column structure of the **CHAINED_ROWS** table, as described in Table 8.4. This table is created by the utlchain.sql script.

Once you have identified the migrated or chained rows, you can use one of two methods to resolve this problem. You can export the table and then either truncate the table or re-create it with more appropriate parameters and import the rows. The alternate way is to reorganize only the rows listed in the **CHAINED_ROWS** table. Before you begin this process, you should have an export of the table in case you encounter a problem and need to start over. The following steps are used to reorganize the chained rows:

1. Execute the **ANALYZE** command to fill in the **CHAINED_ROWS** table:

```
ANALYZE TABlF employee LIST CHAINED ROWS;
```

2. Create a new table to temporarily store the chained rows:

```
CREATE TABLE chained_employee AS
SELECT * FROM employee
WHERE rowid IN
    (SELECT head_rowid FROM chained_rows);
```

**Table 8.4  Data dictionary view for information on chained and migrated rows.**

| Column | Definition |
| --- | --- |
| owner_name | Table owner |
| table_name | Name of the table |
| cluster_name | Name of the cluster, if applicable |
| head_rowid | The row ID of the chained row |
| timestamp | The date and time when the **ANALYZE** command was used to obtain this information |

3. Delete the chained rows from the table:

```
DELETE FROM employee
WHERE rowid in
      (SELECT head_rowid FROM chained_rows);
```

4. Insert the rows back into the table:

```
INSERT INTO employee
SELECT * FROM chained_employee;
```

5. Drop the intermediate table:

```
DROP TABLE chained_employee;
```

To prevent further row migration, you should adjust the **PCTFREE** parameter to allow sufficient space for updates to the rows.

Although indexes do not have chained or migrated rows, you will have increased I/O if the number of levels for a B-tree index exceeds 2. You can analyze your indexes and then look at the **BLEVEL** column in **DBA_INDEXES**, **ALL_INDEXES,** or **USER_INDEXES.** If **BLEVEL** is zero, the root blocks contain the entire index. If **BLEVEL** is greater than 2, you can rebuild the index to reduce the number of levels. Rebuilding your indexes regularly can decrease I/O and improve performance significantly.

The **VALIDATE STRUCTURE** keyword in the **ANALYZE** command is another way to obtain information on the space used by your indexes. The following is an example of this syntax:

```
ANALYZE INDEX employee_name_ind VALIDATE STRUCTURE;
```

This command will check for corruption and provide important statistics on the index. If your index is corrupted, you should drop and rebuild it. Statistical information on your indexes can be found in the **INDEX_STATS** view, described in Table 8.5. Depending on the type of application, you might want to rebuild the index if the total number of deletions is more than 20 percent of the total number of current rows. You can use the following code to determine this percentage:

```
SELECT (del_lf_rows_len / lf_rows_len) * 100 FROM index_stats;
```

When building an index, you can reduce the required I/O with the **UNRE-COVERABLE** option. This option builds the index without using the redo logs and therefore reduces I/O. When you build an index with this option, any

| Table 8.5 | Data dictionary view for statistical information on indexes. |
|---|---|
| **Column** | **Description** |
| **height** | Height of the B-tree index (levels) |
| **blocks** | Number of blocks allocated to this index |
| **name** | Name of the index |
| **lf_rows** | Number of values (leaf rows) in the index |
| **lf_blks** | Number of B-tree leaf blocks |
| **lf_rows_len** | Total length (in bytes) of all the rows in the B-tree index |
| **lf_blk_len** | Usable space in a leaf block |
| **br_rows** | Number of branch rows in the B-tree index |
| **br_blks** | Number of branch blocks in the B-tree index |
| **br_rows_len** | Total lengths of all the branch blocks in the B-tree index |
| **br_blk_len** | Usable space in a branch block |
| **del_lf_rows** | Number of deleted rows |
| **del_lf_rows_len** | Total length (in bytes) of the deleted rows |
| **distinct_keys** | Number of distinct keys (sometimes includes deleted rows) |
| **most_repeated_key** | Number of repetitions for the most repeated key (sometimes includes deleted rows) |
| **btree_space** | Total allocated space for the B-tree index |
| **used_space** | Total space used for the B-tree index |
| **pct_used** | Percentage of allocated space being used |
| **rows_per_key** | Average number of rows per distinct key |
| **blks_gets_per_access** | An estimate for the number of consistent mode block reads necessary to access a row in the B-tree index |

failure will mean that you must reexecute the SQL command to build the index. Because indexes do not contain data, you can easily rebuild the index with an SQL command.

# High-Water Mark

The *high-water mark* is the top limit for the number of blocks that have been used for a table. The high-water mark is recorded in the segment header and is incremented five Oracle blocks at a time as rows are inserted into blocks. The high-water mark is important because of the effect it has when a full-table scan is performed. When performing a full-table scan, Oracle will read all the blocks below the high-water mark even if they're empty blocks. Having many unused blocks below the high-water mark degrades performance for full-table scans with additional, unnecessary I/O.

You should use the **ANALYZE** command to obtain statistics on your tables. Table 8.2 earlier in the chapter lists the relevant columns in the **DBA_TABLES** view. Compare the number of blocks that contain rows with the number of blocks that are available below the high-water mark. This will help you determine the proportion of underused space below the high-water mark. You can use the following formula:

$$1- r/h$$

Here, $r$ represents the number of blocks with rows and $h$ represents the number of blocks below the high-water mark.

You can find the number of blocks with rows with the following statement:

```
SELECT count(distinct substr(rowid, 15,4) || substr(rowid, 1,8) )
FROM schema.table;
```

The number of blocks below the high-water mark is in the **BLOCKS** column in the **DBA_TABLES** view.

If the result from the formula is zero, you do not need to rebuild your table. If the result is greater than zero, you should consider your environment and application before deciding whether to reorganize your table.

If your application is well indexed and rarely performs full-table scans, empty blocks below the high-water mark, although consuming space, are not being accessed. If you receive different results from this formula at different times, this might be only a temporary problem that does not require reorganization. You also need to consider the time you have, the available space, and whether rebuilding the table is a priority.

Oracle also provides the built-in **DBMS_SPACE** package, which can be used to help you determine your high-water mark and space usage. The **DBMS_SPACE** package is created with the dbmsutil.sql script, which is called by the catproc.sql script.

The **DBMS_SPACE** package contains two procedures: **UNUSED_SPACE** and **FREE_BLOCKS**. Listing 8.1 shows **DBMS_SPACE.UNUSED_SPACE**

and Listing 8.2 shows **DBMS_SPACE.FREE_BLOCKS**. The **UNUSED_
SPACE** procedure returns information on the unused space for a segment. The
**FREE_BLOCKS** procedure returns information on the free blocks for a segment. To execute these procedures, the user must have the **ANALYZE ANY**
system privilege.

### Listing 8.1   **DBMS_SPACE.UNUSED_SPACE**.

```
unused_space(
        segment_owner               IN      varchar2,
        segment_name                IN      varchar2,
        segment_type                IN      varchar2,
        total_blocks                OUT     number,
        total_bytes                 OUT     number,
        unused_blocks               OUT     number,
        unused_bytes                OUT     number,
        last_used_extent_file       OUT     number,
        last_used_extent_block_id   OUT     number,
        last_used_block             OUT     number
                )
```

### Listing 8.2   **DBMS_SPACE.FREE_BLOCKS**.

```
free_blocks(
        segment_owner               IN      varchar2
        segment_name                IN      varchar2,
        segment_type                IN      varchar2,
        treelist_group_id           IN      varchar2,
        free_blks                   OUT     number,
        scan_limit                  IN      number      DEFAULT NULL
                )
```

The high-water mark is set at the beginning of the segment when the table is
created. Deleting rows will never reset the high-water mark even if all the rows
are deleted from the table. Only the **TRUNCATE** command will reset the
high-water mark. You can delete empty blocks that have never been used (blocks
that are above the high-water mark) with the **ALTER TABLE** command.
Here's the syntax for this command:

```
ALTER TABLE table_name DEALLOCATE UNUSED;
```

Blocks above the high-water mark are ignored and have no effect on performance. However, this wastes space. If space is an issue, you should reclaim the
empty blocks.

# INITIAL EXTENT

The **INITIAL EXTENT** parameter specifies the space allocated for the very first extent of an object when it's created. Once an object is created, you cannot change the initial extent size. You can, however, change the tablespace default storage parameter for initial extents. The new tablespace default storage parameter will be used for any new tables that are created without a storage specification.

If your **INITIAL EXTENT** parameter is sized for full expected growth of each object, you'll waste space in the early stage of database population and will not improve performance. Instead, Oracle recommends that **INITIAL EXTENT** and **NEXT EXTENT** be sized the same.

# NEXT EXTENT

The **NEXT EXTENT** parameter specifies the size of the next extent that's allocated for the object. When a block cannot be found in which to insert a new row or to place a migrated row, Oracle will add an extent to the object on the basis of the size specified in this parameter. The space for each **NEXT EXTENT** must be one contiguous section of disk. An extent map is used to track the location of all the extents allocated to an object. This extent map is located in the segment header and contains the disk address for each extent allocated to an object.

Oracle does not view the total number of extents as impacting I/O for an index or a table. To improve performance, you should make all extents (both initial and next for indexes and tables) a multiple of the database initialization parameter for **DB_FILE_MULTIBLOCK_READ_COUNT** multiplied by the **DB_BLOCK_SIZE** parameter. The only SQL command that will take longer if there are multiple extents is the **DROP TABLE** command.

# MINEXTENTS

The **MINEXTENTS** parameter is the minimum number of extents that will be allocated when the segment is initially created. You can reduce the overhead involved in creating new extents by allocating additional extents when an object is created. Rollback segments are always created with a minimum of two extents.

# MAXEXTENTS

The **MAXEXTENTS** parameter specifies the maximum number of extents that can be allocated for a segment. Once this number is reached, no new extents can be created, and the user will receive an error message. Oracle8 also allows this to be set to **UNLIMITED**.

# PCTINCREASE

The **PCTINCREASE** parameter is used to determine the percent by which the extents will increase as new extents are allocated. Once the **NEXT EXTENT** parameter is allocated, the new value for **NEXT EXTENT** is determined by multiplying **PCTINCREASE** by the value of **NEXT EXTENT**. The **PCTINCREASE** parameter for rollback segments is always set to zero and cannot be increased. If the **PCTINCREASE** parameter is set to zero at the tablespace level, Oracle will not automatically coalesce space for that tablespace. **PCTINCREASE** should normally be set to zero for most application tables.

# FREELISTS

The **FREELISTS** parameter specifies the number of free lists. A *free list* is a list of the free blocks available for the insertion of new rows into an object. At least one free list is maintained in every segment header. When the amount of space in a block drops below **PCTUSED**, that block is added to the free lists. If the high-water mark for a table changes, blocks can also be added to the free lists. When the space available reaches **PCTFREE**, new rows are no longer inserted into that block, and the block is removed from the free lists. If the size of a new row would fill the block over the **PCTFREE** parameter, the row is not inserted into that block.

Oracle will search through all blocks on the free lists until it finds a block where the row can be inserted. If no block will allow the row to be inserted without exceeding the **PCTFREE** parameter, a new extent will be created. Because Oracle will search through all the free lists for a block to hold the new row, it's important that the **PCTFREE** and **PCTUSED** parameters be sized correctly; otherwise, the free lists will contain a growing number of blocks that cannot be used. The resulting overhead negatively affects performance when new rows are inserted. There will also be additional overhead if blocks are continuously placed on and then removed from the free lists. If the **PCTFREE** and **PCTUSED** parameters equal 100 percent, blocks will be continuously placed on and taken off the free lists. The gap between **PCTFREE** and **PCTUSED** should be greater than the average row size for the segment. If no space is left in the blocks and no empty transaction slots exist, the application will hang. Although this might appear to be a locking problem, it's actually a space problem.

If there are many inserts and deletes for a table, contention for access to the free lists can result in waits for the free lists. The **V$WAITSTAT** view indicates whether contention exists for the free lists. However, this view does not indicate which table or index has the problem. The following SQL statement can be used to obtain the number of waits for free lists:

```
SELECT class, count  FROM v$waitstat
WHERE class = 'free list';
```

The following SQL statement can be used to obtain the total number of requests:

```
SELECT sum(value)  FROM v$sysstat
WHERE name in ('db block gets', 'consistent gets');
```

You should compare the number of free block waits with the total number of requests. If this is more than 1 percent, you need to determine which tables have a problem with free lists and increase the **FREELISTS** parameters for those tables. You must rely on your knowledge of the application to determine which tables have a high number of inserts and deletes and would therefore be candidates for free lists contention.

The number of free lists associated with a table or index cannot be changed with an **ALTER** command. The maximum value depends on the **DB_ BLOCK_SIZE** parameter. If you attempt to create an object with a **FREELISTS** value that's too high, Oracle will generate an error message. To change the number of free lists, you must export the table, drop the table, re-create the table with the new value for **FREELISTS**, and import the data.

Free lists for index segments are handled slightly different than free lists for tables. When an index block becomes empty, it's placed on the free lists. As long as the block contains even one entry, it will be maintained separately and not placed on the free lists.

## FREELIST GROUPS

The **FREELIST GROUPS** parameter is valid only if you're using the Parallel Server option in parallel mode. This parameter specifies the number of free list groups that can be associated with a segment.

## OPTIMAL

The size a rollback segment will dynamically shrink back to is specified by the **OPTIMAL** parameter. This can be specified in bytes, kilobytes, or megabytes. The minimum for **OPTIMAL** cannot be less than the space initially allocated with the **INITIAL**, **NEXT**, and **MINEXTENTS** parameters, as specified in the **CREATE ROLLBACK SEGMENT** command. You need to combine the space requirements specified in these storage parameters to determine the minimal **OPTIMAL** setting. The maximum value is operating-system dependent.

If **OPTIMAL** is not specified, Oracle will still allocate extents for active transactions, as needed, but will not deallocate extents when they're no longer needed. If the **OPTIMAL** setting is used, Oracle will deallocate extents only down to the **OPTIMAL** setting. You can use the **OPTIMAL** parameter to allow more efficient use of disk space for infrequent, large transactions. If **OPTIMAL** is used, it must be set high enough to accommodate the majority of the transactions. If **OPTIMAL** is set too low, the rollback segment will continually allocate and deallocate extents causing additional overhead.

# INITRANS

The **INITRANS** parameter specifies the initial number of transaction entries that are allocated for each block associated with a table. This value should usually remain at the default value of 2 for indexes and clusters and 1 for other objects. Each update requires a transaction entry in the block header. Transaction entries are used to control the number of concurrent updates to a block. The number of transactions is allocated and deallocated dynamically. The size of a transaction is operating-system dependent.

# MAXTRANS

The **MAXTRANS** parameter is the maximum number of transactions updating a block concurrently. You should not change the value for **MAXTRANS**. When the **MAXTRANS** value is reached, Oracle will not make additional updates to the block even if additional free space is available.

# PCTFREE And PCTUSED

The **PCTFREE** (percent free) and **PCTUSED** (percent used) parameters allow you to control the amount of space allocated for updates and inserts into a block. These parameters are used together to optimize space utilization for blocks. It is important that you consider both **PCTFREE** and **PCTUSED** when you plan the storage parameters for each object in your database.

## PCTFREE

The **PCTFREE** parameter specifies the percentage of the block that is to be retained for updates to rows in the block. Row migration will result if the **PCTFREE** parameter is insufficient for the increased size of the rows in the block. When inserting rows into a table, the **PCTFREE** parameter controls when new rows can be inserted and when they must be placed in a new block or a block that's on the free lists. For very static tables with very few updates, the **PCTFREE** parameter should be lower to allow more rows to be inserted into each block. Because all the blocks below the high-water mark for a table are read for full-table scans, performance will be improved and I/O decreased if each block contains the maximum amount of data. However, if **PCTFREE** is set too low, rows that are updated will become chained, and performance will be negatively affected.

Use the following formula to determine a correct setting for **PCTFREE**:

```
PCTFREE = 100 * a/(a+b)
```

Here, *a* represents the average amount added for an update and *b* represents the average size of the initial row.

**PCTFREE** can be changed with the **ALTER** command. Changing **PCTFREE** does not affect existing blocks. However, all future DML will use the new **PCTFREE** parameter.

## PCTUSED

The **PCTUSED** parameter specifies the percentage of the block below which the block usage must drop in order for the block to be added to the free lists. **PCTUSED** is relevant only to tables in which rows are deleted. For example, data is inserted into a block until it reaches the specified **PCTFREE** amount. That block is taken off the free lists until data is deleted down to the setting for **PCTUSED**. When the **PCTUSED** setting is reached again, the block is placed back on the free lists, and data is once again inserted into the block until the **PCTFREE** setting is reached. A high **PCTUSED** setting, in conjunction with a low **PCTFREE** setting, can lead to blocks being taken on and off the free lists continually, which increases overhead.

For tables that have many inserts and few deletes, you should set the **PCTUSED** parameter to a higher number. A higher **PCTUSED** number in conjunction with a lower **PCTFREE** number will pack each block and increase performance by decreasing the number of blocks that need to be read for full-table scans (decreasing I/O).

**PCTUSED** can be changed with the **ALTER** command. Changing **PCTUSED** does not affect existing blocks. However, all future DML will use the new **PCTUSED** parameter.

# Other Database Configuration Options

File placement, striping, and adjusting object storage parameters are important to database configuration. There are several other advanced database configuration options that can be used for specific types of database environments. This includes the use of raw devices, clustering tables, parallelism, multithreaded server (MTS), pinning packages, and caching tables. It is important to carefully review your application server and individual requirements before using any of these options.

## Raw Devices

A *raw device* is a Unix-character special file that Oracle can read from and write to directly without Unix I/O buffering. From Oracle's perspective, tablespaces are created the same regardless of whether the operating system file is a raw device or a data file. Oracle addresses the advantages and disadvantages of using raw devices in its OFA. Raw devices require expert system and database administration to set up and administer. It's possible to mix the use of raw devices for highly active OLTP-related tablespaces with standard file systems for other tablespaces and files.

In a few specific situations, Oracle recommends the use of raw devices. If you are using the Oracle Parallel Server for multiple nodes that are using a single database on a shared disk array, you must use Unix raw devices. You cannot mount a shared disk simultaneously on multiple servers. If you are using a non-Unix server that does not have asynchronous I/O, a raw device will enhance performance. Raw devices can also be used to improve performance for write-intensive redo logs.

There are several disadvantages to using raw devices. Raw devices are much more difficult to administer. The following operations are much more complex when raw devices are used:

➤ Backup and recovery

➤ I/O load balancing

➤ Adding files to the database

Oracle discourages the use of raw devices in any database environment in which you cannot practice backup and recovery operations before the database is used for production. In addition, you must be able to leave two or more large, unformatted disk slices available to accommodate an increase in the size of your database or to perform load balancing. You should always try to identify and resolve I/O bottlenecks as much as possible before you consider using raw devices. Remember that using raw devices does not negate the recommendations for placement of Oracle files on the server.

# Clustering Tables

*Clustering* allows the rows in two tables to be stored together in the same block on the basis of the common value in both tables. The deciding factor for determining whether to cluster tables is how they're accessed by users of your application. Tables should be clustered only if they're referenced in the same SQL statement using a join with an equality condition.

If you often perform full-table scans of the individual tables, a cluster will actually increase I/O. When a full-table scan is performed on a cluster, it will be necessary to read all the blocks associated with the cluster even if the block is empty. If the clustered tables are accessed separately in an SQL statement, clustering will negatively affect performance because many more blocks will need to be read.

Another deciding factor is the size of your data blocks in relation to the size of the cluster key. When Oracle reads data from a cluster, it must read all the blocks that are associated with that cluster key. If it is necessary to read several blocks of data to read one row, using a cluster will involve more physical reads than accessing an unclustered table with a primary key index.

It is important to determine a baseline for performance of SQL statements using a join and indexes before clustering tables. This baseline will give you a basis by which to compare the effect of using a cluster. The application code should be thoroughly tested to determine whether using a cluster will increase performance in one area but negatively affect other application code.

To cluster two tables, you must first decide on the cluster key for your data. A cluster key should consist of the common column or columns that are used in the **WHERE** clause with an equality condition. In addition, the cluster key should be composed of columns that are rarely, if ever, updated. The time required to modify the cluster can be significant if the change to the key causes the data to be moved to another block in the cluster. If too few cluster keys are specified, you'll have collisions (that is, two rows having the same cluster key value). For Oracle to identify the correct row for clusters with the same cluster key value, it's necessary to evaluate all the rows in all the blocks with that value. This slows the performance for scans of clustered tables.

# Parallelism

If your server has more than one CPU, you can take advantage of the parallel query option. This option allows multiple processes to work on retrieving the data. The application of parallelism on massively parallel, clustered, symmetric multiprocessing (SMP) servers or on tables that take advantage of striping can significantly improve performance. The default degree of parallelism is **NOPARALLEL**.

A parallel query is performed using a query coordinator and multiple query servers. Parallelism is used for both scanning and sorting. Separate query servers are used for these operations. The number of query servers for each process is equal to the degree of parallelism specified in **DEGREE**. Because there are two processes (sorting and scanning), the number of parallel query processes is two multiplied by the degree of parallelism specified in **DEGREE**. The query coordinator dispatches the query servers to perform the query against parts of the table and coordinates the results of the multiple query servers. This speeds up full-table scans and sort operations. You can alter the degree of parallelism for a table with the following syntax:

```
ALTER TABLE table_name PARALLEL (DEGREE Integer);
```

Here's an example:

```
ALTER TABLE employee PARALLEL (DEGREE 5);
```

This example would enable queries against the **employee** table to use 5 query servers for sorting and 5 query servers for scanning, for a total of 10 query processes.

The following types of SQL statements can be performed with the parallel query option:

➤ SELECT

➤ Subqueries in **UPDATE, INSERT**, and **DELETE**

➤ CREATE TABLE...AS SELECT

➤ CREATE INDEX

➤ REBUILD INDEX

The syntax for the parallel clause is shown in Figure 8.1.

The query server is responsible for determining which parts of an SQL statement can be performed in parallel. The query server will determine what can

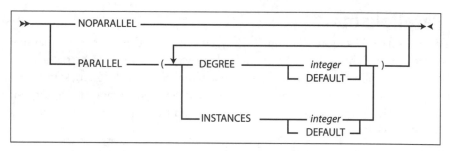

**Figure 8.1**   Syntax for defining parallelism.

be performed in parallel on the basis of hints, the database initialization file parameters, and the table definition. Table 8.6 specifies the relevant database initialization file parameters. The default is operating-system dependent with the exception of **PARALLEL_MIN_PERCENT** and **PARALLEL_MIN_ SERVERS**, both of which default to zero.

You can also take advantage of Oracle's parallel query option to build indexes. Two sets of query servers are used when building an index in parallel. One set retrieves the column and row information from the table. The other set performs the sorting and builds the B-tree index.

When parallelism is used in creating a table or an index, the storage allocated by Oracle for the initial extent is equal to the degree of parallelism multiplied by the size of the **INITIAL EXTENT** parameter. Each of the query servers will be allocated disk space equal to the size of the initial extent. When the query servers return the results to the query coordinator, all the results will be combined into one initial extent and trimmed, as determined by the query coordinator. For example, if you create a table with **INITIAL 10M** using **PARALLEL DEGREE 5**, the resulting initial extent could be as much as 50MB.

| Table 8.6    Database initialization parameters for parallelism. | |
|---|---|
| **Parameter** | **Description** |
| **PARALLEL_DEFAULT_MAX_ INSTANCES** | The number of instances to be used for the parallel operation |
| **PARALLEL_MAX_SERVERS** | The maximum number of servers |
| **PARALLEL_MIN_PERCENT** | The minimum number of query servers (slaves) required |
| **PARALLEL_MIN_SERVERS** | The number of query servers initiated at startup |
| **PARALLEL_SERVER_IDLE_TIME** | The number of minutes a query server can be idle before it is terminated |

The parallel server option is different from the parallel query option in that the former supports multiple servers accessing the same database. The database is placed on a shared disk array that can be accessed by multiple servers in a parallel server configuration. In such a configuration, placing data is even more important. Because all the nodes can access the same data, data contention becomes a key point, and distribution of the data files is vital.

# Multithreaded Server Configuration

Oracle supports two types of database connections: dedicated and shared. Each dedicated connection to Oracle requires a process on the server. Dedicated connections are required for Server Manager. Application connections can use either dedicated connections or shared connections. Shared connections are made using the multithreaded server (MTS) configuration. Connections using MTS reduce the number of processes executing on the server. This is especially useful when many end users are accessing the system at the same time and the server is approaching the limits for processes and semaphores. Users performing large batch processes or database-intensive work will find no advantage to using MTS. The use of MTS affects the shared pool.

> *Note: For information on tuning the shared pool for an MTS configuration, see Chapter 5.*

If you look at the users who are connected to a database, you will see that the session is usually inactive. The only time the session is active is when Oracle is executing a **SELECT, INSERT, UPDATE,** or **DELETE** command. The time period during which a user process is inactive is usually referred to as *think time*. Think time is when a user is typing data onto a screen, composing an SQL query, reviewing the data returned by an SQL query, and so on. The shared server concept is based on the idea of optimizing the active time for all connections. With MTS, users share database servers, and database dispatchers coordinate the process.

To use MTS, you must set the database initialization parameters and then shut down and start up the database. Table 8.7 lists the database initialization parameters that are associated with MTS. The MTS option requires the use of SQL*Net version 2. The SQL*Net listener process should always be started before the database using MTS is started so that the database can register with the listener process on startup. Once the database is started using MTS, all connections will use shared servers and dispatchers automatically, unless the connection is specified as a dedicated connection. The only exception is Server Manager, which always creates a dedicated connection.

## Table 8.7 Multithreaded server database initialization parameters.

| Parameter | Default | Description |
|---|---|---|
| MTS_DISPATCHERS | Null | The number of dispatchers at database startup for each network protocol supported. |
| MTS_LISTENER_ADDRESS | Null | The network protocol address as specified in the SQLNET listener.ora file. |
| MTS_MAX_DISPATCHERS | 5 | The maximum number of dispatcher processes. |
| MTS_MAX_SERVERS | 20 | The maximum number of shared server processes. |
| MTS_MULTIPLE_LISTENERS | FALSE | Indicates multiple **MTS_LISTENER_ ADDRESS** parameters in one consolidated list. |
| MTS_SERVERS | 0 | The number of shared server processes at database startup. |
| MTS_SERVICE | DB_NAME | The connect string to be used if no dispatcher is available. This is the value of the SID in the **CONNECT_ DATA** clause of the tnsnames.ora file. |

When a user logs on to a database that is using MTS, a dispatcher picks up the connection request from the listener and places it in a request queue located in the system global area (SGA). Shared server processes constantly check the request queue for new requests. A shared server picks up the request and performs all the calls necessary to satisfy that request. The results are placed in a response queue for the dispatcher from which the request was initiated. The dispatcher process picks up the response and sends the information to the user. As more users log on to the database, additional dispatchers and servers will be created dynamically up to the **MTS_MAX_DISPATCHERS** and **MTS_MAX_SERVERS** limits. As users log off the database, the number of dispatchers and servers is dynamically decreased down to the number specified by the **MTS_SERVERS** and **MTS_DISPATCHERS** database initialization parameters.

The **V$MTS** view, described in Table 8.8, contains information on the MTS connections. If the **SERVERS_HIGHWATER** column is equal to the **MTS_ MAX_SERVERS** value in the database initialization parameter file, you should consider increasing the value of the **MTS_MAX_SERVERS** parameter.

| Table 8.8    V$MTS data dictionary view. | |
| --- | --- |
| **Column** | **Description** |
| maximum_connections | The maximum number of connections each dispatcher can support (based on the operating system) |
| servers_started | The total number of additional shared servers started since the database started (excluding those specified during startup) |
| servers_terminated | The total number of shared servers stopped since instance startup |
| servers_highwater | The highest number of servers at any time |

When using MTS, you need to be aware that you could encounter artificial deadlocks. When a user tries to commit and the process hangs, it might appear to the end user that there is a deadlock situation. However, the real problem is that the **COMMIT** command cannot be executed because of a problem with MTS. Artificial deadlocks are encountered when the maximum number of shared servers has been reached and no additional requests can be processed (including **COMMIT** and **ROLLBACK** statements).

If the database is configured to use the MTS option, you need to monitor the dispatchers and shared servers. You should establish a baseline and then monitor the MTS dispatchers and shared servers when users are accessing the database. You should increase the maximum number of dispatchers and shared servers when contention exists for these processes. The following three views are important in monitoring your dispatchers and shared servers for MTS:

➤ V$DISPATCHER

➤ V$QUEUE

➤ V$SHARED_SERVER

These views are available only to the SYS user and to users with the **SELECT ANY TABLE** system privilege.

Remember that these **V$** views represent cumulative statistics since the last time the database was shut down and restarted.

## V$DISPATCHER

You can use the **V$DISPATCHER** view to monitor your dispatchers. Table 8.9 describes the **V$DISPATCHER** view, and Table 8.10 lists the possible values for the **STATUS** column of the **V$DISPATCHER** view and the meaning for each. The **IDLE** and **BUSY** columns are the most important items to monitor for the dispatcher. The following query can be used to determine the total busy rate for the dispatcher for each network:

```
SELECT network,
       sum(busy) / (sum(busy) + sum(idle) )
FROM V$DISPATCHER
GROUP BY network;
```

If the total busy rate is greater than 50 percent, you should add additional dispatcher processes. You can do this with the following command:

```
ALTER SYSTEM SET mts_dispatchers = 'protocol, number';
```

### Table 8.9    V$DISPATCHER data dictionary view.

| Column | Description |
| --- | --- |
| name | The name of this dispatcher process. |
| network | The network protocol (that is, TCP or DECNET). |
| paddr | The process address. |
| status | The status of the dispatcher. |
| accept | **YES** indicates that this dispatcher is accepting new connections; **NO** indicates that this dispatcher is not accepting new connections. |
| messages | The number of messages processed by this dispatcher. |
| bytes | The total number of bytes for the messages processed by this dispatcher. |
| breaks | The number of breaks that have occurred in this connection. |
| owned | The number of circuits owned by this dispatcher. |
| created | The number of circuits created by this dispatcher. |
| idle | The total idle time (in hundredths of a second). |
| busy | The total busy time (in hundredths of a second). |
| listener | The last error number received from the listener process. |

### Table 8.10    Status column values for the V$DISPATCHER view.

| Status | Meaning |
|---|---|
| WAIT | Idle |
| SENT | Currently sending a message |
| RECEIVE | Currently receiving a message |
| CONNECT | Establishing a connection |
| DISCONNECT | Processing a request to disconnect |
| BREAK | Processing a break |
| OUTBOUND | Establishing an outbound connection |

This will increase the number of dispatchers for use by new connections. However, it will not increase the number of dispatchers available to users who are already logged on to the database.

## V$SHARED_SERVER

Table 8.11 describes the columns in the **V$SHARED_SERVER** view. Table 8.12 lists the possible values for the **STATUS** column of the **V$SHARED_SERVER** view and the meaning for each. You can determine the number of shared servers that are currently running with the following query:

### Table 8.11    V$SHARED_SERVER data dictionary view.

| Column | Description |
|---|---|
| name | The name of this server process |
| paddr | The process address |
| status | The status of this shared server |
| messages | The number of messages processed by this server |
| bytes | The total number of bytes in all the messages |
| breaks | The number of breaks |
| owned | The number of circuits |
| circuit | The address for the current circuit being served |
| idle | The total idle time (in hundredths of a second) |
| busy | The total busy time (in hundredths of a second) |
| requests | The total number of requests serviced from the common queue since this server was created |

| Table 8.12 | Status column information for the V$SHARED_SERVER view. |
|------------|----------------------------------------------------------|
| **Status** | **Meaning** |
| **EXEC** | Executing an SQL statement |
| **WAIT(ENQ)** | Waiting for a lock |
| **WAIT(SEND)** | Waiting to send data to a user |
| **WAIT(COMMON)** | Waiting for a user request to service |
| **WAIT(RESET)** | Waiting for a circuit to reset after a break |
| **QUIT** | Terminating |

```
SELECT COUNT(*) FROM V$SHARED_SERVER
WHERE status != 'QUIT';
```

If the number of shared servers is approaching the **MTS_MAX_SERVERS** limit, you might be able to improve performance by increasing this database initialization parameter. If you determine that you have set too many shared servers at database startup, you can reduce the number of shared servers. The syntax to increase or reduce the number of shared servers is:

```
ALTER SYSTEM SET MTS_SERVERS = integer;
```

Because Oracle will increase the number of shared servers dynamically, Oracle recommends starting with a low number of servers (1 per 100 users) and increasing the number of shared servers as needed.

## V$QUEUE

V$QUEUE provides information on the MTS queues for the dispatcher and shared servers. Table 8.13 describes the V$QUEUE view. The following query can be used to determine the average wait time for a connection that's waiting in the response queue for a dispatcher process:

```
SELECT network,
       DECODE (SUM(totalq), 0, 'NO RESPONSES',
              SUM(wait)/SUM(totalq) )
FROM V$QUEUE, V$DISPATCHER
WHERE v$queue.type = 'DISPATCHER'
AND    v$queue.paddr = v$dispatcher.paddr
GROUP BY network;
```

| Table 8.13    V$QUEUE data dictionary view. | |
|---|---|
| **Column** | **Description** |
| paddr | The address of the process that owns the queue |
| type | **COMMON** for queues processed by servers; **OUT-BOUND** for queues used by the remote server's dispatcher |
| queued | The number of items in the queue |
| wait | The total time that all items have been queued |
| totalq | The total number of items that have been in the queue |

To determine the average wait time for each shared server request, you can execute the following query:

```
SELECT DECODE( totalq, 0, , 'NO RESPONSES',
                wait/totalq)
FROM V$QUEUE
WHERE type = 'COMMON';
```

Both the **MTS_DISPATCHERS** and the **MTS_SERVERS** parameters can be changed with the **ALTER SYSTEM** command. However, you cannot interactively change the **MTS_MAX_DISPATCHERS** and **MTS_MAX_SERVERS** parameters.

## V$CIRCUIT

If there is a problem with a specific process in the database, you can use the **V$CIRCUIT** view to obtain information on the specific user. Table 8.14 describes the **V$CIRCUIT** view. The **SADDR** column of the **V$CIRCUIT** view provides the session address that corresponds to the **SADDR** column in the **V$SESSION** view. The **V$SESSION** view contains the user name and operating system user information.

If you're using MTS, you should never kill a user process at the operating system prompt. Because connections are shared, other user processes will be killed as well. In addition, you need to be sure that the setting for the **PRO-CESSES** database initialization file parameter includes the total number of all the dispatchers and shared servers that might be active (up to the maximum).

| Table 8.14 V$CIRCUIT data dictionary view. | |
|---|---|
| **Column** | **Description** |
| circuit | The circuit address |
| dispatcher | The current dispatcher process address |
| server | The current server address |
| waiter | The address of the server process waiting for an available circuit |
| saddr | The address of the session |
| status | Set to **BREAK** for "interrupted," **EOF** for "about to be removed," **OUTBOUND** for "outward link to a remote database," or **NORMAL** for "none of the above" |
| queue | Set to **COMMON** if waiting to be picked up by a shared server, **SERVER** if currently being serviced, **OUTBOUND** if waiting to establish a connection, **DISPATCHER** if waiting for a dispatcher, or **NONE** if idle |
| message0 | The size in bytes of the first message buffer |
| message1 | The size in bytes of the second message buffer |
| messages | The total number of messages that have gone through this circuit |
| bytes | The total number of bytes that have gone through this circuit |
| breaks | The total number of interruptions for this circuit |

# Pinning Packages In The Shared Pool

Oracle provides a built-in package, **DBMS_SHARED_POOL**, that can be used to pin packages into the shared pool, thus reducing I/O. The **DBMS_SHARED_POOL** package is created with the dbmspool.sql and prvtpool.plb scripts, which are located in the $ORACLE_HOME/rdbms/admin directory on a Unix server.

The **DBMS_SHARED_POOL.KEEP** procedure will pin the package in the shared pool and prevent it from being aged out or flushed out of the shared pool. The package is not immediately read into the shared pool when this procedure is executed. Rather, it's kept in the shared pool once it has been accessed. The package will stay in the shared pool until the **DBMS_SHARED_POOL.UNKEEP** procedure is executed or the database is shut down. Once the **UNKEEP** procedure has been executed, the package will age out of the shared pool normally.

*Note: For more information on pinning and unpinning objects in the shared pool, see Chapter 5.*

## Caching Tables In The Shared Pool

If you have a table that is frequently accessed, especially with a full-table scan, you can cache the table in the shared pool. This does not permanently read the table into the shared pool or prevent it from being aged out. Full-table scans usually result in the table being placed at the least recently used end of the LRU list and then being quickly aged out. Caching the table will place it on the most frequently used end of the LRU list instead of the least recently used end. The **CACHE** keyword can be used when creating the table to cache it in the shared pool. You can also use hints (for detailed information on hints, see Chapter 5) or the **ALTER TABLE** command to cache a table in the shared pool. The following is an example of how to cache a table in the shared pool with an **ALTER TABLE** command:

```
ALTER TABLE state_codes CACHE;
```

# Practice Questions

## Question 1

> Which two conditions might make it worthwhile for you to manually stripe tablespaces across the file system? [Choose two]
>
> ❑ a.  The application is performing many full-table scans.
>
> ❑ b.  There is limited operating system memory.
>
> ❑ c.  The application is performing few full-table scans.
>
> ❑ d.  The server is running in parallel query mode.

The correct answers are a and d. Manually striping tablespaces across a file system is very labor intensive and complex. Striping will increase performance only if there are many full-table scans and if the degree of parallelism is greater than 1 (parallel query mode). If the operation is performing well and not executing many full-table scans, the time and effort involved in striping is not justified. Therefore, answer c is incorrect. Operating system memory has nothing to do with striping. Therefore, answer b is incorrect.

## Question 2

> What should be your goal when tuning I/O?
>
> ○ a.  Distribute I/O as much as possible
>
> ○ b.  Keep Oracle I/O limited to one area of the system
>
> ○ c.  Do not place any non-Oracle files on the system
>
> ○ d.  Reduce writes as much as possible

The correct answer is a. Oracle recommends that the files be distributed across as many drives as possible. Keeping Oracle I/O limited to one area would mean limiting the number of drives for Oracle files and is opposite to Oracle's recommendations. Therefore, answer b is incorrect. Although it is beneficial to have only Oracle files on a system, this might not be realistic. Therefore, answer c is incorrect. Reducing the number of writes would not reduce the number of physical reads. Therefore, answer d is incorrect.

# Question 3

Which strategy should you follow when your system contains Oracle and non-Oracle files?

○ a.  Store the files on separate devices

○ b.  Store the files in separate directories

○ c.  Make sure that the files contain distinct names

○ d.  Remove all non-Oracle files from the system as soon as possible

The correct answer is a. The best answer is to separate Oracle and non-Oracle files on different physical drives whenever possible. Storing Oracle and non-Oracle files in separate directories will not reduce the I/O contention if both directories are on the same physical disk. Therefore, answer b is incorrect. Naming conventions will not affect I/O, and removing non-Oracle files might not be reasonable for most applications. Therefore, answers c, and d are incorrect.

# Question 4

When you're designing a database, which objects, other than rollback segments, should be stored in the **RBS** tablespace?

○ a.  User-created objects

○ b.  Database triggers

○ c.  Temporary segments

○ d.  None

The correct answer is d. Rollback segments tend to have high I/O and should be stored on separate disks whenever possible. Oracle recommends separate tablespaces for user-created objects for ease of maintenance. Database triggers are stored in the **SYSTEM** tablespace. Temporary segments should be stored in their own tablespace, which should be designated as a temporary tablespace. Therefore, answers a, b, and c are incorrect.

## Question 5

You want to prevent row migration on the **PARTS** table. Which action should you take?

○ a. Increase **PCTUSED**

○ b. Decrease **PCTUSED**

○ c. Increase **PCTFREE**

○ d. Decrease **PCTFREE**

The correct answer is c. Row migration results from insufficient free space for updates. Therefore, the obvious answer is to increase the **PCTFREE** parameter to allow more space for updates. The **PCTUSED** parameter is relevant only to deletions. Therefore, answers a and b are incorrect. Decreasing **PCTFREE** would only increase row migration. Therefore, answer d is incorrect.

## Question 6

Which view can you query to determine whether contention for the free list is high?

○ a. **V$SESSION**

○ b. **V$WAITSTAT**

○ c. **V$RESOURCE**

○ d. **V$LOADSTAT**

The correct answer is b. The **V$WAITSTAT** view will provide information on waits for the free list. However, this view will not indicate which tables are affected by waits for the free list. It is up to the DBA to review the application and determine which tables are performing multiple insert and delete operations. Answers a, c, and d are all incorrect.

## Question 7

What is increased when the database contains migrated rows?

○ a. **PCTUSED**

○ b. **I/O**

○ c. **SHARED_POOL_SIZE**

○ d. **PCTFREE**

The correct answer is b. It is important to read this question carefully. It's asking what is increased by row migration, not how to reduce row migration. The **PCTUSED** and **PCTFREE** parameters are not increased by migrated rows. Therefore, answers a and d are incorrect. The **SHARED_POOL_SIZE** parameter is also not increased automatically by row migration. Therefore, answer c is incorrect.

When a row is migrated, an indicator is set at the previous block location to point to the new location. This increases I/O because the original block in which the row was located must be read, as must the new block containing the row. The **PCTUSED** and **PCTFREE** parameters are used to regulate space in blocks, and inappropriate settings can lead to row migration problems.

## Question 8

You issue this command:

```
ANALYZE TABLE inventory.item COMPUTE STATISTICS;
```

Which column in the **DBA_TABLES** view can you query to see the number of migrated rows in the **inventory.item** table?

○ a. **BLOCKS**

○ b. **CHAIN_CNT**

○ c. **AVG_ROW_LEN**

○ d. **NUM_ROWS**

The correct answer is b. The **CHAIN_CNT** column lists the number of both chained and migrated rows. Chained rows result from having a block size that is too small for the row to fit into a single block. Because the block size can be changed only by re-creating the database, this problem is not easily fixed. Migrated rows are the result of insufficient space in a block for updates. Once the migrated rows have been identified, they can be removed and reinserted. BLOCKS gives the number of blocks for the table. Therefore, answer a is incorrect. AVG_ROW_LEN shows the average row length for the rows in the table. Therefore, answer c is incorrect. NUM_ROWS is the number of rows in the table. Therefore, answer d is incorrect.

# Question 9

Which statement type can you use to reset the high-water mark on a table?

○ a. **DELETE**

○ b. **TRUNCATE**

○ c. **UPDATE**

○ d. **INSERT**

The correct answer is b. You need to read this question carefully. The DELETE command will remove all the rows but will not reset the high-water mark. Therefore, answer a is incorrect. Inserting and updating data in a table can cause the high-water mark to change (increase). However, this is done implicitly, only when Oracle determines that it's necessary, and does not reset the high-water mark. Therefore, answers c and d are incorrect. The only SQL command that will reset the high-water mark is the TRUNCATE command.

# Question 10

Manual striping is easier to manage than operating system striping.

○ a. True

○ b. False

The correct answer is b. In addition to being harder from a maintenance standpoint, manual striping requires an in-depth knowledge of the tables and data usage.

# Question 11

> Your database does not contain a separate tablespace for indexes. In which of the following tablespaces should you place them?
>
> ○ a. **SYSTEM**
>
> ○ b. **TEMPORARY**
>
> ○ c. **DATA**
>
> ○ d. **USER**
>
> ○ e. **ROLLBACK**

The correct answer is d. You never place anything but the data dictionary and objects owned by the users SYS or SYSTEM in the **SYSTEM** tablespace. Therefore, answer a is incorrect. The **TEMPORARY** tablespace is subject to fragmentation and index data cannot be placed there. Therefore, answer b is incorrect. Placing index data in the same tablespace as the **DATA** tablespace will result in contention, and nothing should ever be placed in the **ROLL-BACK** segments except rollback segments. Therefore, answers c and e are incorrect.

# Need To Know More?

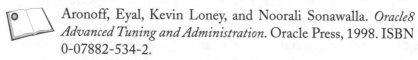 Aronoff, Eyal, Kevin Loney, and Noorali Sonawalla. *Oracle8 Advanced Tuning and Administration*. Oracle Press, 1998. ISBN 0-07882-534-2.

Ault, Michael R. *Oracle8 Black Book*. The Coriolis Group, 1998. ISBN 1-57610-187-8. (Be sure to read Chapters 9 and 11 carefully.)

Ault, Michael R. *Oracle8i Administration and Management*. Wiley Computer Publishing, 1999. ISBN 0-471-35453-8.

Corey, Michael, Michael Abbey, and Daniel J. Dechichio, Jr. *Oracle8 Tuning*. Oracle Press, 1997. ISBN 0-07882-390-0.

The first place to go for more information is the *Oracle8 Tuning Manual* and the *Oracle8 Server Reference Manual*.

# Tuning Oracle Sorts

**9**

### Terms you'll need to understand:

√ Disk sort

√ Memory sort

√ **SORT_DIRECT_WRITES**

√ Program global area (PGA)

√ System global area (SGA)

√ User global area (UGA)

√ Shared pool

√ Temporary tablespace

√ Sort extent pool (SEP)

√ **DISTINCT**

√ **ORDER BY**

### Techniques you'll need to master:

√ Using initialization parameters to control sorts

√ Tuning direct write sorts

√ Monitoring sort activity with **V$SYSSTAT** and **V$SORT_SEGMENT**

√ Configuring temporary tablespaces

√ Using **SELECT** statements to control sorts

Although data, by definition, is stored unsorted in a relational database, result sets that are unsorted are frustrating and difficult to deal with. To return an ordered set of values, Oracle performs sorts. Some operations, such as forced uniqueness or distinctiveness of returned data sets, will always cause a sort operation.

Sorts are of two general types: disk sorts, which are the most expensive in terms of resources, and memory sorts, which are the least expensive. You control the number of sorts done on disk and the number done in memory through the proper setting of several Oracle initialization file parameters. You can determine how efficiently sorts that must be done on disk are accomplished through a combination of temporary tablespace storage setup and special initialization parameter settings.

The Oracle8: Performance Tuning exam will contain several questions regarding sorts and the tuning and monitoring of sorts. After you study the material in this chapter, you should have no problem facing the questions on the exam that cover sorting.

# Types Of Oracle Sorts

As mentioned previously, Oracle uses disk sorts and memory sorts. Because disk accesses are usually an order of magnitude longer in duration than memory-based operations, any operations that require the reading, writing, and access of data on disk can be a major performance hit. Memory sorts are done entirely with the process memory area preallocated for sorting. Memory sorts are cheap in terms of resources, and they should be the target for tuning (making all sorts memory sorts).

## Disk Sorts

If a sort exceeds the size of the **SORT_AREA_SIZE** initialization parameter (the area used for memory sorts), it will require a disk sort. (**SORT_AREA_SIZE** will be discussed later in this section.) Disk sorts are always performed in the user's designated temporary tablespace. Because sorts are always performed in the temporary tablespace for a user, the database administrator (DBA) must be sure that no user has the **SYSTEM** tablespace assigned as a temporary tablespace. If the value of **SORT_AREA_SIZE** is greater than 10 times the size of **DB_BLOCK_SIZE**, memory area from the sort area is allocated to perform direct writes to disk if **SORT_DIRECT_WRITES** is set to **AUTO**. One exception is when sorts are being used during the creation of indexes. In this case, the sorts are done in the target tablespace for the index. You especially need to be aware of when index creations are performed on tables in parallel. These types of index creations will involve multiple initial extents that are then consolidated into the final set of extents.

If the default and temporary tablespaces are not explicitly assigned when a user is created, the assignment will default to the **SYSTEM** tablespace. Always explicitly assign users their default and temporary tablespaces. Fragmentation and excessive **SYSTEM** tablespace I/O are prime indicators that a user's temporary tablespace assignment has been set to **SYSTEM**.

In environments rich in disk space but poor in memory, you might want to perform disk sorts rather than tie up memory resources. Forced disk sorting is accomplished by setting the **SORT_DIRECT_WRITES, SORT_WRITE_ BUFFERS, SORT_BUFFER_SIZE, SORT_SPACEMAP_SIZE**, and **SORT_READ_FAC** initialization parameters correctly.

*Note: The initialization parameters SORT_DIRECT_WRITES, SORT_WRITE_BUFFERS, SORT_BUFFER_SIZE, SORT_ SPACEMAP_SIZE, and SORT_READ_FAC have been, to use Oracle's term, "obsoleted," as of Oracle version 8.1.3. However, because they're still used in some of the versions of Oracle8, a complete discussion of their use is given here.*

Here are some general guidelines for setting these parameters:

➤ **SORT_DIRECT_WRITES**—This parameter turns on forced disk sorts when set to **TRUE**; its default setting is **AUTO**. This controls whether sort writes pass through the buffer caches. Bypassing the buffer caches means that sort speed can be increased by a factor of six or more.

➤ **SORT_WRITE_BUFFERS**—This parameter determines the number of sort direct write buffers; it's set at 2 by default and can be increased as needed to a maximum of 8 to improve sort speeds. Each process has its own set of sort write buffers.

➤ **SORT_BUFFER_SIZE**—This parameter determines the size of each sort write buffer and is initially set at 32,768 bytes. You can increase this setting as needed, up to 65,536 bytes, to improve sort speed.

➤ SORT_SPACEMAP_SIZE—This parameter determines the size of the disk map used to map disk areas used for sorting. The default is 512 bytes, which is usually enough, unless you have extremely large sorts, such as during index builds. The suggested setpoint is

```
(total sort bytes / SORT_AREA_SIZE) + 64
```

where **total sort bytes** is equal to (number of records) * (sum of column sizes + (2 * number of columns)).

➤ SORT_READ_FAC—This parameter determines the number of blocks read from disk in a single operation for a sort. The default is 20, which is usually enough but can be increased if you perform numerous large sorts. The calculation for this parameter is

```
(avg_seek_time + avg_latency + blk_transfer_time) /
blk_transfer_time
```

Therefore, if you have abundant memory and temporary disk space on your system, using **SORT_DIRECT_WRITES** to bypass the buffer cache and to write directly to disk for large sorts (through sort buffers defined for each process) can increase the speed of large sorts by up to six times. Because we're talking about increasing disk I/O load by using **SORT_DIRECT_WRITES**, I/O should be properly tuned for your system as well.

As noted earlier, the initialization parameter **SORT_DIRECT_WRITES** and the other associated initialization parameters—**SORT_WRITE_BUFFERS**, **SORT_BUFFER_SIZE**, **SORT_READ_FAC**, and **SORT_SPACEMAP_SIZE**—have been obsoleted. Their functionality has been replaced somewhat by the initialization parameter **SORT_MULTIBLOCK_READ_COUNT**.

The **SORT_MULTIBLOCK_READ_COUNT** initialization parameter, introduced in Oracle8i, works with temporary tablespace segments in much the same way that **DB_FILE_MULTIBLOCK_READ_COUNT** works with data tablespace segments—that is, it controls the number of blocks read from disk into memory for each sort run that was written to disk. Increasing this value increases the number of blocks that are read from the temporary segments into memory, thus decreasing the number of disk accesses required for the sort runs. The adverse effect of this is that it may decrease the number of sort runs that can be merged in one merge pass, thereby increasing the amount of I/O for the merge runs. **SORT_MULTIBLOCK_READ_COUNT** needs to be carefully tuned to balance the increase in speed for sorts to the possible increase in I/O costs associated with an increase in the number of merge runs.

# Memory Sorts

Ideally, all sorts should be done in memory because memory provides the fastest data sorting and access capabilities. Doing all sorts in memory, except for a few small databases, is not a very realistic possibility. However, you can tune sorts using the **SORT_AREA_SIZE** and **SORT_AREA_RETAINED_SIZE** initialization parameters to minimize disk sorts and to reduce memory requirements for sorts.

By monitoring the **V$SYSSTAT** table through use of a query similar to

```
SELECT name, value FROM v$sysstat WHERE name like '%sort%';
```

you can determine how many sorts are being done to disk and how many sorts are being done in memory. For example, running the previous query against a 20GB production database that mixes online transaction processing (OLTP) and batch system processes with a 3MB **SORT_AREA_SIZE** and a 2MB **SORT_AREA_RETAINED_SIZE** produced the following results:

```
SQL> SELECT name, value FROM v$sysstat WHERE name LIKE '%sort%';

NAME                                                    VALUE
- - - - - - - - - - - - -                            - - - - - - - - - -
sorts (memory)                                         234126
sorts (disk)                                               30
sorts (rows)                                          75234036
```

Therefore, in this system, you're seeing 0.013 percent of the sorts going to disk (not a bad ratio). The 0.013 percent ratio is especially good when you realize that several large batch jobs (for example, snapshot builds and table analysis operations) were run since the last time this database was restarted. Your goal should be to reduce disk sorts to less than 10 percent—and generally less than 1 percent is attainable. Some basic guidelines for setting **SORT_AREA_SIZE** and **SORT_AREA_RETAINED_SIZE** follow:

➤ For **SORT_AREA_SIZE**, the default setting usually is insufficient, except in the most minimal of OLTP environments. If you can quantify the average sort done on your system, set this parameter to that value or a multiple of that value; otherwise, monitor the sort statistics in **V$SYSSTAT** and adjust this parameter up until disk sorts are less than 10 percent of total sorts, as a minimum. For non-multithreaded server (non-MTS) systems, this memory is taken from the user's process global area (PGA). For systems using MTS, this memory is taken from the shared pool area of the system global area (SGA), which is referred to as the *user global area (UGA)*. If a sort is larger than **SORT_AREA_SIZE**, it's broken into **SORT_AREA_SIZE** chunks and done on disk.

➤ The **SORT_AREA_RETAINED_SIZE** parameter sets the initial size of the sort area allocated per user. In memory-poor environments, set this parameter to a fraction of the value of **SORT_AREA_SIZE**. Users will be allocated **SORT_AREA_RETAINED_SIZE** for initial sorting, and their space will grow to **SORT_AREA_SIZE**. Any memory in addition to **SORT_AREA_RETAINED_SIZE** that is allocated for a large sort will be returned to the user's UGA after the sort.

Whenever possible, sorting should be done in memory rather than disk. By properly analyzing your sort activities, you can reduce the number and size of sorts such that most, if not all, are done in memory.

# Sorts And The Temporary Tablespace

All disk sorts are done in the user's assigned temporary tablespace. If users are not assigned default and temporary tablespaces when they're created, these items will default to the **SYSTEM** tablespace. All users, including SYS and SYSTEM, should have their temporary tablespace reassigned to one other than **SYSTEM**. Sorts that are allowed to occur in the **SYSTEM** tablespace can cause excessive fragmentation of the **SYSTEM** tablespace. In addition, allowing large sorts in the **SYSTEM** tablespace could result in the database hanging if the **SYSTEM** tablespace runs out of space. Another consideration is that the default storage parameters are not optimized for sorting in the **SYSTEM** tablespace, and this will result in inefficient sorting operations.

## Temporary Tablespace Storage Considerations

Temporary tablespaces exist entirely to support sorting operations. The temporary tablespace default storage clause must be based directly on how you have designated sorting to be done on your system.

In all systems, even where direct writes are being done, the **INITIAL** and **NEXT** values for the temporary tablespace default storage clause should be the same and should equal the value of the **SORT_AREA_SIZE** initialization parameter. The **PCTINCREASE** default storage parameter for a temporary tablespace should always be set to zero. Setting **PCTINCREASE** to zero for a temporary tablespace does two things. First, it prevents automatic coalescing of unused extents. Second, it ensures that the extent size always matches **SORT_AREA_SIZE** and therefore wastes little space.

Why wouldn't you want automatic coalescing of the unused extents in a temporary tablespace? Because if **INITIAL** is equal to **NEXT** and **PCTINCREASE** is equal to zero, all extents in a temporary tablespace will be of equal size. If all extents in a temporary tablespace are of equal size, any used extent that is returned to the free extent pool will be the proper size for the next sort operation that requires an extent. Having unused extents already available in the temporary tablespace by setting **PCTINCREASE** to zero and not allowing automatic coalescing reduces the time required to reallocate extents.

Use the **TEMPORARY** clause for creating temporary tablespaces. A tablespace designated as **TEMPORARY** will not allow the creation of nontemporary segments (such as tables, indexes, and clusters) and is optimized for sorting. The actual sort segment in a tablespace designated as **TEMPORARY** is not created until the first sort request is issued.

The extents in a temporary tablespace are mapped into a sort extent pool (SEP) when the first sort operation occurs against that temporary tablespace. Once a tablespace is mapped into a SEP, subsequent sorts will use the SEP to locate available sort extents. The **V$SORT_SEGMENT** dynamic performance view is used to view information about sort extents in the SEP. The contents of the **V$SORT_SEGMENT** view are shown in Table 9.1.

| Table 9.1   Contents of the V$SORT_SEGMENT view. | |
| --- | --- |
| **Column** | **Description** |
| TABLESPACE_NAME | Name of the temporary tablespace |
| SEGMENT_FILE | Number of the data file that contains the segment |
| SEGMENT_BLOCK | Number of the block in the data file where the segment begins |
| EXTENT_SIZE | Size of the temporary segment extent |
| CURRENT_USERS | Number of users using the tablespace |
| TOTAL_EXTENTS | Total number of extents available in this tablespace |
| TOTAL_BLOCKS | Total number of blocks available in this tablespace |
| USED_EXTENTS | Total number of extents being used in this tablespace |
| USED_BLOCKS | Total number of blocks being used in this tablespace |
| FREE_EXTENTS | Total number of free extents in this tablespace |
| FREE_BLOCKS | Total number of free blocks in this tablespace |
| ADDED_EXTENTS | Total number of extents added to this tablespace |
| EXTENT_HITS | Total times this unused extent has been found in the SEP |

*(continued)*

| Table 9.1 Contents of the V$SORT_SEGMENT view (continued). | |
| --- | --- |
| **Column** | **Description** |
| FREED_EXTENTS | Number of extents released to the SEP |
| FREE_REQUESTS | Number of times a request was made for a free extent |
| MAX_SIZE | Maximum size available for a segment to use |
| MAX_BLOCKS | Maximum blocks available for a segment to use |
| MAX_USED_SIZE | Maximum size area currently used by a segment |
| MAX_USED_BLOCKS | Maximum number of blocks currently used by a segment |
| MAX_SORT_SIZE | Largest sort done to date in bytes |
| MAX_SORT_BLOCKS | Largest sort done to date in blocks |

The use of **SORT_DIRECT_WRITES** can increase the required temporary tablespace disk space. Therefore, when you're going from a system where **SORT_DIRECT_WRITES** is not configured to one where it's used, be sure to allow for more temporary tablespace storage space.

# Controlling Sorts

By properly tuning SQL statements and understanding which type of operations produce which sorts, you can reduce the number and size of sort operations and therefore allow more sorts to be performed in memory. The following operations always require a sort:

➤ SELECT DISTINCT

➤ SELECT UNIQUE

➤ SELECT...ORDER BY

➤ SELECT...GROUP BY

➤ CREATE INDEX

➤ CREATE TABLE...AS SELECT with primary key specification

➤ INTERSECT, MINUS, and UNION set operators

➤ Un-indexed table joins

➤ Some correlated subqueries

Proper indexing often can reduce sorts. If a **SELECT** operation uses an index, it will normally return the values in indexed order. By creating an index on the column by which you want the query to be ordered, you can eliminate the need for an **ORDER BY** clause. Avoid using **SELECT DISTINCT** and **SELECT UNIQUE** operations unless absolutely necessary. An example of an unneeded **DISTINCT** or **UNIQUE** might be a **SELECT** that includes the primary key value because, by definition, a row including a primary key will always be distinct or unique.

# Practice Questions

## Question 1

> Which initialization file parameter can you set to prevent sort writes to the buffer cache?
>
> ○ a. **SORT_AREA_SIZE**
>
> ○ b. **SORT_DIRECT_WRITES**
>
> ○ c. **SORT_WRITE_BUFFERS**
>
> ○ d. **SORT_WRITE_BUFFER_SIZE**

The correct answer is b. **SORT_DIRECT_WRITES** can be set to **TRUE, FALSE,** or **AUTO. TRUE** sets all sorts to bypass the buffer cache and write through the **SORT_WRITE_BUFFERS. FALSE** turns off direct writes, and all sorts go through the buffer cache. If **SORT_DIRECT_WRITES** is set to **AUTO,** the decision on bypassing the buffer cache is based on **SGA** and **DB_BLOCK_SIZE** settings.

Answer a is incorrect because **SORT_AREA_SIZE** determines the size of the normal sort area but has nothing to do with direct writes; in fact, it can be reduced in size if direct writes are enabled. Answer c is incorrect because, although **SORT_WRITE_BUFFERS** sets the number of sort write buffers, it does not turn on or off the direct writes option. Answer d is incorrect because, although **SORT_WRITE_BUFFER_SIZE** controls the size of sort write buffers, it does not turn on or off the direct writes option.

## Question 2

> Which SQL clauses will cause a sort operation? [Choose two]
>
> ❑ a. **INTO**
>
> ❑ b. **WHERE**
>
> ❑ c. **ORDER BY**
>
> ❑ d. **DISTINCT**

The correct answers are c and d. **ORDER BY, DISTINCT, UNIQUE,** and **GROUP BY** clauses will always result in sorts. Answer a is incorrect because **INTO** is used in embedded SQL to place a value into a variable. Answer b is incorrect because **WHERE** simply shows the beginning of a restriction clause.

# Question 3

> Which dynamic performance view can you query to see whether sorts are being done in memory or on disk?
>
> ○ a.  **V$ROWCACHE**
>
> ○ b.  **V$SESSION**
>
> ○ c.  **V$SYSSTAT**
>
> ○ d.  **V$SQLAREA**

The correct answer is c. The **V$SYSSTAT** view contains entries for the **sorts (disk)** and **sorts (memory)** statistics, which give the total number of those types of sorts since the database was started. Answer a is incorrect because the **V$ROWCACHE** view contains statistics about the data dictionary cache but not about sorts. Answer b is incorrect because **V$SESSION** contains statistics about user sessions but not about sorts. Answer d is incorrect because **V$SQLAREA** contains information about SQL statements that have been placed in the shared pool but not about sorts.

# Question 4

> Where will a process look for sort space if needed?
>
> ○ a.  UGA
>
> ○ b.  PGA
>
> ○ c.  SEP

The correct answer is c. The SEP (sort extent pool) tracks available sort extents. Answers a and b are incorrect because both the UGA (user global area) and the PGA (process global area) might contain sort data, but they do *not* track free sort extent areas.

# Question 5

What is one purpose of the **SORT_AREA_SIZE** initialization parameter?

○ a.  It gives the size that a sort area will shrink to when not needed.

○ b.  It determines whether a sort can be done in memory or must be done in sort sets on disk.

○ c.  It forces sorts to bypass the buffer cache.

○ d.  It sets the size of direct sort buffers.

The correct answer is b. **SORT_AREA_SIZE** sets the size of the memory sort area for a process; if a sort exceeds the **SORT_AREA_SIZE** setting, it's done in **SORT_AREA_SIZE** sections on disk. Answer a is incorrect because this is a function of the **SORT_AREA_RETAINED_SIZE** parameter. Answer c is incorrect because this is a function of the **SORT_DIRECT_WRITES** parameter. Answer d is incorrect because this is a function of the **SORT_ WRITE_BUFFER_SIZE** parameter.

# Question 6

In Oracle8, which dynamic performance view can be queried to determine the value of the **TOTAL_EXTENTS** column for the temporary tablespaces?

○ a.  **V$TYPE_SIZE**

○ b.  **V$SQLTEXT**

○ c.  **V$SORT_SEGMENT**

○ d.  **V$DB_OBJECT_CACHE**

The correct answer is c. The **V$SORT_SEGMENT** view contains statistics on all temporary tablespaces used for sorting. Answer a is incorrect because **V$TYPE_SIZE** contains information on the sizes of various data type sizing parameters. Answer b is incorrect because **V$SQLTEXT** contains information about SQL that has been placed in the shared pool. Answer d is incorrect because **V$DB_OBJECT_CACHE** contains data about stored objects in the shared pool.

# Question 7

What is the purpose of the **EXTENT_HITS** column in the **V$SORT_SEGMENT** dynamic performance view?

- ○ a. It shows the maximum number of blocks available for sorting in the tablespace.
- ○ b. It shows the number of extents currently used in the tablespace for sorting.
- ○ c. It shows the number of times an unused extent was found in the SEP (sort extent pool).
- ○ d. It shows the total extents in the tablespace.

The correct answer is c. The **EXTENT_HITS** column shows the number of times an unused extent was found in the SEP. Answer a is incorrect because this is the description of the **MAX_SORT_BLOCKS** column. Answer b is incorrect because this is the description of the **USED_EXTENTS** column. Answer d is incorrect because this is the description of the **TOTAL_EXTENTS** column.

# Question 8

**PCTINCREASE** should be set to which value for a temporary tablespace?

- ○ a. 10
- ○ b. 0
- ○ c. 50
- ○ d. 20

The correct answer is b. You should set **PCTINCREASE** to zero for a temporary tablespace. Setting **PCTINCREASE** to zero when **INITIAL** and **NEXT** are set correctly in a temporary tablespace prevents fragmentation and limits the need for coalescing the temporary tablespace by ensuring that each extent in the tablespace is of uniform size. Because answer b is correct, all other answers are therefore incorrect.

# Question 9

> When should you consider setting **SORT_DIRECT_WRITES** to **TRUE**?
>
> ○ a. When you have little memory or disk space available for sorting
>
> ○ b. When you have a lot of disk space and low memory
>
> ○ c. When ycou have a lot of temporary disk space and a lot of memory
>
> ○ d. When you have a lot of memory and little temporary disk space for sorting

The correct answer is c. When **SORT_DIRECT_WRITES** is set to **TRUE**, each user receives **SORT_WRITE_BUFFERS** * **SORT_BUFFER_SIZE** memory allocation to write through sort data to disk, bypassing the buffer cache. In addition, because of the way in which **SORT_DIRECT_WRITES** is allocated disk area, it will require more disk space than standard sorting. The added disk memory requirements make answers a and d incorrect, and the added memory requirements make answer b incorrect.

# Question 10

> When will a sort be separated into sort runs and written to disk?
>
> ○ a. When the sort data exceeds **SORT_AREA_RETAINED_SIZE** in size
>
> ○ b. When **SORT_DIRECT_WRITES** is set to **FALSE**
>
> ○ c. When the sort data exceeds **SORT_AREA_SIZE** in size
>
> ○ d. With every sort

The correct answer is c. When sort data exceeds the **SORT_AREA_SIZE**, it is separated into sort runs and written to disk. Answer a is incorrect because this only results in more memory being allocated to **SORT_AREA_SIZE**. Answer b is incorrect because this turns direct writes off. Answer d is incorrect because if the size of the sort is less than **SORT_AREA_SIZE**, it is performed in memory.

# Need To Know More?

 Aronoff, Eyal, Kevin Loney, and Noorali Sonawalla. *Oracle8 Advanced Tuning and Administration*, Oracle Press, 1998. ISBN 0-07882-534-2.

 Ault, Michael R. *Oracle8 Black Book*, The Coriolis Group, 1998. ISBN 1-57610-187-8. (Be sure to read Chapters 9 and 11 carefully.)

 Ault, Michael R. *Oracle8i Administration and Management*, Wiley Computer Publishing, 1999. ISBN 0-471-35453-8.

 Corey, Michael, Michael Abbey, and Daniel J. Dechichio, Jr. *Oracle8 Tuning*, Oracle Press, 1997. ISBN 0-07882-390-0.

 The first place to go for more information is the *Oracle8 Tuning Manual* and the *Oracle8 Server Reference Manual*.

# Latches, Locks, And Contention Issues

### Terms you'll need to understand:

√ Lock

√ Deadlock

√ Row-level lock

√ Table-level lock

√ Latch

√ Lock tree

√ Spin

### Techniques you'll need to master:

√ Detecting lock and latch problems

√ Tuning locks

√ Freeing locks

√ Tuning latches

√ Detecting latch contentions

√ Detecting other contention problems

Oracle uses latches (a form of low-level locking) and locks to protect both data structures and memory structures. Generally, a latch always protects a memory structure, and a lock always protects a data structure. Locks and latches are usually controlled automatically, although you can tune them for peak efficiency. Oracle protects these structures by requiring a process to acquire the protecting lock or latch before granting it access to the underlying structure. Contention arises when a process is trying to acquire the latch or lock and must wait for previous processes to release the latch or lock. Most locking problems can be traced to application-forced locking that's not properly applied. This chapter discusses discovering and resolving lock and latch contention issues. Some contention issues that do not fall into the locks and latches categories will also be discussed.

# Oracle Locks

Locks are used to protect data. Locks default to the row level, but they can be forced—through either initialization parameters or program statements—to occur at other levels as well. Oracle automatically assigns the lowest level of lock to achieve the statement's implicit goal. Therefore, as long as transactions are properly designed, Oracle should automatically invoke the proper locking strategy. Incorrect locking will result in deadlock situations.

Locks consist of several types, for example, DML (Data Manipulation Language), DDL (Data Definition Language), table, and row locks, and can be either exclusive locks or share locks. Only one exclusive lock can be placed at any time on a given resource. Multiple share locks are possible against the same resource at the same time. Queries are always allowed, even on locked resources, but other activities are prohibited, depending on the type of lock.

Locks are held for the duration of the transaction. This prevents destructive interactions from other processes or transactions, thus maintaining data integrity for the length of a specific transaction. A **COMMIT** or **ROLLBACK** will release all locks held by a transaction. Locks acquired from the time a **SAVEPOINT** is issued will be released when the transaction is rolled back to that **SAVEPOINT**; locks acquired before the **SAVEPOINT** are not affected. However, if a resource is locked in a **SAVEPOINT** and then the transaction is rolled back to that **SAVEPOINT**, only transactions without current lock waits can acquire locks on those resources on which the locks were released. Transactions with active waits will still wait until the entire transaction is complete.

Lock conversion happens automatically in Oracle databases. A lower-level table lock will convert to a higher-level lock, as required. Row-exclusive locks are the highest level of locks and therefore cannot be converted. Exclusive locks are held for rows participating in all **INSERT**, **UPDATE**, and **DELETE** trans-actions. A **SELECT FOR UPDATE** statement assigns row-exclusive locks to rows referenced by the **SELECT** statement and a row-share table lock. The row-share table lock is automatically updated to an exclusive lock once a row is updated.

Lock escalation is never done in Oracle because it increases the chance that a deadlock will occur. Oracle attempts to avoid deadlocks by using the highest granularity of locking possible for a transaction.

Even fine-grain locks can participate in a deadlock. Deadlocks occur when two processes compete for the same data resource. Oracle has provided several scripts and packages of procedures that should be used to monitor and control locks. The statement that detects a deadlock is the one that's rolled back auto-matically by Oracle. The rolled-back statement receives an error.

Locks are controlled by means of *enqueues*. Enqueues are controlled by setting the **ENQUEUE_RESOURCES** initialization parameter, which controls the size of the internal locking table. Therefore, the total number of enqueues controls the total number of locks. Some forms of lock contention are resolved by increasing the **ENQUEUE RESOURCES** initialization parameter.

# Types Of Locks

Oracle has several types of locks and automatically uses the proper type of lock for a transaction. All Oracle locks fall into one of the following categories:

➤ *DML (data) locks*—DML locks protect the data. They can be either table level or row level.

➤ *DDL (dictionary) locks*—DDL locks protect the structure of objects, such as a definition of a table or view.

➤ *Internal locks and latches*—Internal locks and latches protect internal structures such as data files. They're entirely automatic.

➤ *Distributed locks*—Distributed locks ensure that structures are consistent across the different instances that participate in the parallel database (used in Oracle Parallel Server). They're held at the instance level, not the transaction level.

➤ *Parallel cache management (PCM) locks*—Instance locks that manage the locking of blocks in data files. Oracle Parallel Server uses these instance locks to coordinate access to shared resources.

# DML Locks

DML locks guarantee the integrity of data accessed simultaneously by multiple transactions. They prevent destructive interference from transactions other than the one holding the lock. Oracle DML locks ensure that a row can be updated by only one transaction at a time and that a table cannot be dropped if an uncommitted transaction exists for the table. DML locks are either row level or table level.

## Row-Level DML Locks (TX Locks)

Row-level locks represent the finest level of granularity for Oracle locking. These locks are the only DML locks acquired automatically. A transaction can have an unlimited number of row locks acquired. DML locks ensure that contention for rows occurs only when two transactions attempt to acquire a lock on the same row or rows at the same time. DML row locks are also known as *TX* or *transaction locks*. The following rules apply to DML row locks:

➤ Readers of data never wait for writers of the same data row.

➤ Writers never wait for readers, unless **SELECT...FOR UPDATE** (explicit locking) is used.

➤ Writers wait for other writers only if they're attempting to update the same data row.

➤ They're always accompanied by table-level share locks.

Notice that a row lock is always accompanied by a table-level share lock, which prevents other transactions from issuing a table-level lock against the table being updated until the transaction with the row lock completes. The table-level share lock also prevents DDL operations against tables participating in the transaction.

## Table-Level Locks (TM Locks)

Oracle uses a number of different levels of table locks to control read, write, and general access to tables. *TM* usually indicates table-level locks in the lock-type column when that column is queried by Server Manager. Table 10.1 shows which statements cause which types of locks as well as which types of locks are permitted against tables undergoing these transaction statements.

The following guides should be used in interpreting Table 10.1:

➤ *Row-share lock (RS)*—This is the least restrictive of the table locks; it's also known as a *subshare lock (SS)*. It allows other transactions to insert,

### Table 10.1   Summary of table locks.

| SQL Statement | Mode of Table Lock | Lock Modes Permitted? | | | | |
|---|---|---|---|---|---|---|
| | | RS | RX | S | SRX | X |
| INSERT | RX | Y | Y | N | N | N |
| UPDATE | RX | Y* | Y* | N | N | N |
| DELETE | RX | Y* | Y* | N | N | N |
| SELECT | None | Y | Y | Y | Y | Y |
| SELECT...UPDATE | RS | Y* | Y* | Y* | Y* | N |
| LOCK TABLE IN ROW SHARE MODE | RS | Y | Y | Y | Y | N |
| LOCK TABLE IN SHARE MODE | S | Y | N | Y | N | N |
| LOCK TABLE IN SHARE ROW EXCLUSIVE MODE | SRX | Y | N | N | N | N |
| LOCK TABLE IN EXCLUSIVE MODE | X | N | N | N | N | N |

* Yes if no conflicting locks are held by another transaction; otherwise, waits occur.

update, delete, or lock other rows in the same table and prevents a
LOCK TABLE...IN EXCLUSIVE MODE operation by another
transaction.

➤ *Row-exclusive lock (RX)*—This lock is almost identical to a row-share
lock but further limits the types of lock operations that other transactions can use; it's also known as a *subexclusive table lock (SX)*. It allows
inserts, updates, deletes, and locks of other rows and prohibits LOCK
TABLE commands with the following options: IN SHARE MODE,
IN SHARE EXCLUSIVE MODE, and IN EXCLUSIVE MODE.

➤ *Share lock (S)*—This lock is explicitly acquired through use of the LOCK
TABLE...IN SHARE MODE command. It allows query, SELECT...
FOR UPDATE, or other LOCK TABLE...IN SHARE MODE
operations. However, it restricts updates from transactions other than the
one holding the share lock. If multiple transactions hold the share lock,
no transaction can update the table. The following are prohibited
operations in tables that have a share lock:

➤ UPDATES

➤ LOCK TABLE...IN SHARE ROW EXCLUSIVE MODE

➤ LOCK TABLE...IN EXCLUSIVE MODE

➤ LOCK TABLE...IN ROW EXCLUSIVE MODE

➤ *Share-row-exclusive lock (SRX)*—This lock is more restrictive than a share lock; it's also known as a *share-subexclusive table lock (SSX)*. This lock is explicitly acquired through the **LOCK TABLE...IN SHARE ROW EXCLUSIVE MODE** command. Only one transaction can acquire an SRX lock on a specific table at any time. Other transactions can query the table or issue **SELECT...FOR UPDATE** commands but cannot update data until the lock is released. This lock prohibits almost all other locking, specifically the following lock operations:

➤ LOCK TABLE...IN SHARE MODE

➤ LOCK TABLE...IN SHARE ROW EXCLUSIVE MODE

➤ LOCK TABLE...IN ROW EXCLUSIVE MODE

➤ LOCK TABLE...IN EXCLUSIVE MODE

➤ *Exclusive lock (X)*—This is the most restrictive of locks. Only a single transaction can lock a table in X mode. A table locked in X mode can be queried only by other transactions; all other operations are prohibited until the X lock is lifted.

DML locks are automatically created by Oracle as they're needed. However, the database administrator can control the number of allowed DML locks with the **DML_LOCKS** initialization parameter. Queries (**SELECTs**) are the DML statements that are least likely to cause interference with other SQL statements because they only read data. A query acquires no data locks (as long as it does not have a **FOR UPDATE** clause). DML locks are always issued implicitly at the row level.

# DDL Locks

DDL locks protect the definition of a schema object while the object is acted on or referred to by an ongoing DDL operation. For example, an index creation will prohibit other DDL operations against the indexed table until the index build is complete. DDL locks are always automatic, and no implicit creation of DDL locks occurs. DDL locks affect only individual data dictionary objects and never the entire data dictionary. DDL locks are either share mode or exclusive mode (most are exclusive). Shared DDL locks are used for operations such as **CREATE PROCEDURE,** which issues share DDL locks on all tables that the procedure references. The entire purpose of a share DDL lock is to ensure that the definition of the locked object does not change while the object is being defined. The following commands acquire a shared DDL lock:

➤ **AUDIT**

➤ **NOAUDIT**

➤ **COMMENT**

➤ **GRANT**

➤ **CREATE** (or **REPLACE) VIEW/PROCEDURE/PACKAGE/ PACKAGE BODY/FUNCTION/TRIGGER**

➤ **CREATE SYNONYM**

➤ **CREATE TABLE** (when the **CLUSTER** parameter is not included)

An exclusive DDL lock is created when statements such as **ALTER** are issued. A DDL lock will not be issued against an object that has exclusive row locks issued against it. Therefore, exclusive DDL locks usually do not cause contention problems.

Another form of DDL lock is a *breakable parse lock*. Such a lock is held by any object in the shared pool on each object it references. Parse locks are held for as long as the SQL statement remains in the shared pool. As its name implies, a breakable parse lock is breakable, thus allowing conflicting DDL operations to acquire and modify the object on which the lock is set. Of all locks, DDL locks are the least likely to cause contention. A breakable parse lock is also called a *PL/SQL user lock (UL)*.

## Lock Utility Scripts And Packages

Oracle provides several utility scripts and utility packages to help DBAs monitor locks. These scripts must be explicitly run by the DBA before their contents can be utilized. These scripts and packages are:

➤ *catblock.sql*—This script builds tables and views used by the other lock utilities. The script creates the following tables and views: **DBA_ KGLLOCK, DBA_LOCK, DBA_LOCK_INTERNAL, DBA_ DML_LOCKS, DBA_DDL_LOCKS, DBA_WAITERS,** and **DBA_ BLOCKERS.** This script must be run before utllockt.sql will execute.

➤ *dbmslock.sql*—This script creates the capability for developers to create and maintain their own locks.

➤ *utllockt.sql*—This script creates a simple wait-for lock tree display. You must have run catblock.sql before running this script for the first time. However, catblock.sql only needs to be run once.

The catblock.sql script is run first. It usually should be run right after running the catproc.sql script when you're building an instance. The catblock.sql script needs to be run only once for an instance, except when you're updating to a newer version of Oracle.

## Monitoring Locks

Locks have several internal sources of information. In addition to the tables created by the catblock.sql script, lock information is stored in several other tables and views. The trace files generated by Oracle processes are great sources of information about lock problems. In fact, the rowid for the row that causes a deadlock will be pinpointed in the session trace file for the session participating in the deadlock. The trace files for a session are located where specified by the **USER_DUMP_DEST** initialization parameter. If you suspect that lock contention is occurring in your instance, you can consult the **V$SESSION** view to see which row in a table is causing the lock contention.

Of the locks discussed here, the TM, TX, and UL types of locks are usually obtained by user applications and should be monitored the most frequently.

If in your monitoring you discover that a user has locked a table or set of rows and has left for vacation or that a user has simply left for the day with locks in place, you should kill the offender's Oracle session using the **ALTER SYS-TEM KILL SESSION** command. To do so, you must obtain the **SERIAL#** and **SID** values from the **V$SESSION** view.

## Parallel Server Locks

A parallel server requires that two or more Oracle instances share data between their SGAs. This sharing of data is accomplished through PCM locks. These locks are used to maintain cache coherency and are explicitly configured by the DBA when the instances are configured. All PCM lock initialization parameters must match between all instances of an Oracle parallel server configuration.

The DBA can use the **GC_DB_LOCKS** and **GC_FILES_TO_LOCKS** parameters to set the total number of available PCM locks and the granularity of those locks. You can never have more PCM locks configured by the **GC_FILES_TO_LOCKS** parameter than are created by the **GC_DB_ LOCKS** parameter. PCM locks require about 115 bytes of memory per lock specified. The granularity of PCM locks refers to the number of database file blocks covered per individual lock. The **GC_FILES_TO_LOCKS** parameter is used to specify granularity as well as whether PCM locks are assigned to contiguous blocks or whether a hashing algorithm is used to randomize the assignment of locks to blocks.

The granularity of PCM locks is based on how the data in the database is to be accessed. Online transaction processing (OLTP) systems generally require fine-grain locking, whereas decision support system (DSS) or data warehouse (DWH) applications generally require coarser locking. A mixed-mode environment (such as one that has OLTP action during the day and large batch reporting done at night) might require a compromise.

If improper granularity is specified, a condition can occur in which instance A has a lock on several blocks and instance B requires a record in one of A's locked blocks so that A must release the PCM lock to allow B to access the record. Instance B might not even be interested in the same block that A was using, but because A and B are covered by the same lock, the lock must be released. When a lock that covers more than one block is released because of interest by another instance in a nonactive block, this is called a *false ping*. If two instances swap locks over the same block, it's simply called a *ping*. The ultimate goal of a proper PCM lock configuration is to minimize all forms of pinging.

# Oracle Latches

Latches are simple, low-level serialization mechanisms that are used to protect internal shared data structures in the SGA, including lists of currently used tables and users accessing the database. They are also used to protect the data structures that describe the contents of the data block buffers. Processes acquire latches when looking at or manipulating these internal structures.

 Although there are numerous latches (142 to be exact) in the Oracle8i database that can be monitored via the **V$LATCH** dynamic view, you should only concern yourself with a small subset of these latches. In addition to being covered extensively in the DBA exam, they're the latches that will be of most interest to you during the tuning process.

# Redo Allocation Latch

Any user process wanting to allocate space to write to the redo log buffer must obtain the redo allocation latch. After acquiring the redo allocation latch, the user process can then copy its entry into the redo log buffer. This is known as *copying on the redo allocation latch*. Because there's only one redo allocation latch in a database instance, only one user process can allocate space in the redo log buffer at one time. Although this arrangement ensures the sequential nature of the entries in the redo log buffer, it does pose some contention problems.

The initialization parameter **LOG_SMALL_ENTRY_MAX_SIZE** can be used to alleviate the contention caused by having only one redo allocation latch. Any user process wanting to copy an entry into the redo log buffer that exceeds the threshold size set by **LOG_SMALL_ENTRY_MAX_SIZE** must obtain a redo copy latch (covered in the next section), which copies the entry, thereby freeing the redo allocation latch for the next process. Decreasing the value of **LOG_SMALL_ENTRY_MAX_SIZE** means that more entries will be required to use the redo copy latch, thus allowing faster access to the redo allocation latch for user processes.

To determine contention for the redo allocation latch, use the following query:

```
SELECT name, gets, misses, immediate_gets, immediate_misses
    FROM v$latch
    WHERE name ='redo allocation';
```

If the ratio of **misses** to **gets** exceeds 1 percent or if the ratio of **immediate_misses** to the sum of **immediate_gets** and **immediate_misses** exceeds 1 percent, you should decrease the value for **LOG_SMALL_ENTRY_MAX_SIZE** until both ratios are under 1 percent.

# Redo Copy Latch

The value of **LOG_SMALL_ENTRY_MAX_SIZE** is used to determine which user process entries must obtain a redo copy latch to copy data into the redo log buffers. Any process with an entry larger than **LOG_SMALL_ENTRY_MAX_SIZE** must acquire a redo copy latch to copy the entry to the redo log buffer. When you increase the value of **LOG_SMALL_ENTRY_MAX_SIZE** to force processes to use the redo copy latch, you might begin experiencing contention for the latch. If this is the case, you can increase the number of redo copy latches by increasing the value of **LOG_SIMULTANEOUS_COPIES**. The default value of **LOG_SIMULTANEOUS_COPIES** is equal to the number of CPUs on your machine. This value can be increased to twice the number of CPUs available on your machine.

To determine contention for the redo copy latch, use the following query:

```
SELECT name, gets, misses, immediate_gets, immediate_misses
     FROM v$latch
     WHERE name ='redo copy';
```

If the ratio of **misses** to **gets** exceeds 1 percent or if the ratio of **immediate_misses** to the sum of **immediate_gets** and **immediate_misses** exceeds 1 percent, you should decrease the value for LOG_SMALL_ENTRY_MAX_SIZE and/or increase the value of LOG_SIMULTANEOUS_COPIES until the ratios for both are less then 1 percent.

# Other Contention: Free Lists

Free lists are used to govern access to the data blocks of tables and indexes. They're lists of data blocks that have been allocated to each segment of the table or index and currently contain free space greater then that set by the object space parameter **PCTFREE**.

Free lists are maintained in each allocated segment of the table or index tablespace. When a record is inserted into a table, Oracle scans the segments of the table by checking the free lists in each segment. Oracle will attempt to insert the record into the first data block indicated as free by the free lists. If the space in the data block is not sufficient to insert the record, Oracle removes the block from the free lists and continues until it finds a data block with adequate space.

In the case of **DELETE** or **UPDATE**, Oracle performs the action and then checks whether the space available in the data block has fallen under the value set by the space allocation parameter **PCTUSED**. If it has, the data block is added to the head of the free lists for the segment.

 Although not easily found in the Oracle manuals, truncating a table will also return data blocks to the head of the free lists.

A table that's experiencing a lot of inserts and deletes can experience contention for the free lists. To alleviate the contention problems, more free lists can be added. Unfortunately, adding free lists involves dropping and re-creating the structure (table or index) and stipulating more free lists in the DML creation statement by indicating a higher value for the **FREELISTS** storage parameter.

> *Note: The maximum value allowed for the FREELISTS storage parameter is determined by the block size. If the value specified is too large, Oracle will generate an error and return the maximum value allowed for the FREELISTS storage parameter.*

Latch contention can also be caused by improperly setting the **SPIN_COUNT** initialization parameter. This parameter controls the number of times a process will loop (or spin) when trying to lock a busy latch before going to sleep and then trying again some time later. The **SPIN_COUNT** parameter is usually set to 2000 on most computers. If you receive an indication of latch contention, increasing this parameter might improve overall performance because latches usually are not held for long.

# Practice Questions

## Question 1

> How does an Oracle8 server resolve deadlocks?
>
> ○ a.  By rolling back the statement that detected the deadlock
>
> ○ b.  By rolling back all statements causing the deadlock
>
> ○ c.  By automatically killing the user process that detected the deadlock
>
> ○ d.  By automatically killing all user processes involved in the deadlock

The correct answer is a. Oracle will roll back the statement that detects the deadlock. Usually, this means the second statement in a series. This is done because a first-come, first-served model is used for this resolution model—that is, the first statement to get a lock deserves to keep it. Answer b is incorrect because only the detecting statement is rolled back. However, if both a and b (the statement that detected the deadlock and the statement causing the deadlock) are part of a single transaction, it might result in the entire transaction rolling back, but usually only the detecting statement is affected. Answers c and d are incorrect because Oracle kills user processes only during shutdowns.

## Question 2

> A PL/SQL procedure is executed within the application, and its objects are placed in the cache. Which type of lock will Oracle place on these objects?
>
> ○ a.  An exclusive DML lock
>
> ○ b.  An exclusive DDL lock
>
> ○ c.  A shared DML lock
>
> ○ d.  A breakable parse lock (UL)

The correct answer is d. Whenever a stored object is placed in the shared pool, a UL (breakable parse) lock is used for it and its objects. Answer a is incorrect because this type of lock is used for rows undergoing DML operations. Answer b is incorrect because this type of lock is used for objects undergoing DDL operations. Answer c is incorrect because this type of lock is used only for objects undergoing DML operations.

# Question 3

How will a table lock be named when the lock-type column is queried in lock
views using Server Manager?

○ a.  TM

○ b.  TX

○ c.  SSX

○ d.  RX

The correct answer is a. TM is the designation for table locks. Answer b is
incorrect because TX is used for a transaction lock. Answer c is incorrect because SSX is used to designate a lock mode (share-subexclusive table lock mode),
not a type of lock. Answer d is incorrect because RX (row-exclusive lock mode)
is also used to indicate a lock mode, not a type of lock.

# Question 4

Which view contains information about the row participating in lock contention?

○ a.  **V$LOCK**

○ b.  **V$SYSSTAT**

○ c.  **V$ROWCACHE**

○ d.  **V$SESSION**

The correct answer is d. Using data contained in **V$SESSION**, a DBA can
determine the row and table participating in lock contention. Answer a is incorrect because it does not contain information on rows. Answer b incorrect
because although **V$SYSSTAT** might contain information on contention, it
contains no row information. Answer c is incorrect because **V$ROWCACHE**
deals with data dictionary cache information, not locks.

# Question 5

Which script must be run before you can use the utllockt.sql script?

○ a.  catexp.sql

○ b.  catblock.sql

○ c.  dbmsutil.sql

○ d.  utlxplan.sql

The correct answer is b. The catblock.sql script must be run to set up the views used by the utllockt.sql script. Answer a is incorrect because the catexp.sql script sets up the tables used by export and import operations and has nothing to do with lock data. Answer c is incorrect because dbmsutil.sql sets up many useful packages but it has none that deal with locks. Answer d is incorrect because utlxplan.sql builds the **EXPLAIN_PLAN** table and has nothing to do with locks.

# Question 6

Which Oracle mechanism maintains all locks in the database?

○ a.  Data dictionary

○ b.  Library cache

○ c.  Enqueues

○ d.  Dispatchers

The correct answer is c. The enqueues maintain all locks in the system and are configured using the **ENQUEUE_RESOURCES** initialization parameter. Answer a is incorrect because the data dictionary might use locks and store data about locks, but it does not maintain them. Answer b is incorrect because, although the library cache might use locks, it does not maintain them. Answer d is incorrect because dispatchers are used in multithreaded servers and have nothing to do with locks and maintaining locks.

# Question 7

When are DML locks held by a transaction released?

- ○ a.  After each DML statement completes
- ○ b.  When the user commits the transaction
- ○ c.  When the user enters a new DML statement
- ○ d.  When the data-entry screen in an application fills

The correct answer is b. Locks are released only after a commit, rollback, or abnormal transaction termination. Answers a and c are incorrect because a large transaction might include multiple DML statements, but no locks are released until a commit, rollback, or termination of the complete transaction. Answer d is incorrect because the simple act of filling a screen forces no database action unless the screen is coded to commit when all the screen is filled, which is not specified in this answer.

# Question 8

A deadlock is detected in statement B of a large transaction after statement A has started but has not completed. What is the state of the transaction?

- ○ a.  Statement A is rolled back and an error message is generated for statement B.
- ○ b.  Statements A and B are rolled back, and the transaction receives an error message.
- ○ c.  The entire transaction is rolled back.
- ○ d.  Statement B is rolled back and an error message is generated for the transaction.

The correct answer is d. When a statement detects a deadlock, the detecting statement is rolled back and an error is generated. Answer a is incorrect because statement A is already active (and presumably holds the lock that B is deadlocking against) and is not rolled back. Answer b is incorrect because only statement B, the detecting statement, is rolled back. Answer c is incorrect because you do not have enough information about the transaction to make this call.

# Question 9

Robyn has an active database connection and leaves for lunch. She did not commit her work, and the table she was accessing has a table-level lock on it. Which action should you take to release the locks so that other users can access this table?

○ a.  Kill Robyn's session

○ b.  Make the users wait until Robyn returns

○ c.  Shut down the instance and restart

○ d.  Kill Robyn's session with an operating system command

○ e.  Commit Robyn's transactions using SQL*Plus

The correct answer is a. Because you do not know the state of Robyn's transaction, answer a is the only solution. Answer b is incorrect because the users might have to wait too long. Imagine what would happen if Robyn were to go home rather than return after lunch. Answer c is incorrect because, although you can kill individual sessions, you wouldn't want to shut down the entire database to fix one user's oversight. Answer d would work, but what if you're using a multithreaded server or Robyn is coming in over a database link? You might not be able to recognize Robyn's process at the operating system level. Therefore, although this will work, you might kill the wrong session. Answer e is incorrect because, again, you do not know whether the data being entered or changed by Robyn is correct or whether she might decide to roll it back after lunch. Besides, she might be in an entirely different location than you.

# Question 10

Which lock types are usually obtained by user applications? [Choose three]

❑ a.  TM

❑ b.  UL

❑ c.  SS

❑ d.  TX

❑ e.  RX

The correct answers are a, b, and d. Users usually obtain TM locks (table locks), UL locks (breakable parse locks), and TX locks (transaction locks). Answer c is the indication for a subshare table lock, otherwise known as a *row–share table lock* (RS lock), and is a lock mode, not a lock. Answer e is the indication for a row–exclusive lock mode. It's also a lock mode, not a lock.

# Question 11

You're experiencing latch contention problems with redo copy latches. Which initialization parameter can you change to reduce contention?

○ a. **LOG_SIMULTANEOUS_COPIES**

○ b. **LOG_BLOCK_CHECKSUM**

○ c. **LOG_SMALL_ENTRY_MAX_COUNT**

The correct answer is a. **LOG_SIMULTANEOUS_COPIES** is used to reduce contention. Answer b, **LOG_BLOCK_CHECKSUM**, is used to verify data blocks written to the redo logs, not redo copy latches. Answer c is not an initialization parameter. Therefore, answers b and c are incorrect.

# Question 12

What types of activities can cause contention for free lists? [Choose three]

❑ a. Inserts

❑ b. Deletes

❑ c. DDL

❑ d. Updates

❑ e. Selects

The correct answers are a, b, and d. During inserts, the free list is checked for available space in the data blocks of the segment. During updates and deletes, the block is added to the head of the free list if the available space falls below **PCTUSED**. DDL and select statements do not access the free lists. Therefore, answers c and e are incorrect.

## Question 13

> What is the ideal hit ratio for latches?
>
> ○ a.  80 percent or over
>
> ○ b.  90 percent or over
>
> ○ c.  95 percent or over
>
> ○ d.  99 percent or over

The correct answer is d. Any latch hit ratio under 99 percent should be addressed and corrective action taken. Because the other answers represent ratios under 99 percent, answers a, b, and c are all incorrect.

## Question 14

> Where are free lists maintained?
>
> ○ a.  Table header
>
> ○ b.  Segment header
>
> ○ c.  Data file header
>
> ○ d.  Tablespace header
>
> ○ e.  Redo log header

The correct answer is b. Free lists are maintained in the segment headers of the segments allocated for the object (table or index). Answers a, c, d, and e are incorrect because the free lists are not stored in them.

## Question 15

> What two events will cause a data block to be moved to the head of the free lists?
>
> ❑ a.  The free space in the block falls below **PCTUSED**.
>
> ❑ b.  The user process terminates.
>
> ❑ c.  The table has been truncated.
>
> ❑ d.  The server process terminates.

The correct answers are a and c. After an update or delete, Oracle checks whether the free space in the block is greater than the value of **PCTUSED**. If it is, Oracle will add the data block to the head of the free lists. Also, if a table has been truncated, the high-water mark for the object is reset, thus making all the data blocks available in the free lists. Answers b and d are incorrect because they have no effect on the free lists.

# Need To Know More?

 Aronoff, Eyal, Kevin Loney, and Noorali Sonawalla. *Oracle8 Advanced Tuning and Administration*. Oracle Press, 1998. ISBN 0-07882-534-2.

 Ault, Michael R. *Oracle8 Black Book*. The Coriolis Group, 1998. ISBN 1-57610-187-8. (Be sure to read Chapters 9 and 11 carefully.)

 Ault, Michael R. *Oracle8i Administration and Management*. Wiley Computer Publishing, 1999. ISBN 0-471-35453-8.

 Corey, Michael, Michael Abbey, and Daniel J. Dechichio, Jr. *Oracle8 Tuning*. Oracle Press, 1997. ISBN 0-07882-390-0.

 The first place to go for more information is the *Oracle8 Tuning Manual* and the *Oracle8 Server Reference Manual*.

# Sample Test

In this chapter, we provide pointers to help you develop a successful test-taking strategy, including how to choose proper answers, how to decode ambiguity, how to work within the Oracle testing framework, how to decide what you need to memorize beforehand, and how to prepare in general for the test. At the end of this chapter, we include a set of 65 questions on subject matter that is pertinent to Exam 1Z0-014, "Oracle8: Performance Tuning." In Chapter 12, you'll find the answer key to this test. Good luck!

# Questions, Questions, Questions

There should be no doubt in your mind that you are facing a test full of specific and pointed questions. The Oracle8: Performance Tuning test consists of 61 questions that you must complete in 90 minutes.

Questions belong to one of two basic types: multiple-choice with a single answer, and multiple-choice with one or more answers.

Always take the time to read a question at least twice before selecting an answer, and always look for an Exhibit button as you examine each question. Exhibits include graphics information that pertains to the question. (An exhibit is usually a screen capture of program output or GUI information that you must examine to analyze the question's scenario and formulate an answer.)

Not every question has only one answer; many questions require multiple answers. Therefore, it's important to read each question carefully—not only to determine how many answers are necessary or possible, but to look for additional hints or instructions when selecting answers. Such instructions often occur in brackets immediately following the question itself (as they do for all multiple-choice questions in which one or more answers are possible).

# Picking Proper Answers

Obviously, the only way to pass any exam is to select enough of the right answers to obtain a passing score. However, Oracle's exams are not standardized like the SAT and GRE exams; they are far more diabolical and convoluted. In some cases, questions are strangely worded, and deciphering them can be a real challenge. In those cases, you may need to rely on answer-elimination skills. Almost always, at least one answer out of the possible choices for a question can be eliminated immediately because it matches one of these conditions:

➤ The answer does not apply to the situation.

➤ The answer describes a nonexistent issue.

➤ The answer is already eliminated by the text of the question.

After you eliminate all answers that are obviously wrong, you can apply your retained knowledge to eliminate further answers. Look for items that sound correct but that refer to actions, commands, or features that are not present or available in the situation that the question describes.

If you're still faced with a blind guess among two or more potentially correct answers, reread the question. Try to picture how each of the possible remaining answers would alter the situation. Be especially sensitive to terminology, because sometimes the choice of words (*remove* instead of *disable*) can make the difference between a right answer and a wrong one.

Only when you've exhausted your ability to eliminate answers should you guess at an answer. An unanswered question offers you no points, but guessing gives you at least some chance of getting a question right. Just don't be too hasty when making a blind guess.

 You can wait until the last round of reviewing marked questions (just as you're about to run out of time, or out of unanswered questions) before you start making guesses.

# Decoding Ambiguity

Exams are meant to test knowledge on a given topic, and the scores from a properly designed test will have the classic bell-shaped distribution for the target audience, meaning a certain number will fail. A problem with this exam is that is has been tailored to Oracle's training materials even though some of the material in the training is hearsay, some is old DBA tales, and some is just incorrect. Where obvious errors in the exam questions exist, the previous chapters have attempted to point them out to you.

The only way to overcome some of the exam's limitations is to be prepared. You will discover that many of the questions test your knowledge of something that is not directly related to the issue raised by the questions. This means that the answers offered to you, even the incorrect ones, are as much a part of the skill assessment as are the questions. If you do not know all the aspects of an exam topic (in this case, database administration) cold, you will not be able to eliminate answers that are obviously wrong because they relate to a different aspect of the topic than the one addressed by the question itself.

Questions can reveal answers, especially when dealing with commands and data dictionary topics. Read a question and then evaluate the answers in light of common terms, names, and structure.

Another problem is that Oracle uses some terminology in its training materials that is found nowhere else in its documentation sets. Whether this was a deliberate attempt to force you to take its classes to pass the exam or simply sloppy documentation is not known.

# Working Within The Framework

The questions will be presented to you randomly. A question on tuning applications might follow one on tuning rollback segments, followed by one on using the UTLESTAT and UTLBSTAT scripts. However, this can work to your advantage in that a future question might unwittingly answer the question you are puzzling over. You might find that an incorrect answer to this question will be the correct answer to a question later in the exam. Take the time to read all the answers for each question, even (or especially) if you spot the right one immediately.

You can revisit any question as many times as you like. If you're uncertain of the answer to a question, check the box that's provided to mark it for easy return later on. You should also mark questions that you think may offer information that you can use to answer other questions. We usually mark somewhere between 25 and 50 percent of the questions. The testing software is designed to let you mark every question if you choose, so use this feature to your advantage. Everything you will want to see again should be marked; the testing software can then help you return to marked questions quickly and easily.

# Deciding What To Memorize

The amount of memorization you will need to do depends on whether you are a visual learner. If you can see the command structure diagrams in your head, you will not need to memorize as much as if you cannot. The exam will stretch your recollection skills through command syntax and operational command sequences used within the Oracle environment, testing not only when you should use a feature but also when you should not.

The important types of information to memorize are:

➤ Commonly used **V$** views

➤ Tuning scripts and their uses

➤ The use of initialization parameters for sort and system global area (SGA) tuning

➤ Restrictions on command use (such as with joins in **SELECT**)

➤ The use of SQL*Plus in tables related to query performance

➤ Tuning rollback segments and redo logs

If you work your way through this book while sitting in front of an Oracle database that you have access to and try out commands and exam answers and play with unfamiliar features, you should have no problem understanding the questions on the exam. Also, don't forget that the Cram Sheet at the front of the book captures the material that is most important to memorize, so don't forget to use it to guide your studies as well.

# Preparing For The Test

The best way to prepare for the test—after you've studied—is to take at least one practice exam. We've included one in this chapter for that reason; the test questions are located in the pages that follow. (Unlike the preceding chapters in this book, the answers don't follow the questions immediately; you'll have to flip to Chapter 12 to review the answers.)

Give yourself 90 uninterrupted minutes to complete the practice exam in this chapter. Use the honor system—you will gain no benefit from cheating. The idea is to see where you are weak and require further study, not to answer all the questions correctly by looking up the answers. When your time is up or when you finish, you can check your answers in Chapter 12. Pay special attention to the explanations for the incorrect answers; these can also help to reinforce your knowledge of the material. Knowing how to recognize correct answers is good, but understanding why incorrect answers are wrong can be equally valuable.

# Taking The Exam

Relax. Once you're sitting in front of the testing computer, there's nothing more you can do to increase your knowledge or preparation. Take a deep breath, stretch, and start reading that first question.

There's no need to rush; you have plenty of time to complete each question and to return to those questions that you skip or mark for return. If you read a question twice and remain clueless, you can mark it. Both easy and difficult questions are intermixed throughout the test in random order. Don't cheat yourself by spending too much time on a hard question early in the test, which deprives you of the time you need to answer the questions at the end of the test.

You can read through the entire test and, before returning to marked questions for a second visit, figure out how much time you've got per question. As you answer each question, remove its mark. Continue to review the remaining marked questions until you run out of time or you complete the test.

That's it for pointers. Here are some questions for you to practice on.

# Practice Questions

## Question 1

What information is contained in the **V$CACHE** view?

○ a.  Objects currently being cached

○ b.  Objects cached since the database was started

○ c.  Objects waiting to be cached

○ d.  Objects too small to be cached

## Question 2

You have a high-volume OLTP system with numerous inserts and updates. For what should you monitor tables with high levels of inserts?

○ a.  Free list contention

○ b.  Row chaining

○ c.  Block fragmentation

○ d.  Index fragmentation

## Question 3

When will the proper addition of indexes improve performance?

○ a.  When you have excessive redo header waits

○ b.  When you have a shortage of memory

○ c.  When SQL statements are performing poorly

○ d.  When you have excessive undo header waits

# Question 4

If you have latch contention and query the **V$LATCH** view, what will the **SLEEPS** column tell you?

- ○ a.  The number of times a process missed getting a lock
- ○ b.  The number of times a process got a latch immediately
- ○ c.  The number of times a process missed getting an immediate latch
- ○ d.  The number of times a process waited on a latch

# Question 5

When would you allocate extents of a table explicitly to separate data files?

- ○ a.  When following OFA guidelines
- ○ b.  When optimizing file placement
- ○ c.  When striping tables by hand
- ○ d.  When you are absolutely sure that your sizing estimates are correct

# Question 6

What exactly is a TM lock?

- ○ a.  The identifier given to an exclusive table lock in the lock-type column of the Server Manager
- ○ b.  The identifier given to a share table lock in the lock-type column of the Server Manager
- ○ c.  The identifier given to a table lock in the lock-type column of the Server Manager
- ○ d.  The identifier given to a row-exclusive lock in the lock-type column of the Server Manager

# Question 7

Which columns contain statistics concerning **WILLING_TO_WAIT** requests in the **V$LATCH** view? [Choose two]

- ☐ a. **HITS**
- ☐ b. **WAITS**
- ☐ c. **SLEEPS**
- ☐ d. **MISSES**
- ☐ e. **GETS**

# Question 8

What can you instruct developers to do to ensure that effective low-level database tuning is possible?

- ○ a. Be sure that all SQL statements are well-written.
- ○ b. Use only ANSI SQL92 standard statements.
- ○ c. Nothing; well-written applications do not require low-level tuning.

# Question 9

You query the **V$WAITSTAT** view and see a value of 215 in the **UNDO HEADER** column. Which problem does this indicate?

- ○ a. An extent shortage for rollback segments
- ○ b. LRU latch contention
- ○ c. Contention for rollback segment header blocks
- ○ d. An excessive number of rollback segment header blocks

# Question 10

What is the purpose of the library cache area of the shared pool?

- ○ a. To store data on data dictionary caches
- ○ b. To store data retrieved from data files
- ○ c. To store shared SQL and PL/SQL
- ○ d. To provide for sort areas

# Question 11

What is the purpose of the report.txt file?

○ a.  It contains information about database errors and alerts.

○ b.  It contains information you would use to tune your database.

○ c.  It preloads temporary tables with database statistics.

○ d.  It calculates the delta values of database statistics for tuning.

# Question 12

Assuming that your initialization parameters are set correctly, what can be done to minimize the number of checkpoints that occur?

○ a.  Use fewer redo log groups

○ b.  Use smaller redo log group members

○ c.  Use more redo log groups

○ d.  Use larger redo log group members

# Question 13

At which level will Oracle resolve deadlocks?

○ a.  Transaction

○ b.  Statement

○ c.  Row

○ d.  Table

# Question 14

What are the only objects that should be stored with rollback segments?

○ a.  User-created objects

○ b.  Database triggers

○ c.  Temporary segments

○ d.  Other rollback segments

# Question 15

The Chemical application has tables that undergo numerous deletes. Which of the following values for **PCTUSED** would be the best for these tables?

○ a. 20

○ b. 10

○ c. 50

○ d. 0

# Question 16

What would sizing the shared pool too small cause?

○ a. Heavy I/O in the system tablespace

○ b. Excessive checkpointing

○ c. Undo header contention

○ d. Latch contention

# Question 17

You are creating the database for a decision support system (DSS). To what value should you set the **DB_BLOCK_SIZE** initialization parameter?

○ a. 10K

○ b. The maximum value for the platform

○ c. 4K

○ d. The minimum value for the platform

○ e. Oracle automatically sets the right size when the database is created.

# Question 18

Which scripts would you run to enable the **DBMS_APPLICATION_INFO** package? [Choose two]

- ❏ a.  UTLESTAT.SQL
- ❏ b.  UTLBSTAT.SQL
- ❏ c.  DBMSAPIN.SQL
- ❏ d.  CATALOG.SQL
- ❏ e.  PRVTAPIN.SQL

# Question 19

Which criteria should you use when determining the number of rollback segments you will need?

- ○ a.  The value of the **DB_BLOCK_BUFFERS** parameter
- ○ b.  The number of concurrent processes on the system
- ○ c.  The number of concurrent DML processes on the system
- ○ d.  The number of indexes in the application

# Question 20

The document-management system was installed several years ago. When installed, the system had several large tables manually striped across several disks. The application was very well tuned and performed excellently. Since installation, data files for the striped tables and other tablespaces have been placed haphazardly around the disk farm in whatever space was large enough to hold them. Which tuning issue should you look at first if the users complain of poor performance?

- ○ a.  Retune the application
- ○ b.  Check memory tuning
- ○ c.  Tune I/O to ensure that the load is balanced evenly across the disk farm
- ○ d.  Tune for latch contention
- ○ e.  Redesign the entire application

# Question 21

You run UTLBSTAT and UTLESTAT. After reviewing the output, you find an indication of a high **GET_MISS/GET_REQ** ratio for the library cache. What can you do to correct this problem?

○ a. Increase the shared pool size

○ b. Decrease the shared pool size

○ c. Pin all the objects in the library cache

○ d. Increase the redo log buffers

# Question 22

Which view do you query to get the value of **TOTAL_EXTENTS** for the temporary tablespace?

○ a. **V$SQLTEXT**

○ b. **V$DB_OBJECT_CACHE**

○ c. **V$TYPE_SIZE**

○ d. **V$SORT_SEGMENT**

# Question 23

When developing a tuning strategy, which area is usually considered most important and will result in the most performance gains?

○ a. I/O

○ b. Design

○ c. Application

○ d. Memory

○ e. Contention

# Question 24

Which change would you make if you wanted to decrease the number of disk sorts?

○ a.  Increase **SORT_AREA_RETAINED_SIZE**

○ b.  Decrease **SORT_AREA_SIZE**

○ c.  Increase **SORT_AREA_SIZE**

○ d.  Decrease **SORT_AREA_RETAINED_SIZE**

# Question 25

Which SQL statement would require a sort?

○ a.  SELECT * FROM nuclides;

○ b.  SELECT nuclide, atomic_no FROM nuclides;

○ c.  SELECT nuclide, atomic_no FROM nuclides

   WHERE atomic no<80;

○ d.  SELECT DISTINCT result FROM samples;

# Question 26

Users have complained that they experience delays when getting results back from ad hoc queries to the document control application. As the DBA, which area should you examine first when troubleshooting the problem?

○ a.  PGA

○ b.  SQL statements

○ c.  I/O

○ d.  SGA

# Question 27

When you increase the number of dispatchers using the **ALTER SYSTEM** command in a system using a multithreaded server (MTS), when are the new dispatchers activated?

○ a. After the **ALTER SYSTEM** command is issued

○ b. As soon as new dispatchers are needed

○ c. After the database is shut down and restarted

○ d. After the listener process is stopped and restarted

# Question 28

Which SQL statement will not require a sort?

○ a. SELECT name, atomic_wt, atomic_mass FROM nuclides

WHERE group = 'I' ORDER BY atomic_wt;

○ b. SELECT * FROM nuclides;

○ c. SELECT name, atomic_wt, atomic_mass FROM nuclides

ORDER BY atomic_wt;

○ d. SELECT DISTINCT(atomic_mass) FROM nuclides

WHERE atomic_wt>53;

# Question 29

What is one of the purposes of the **DBMS_SHARED_POOL** package?

○ a. To create functions needed for PL/SQL

○ b. To create procedures and packages needed to create other procedures and packages

○ c. To create utilities used by the DIANA routines

○ d. To pin large or frequently used packages in the library cache

# Question 30

What is the purpose of the Oracle8 SQL*Trace facility?

○ a.  To generate a set of delta reports for database tuning

○ b.  To generate a human-readable report from a trace file

○ c.  To generate an execution plan for an SQL statement

○ d.  To identify SQL areas that might be causing performance problems

# Question 31

What is the common characteristic of the TM, UL, and TX lock types?

○ a.  They are table-level locks.

○ b.  They are share locks.

○ c.  They are lock types obtained usually by user applications.

○ d.  They are lock types used only by Oracle8 internal processes.

# Question 32

You have tuned the application, and your manager still wants an extra bit of performance. What should you tune next?

○ a.  Memory

○ b.  I/O

○ c.  Contention

○ d.  Design

# Question 33

What is the purpose of the Oracle Expert tool?

○ a.  To configure the Oracle database

○ b.  To monitor Oracle performance

○ c.  To monitor tablespaces

○ d.  To monitor the user sessions that are using the most resources

# Question 34

Which Enterprise Manager tool can you use to collect data about application events?

○ a. Oracle Trace

○ b. Oracle Expert

○ c. Oracle Tablespace Manager

○ d. Oracle Performance Manager

# Question 35

When tuning the shared pool, which structure should be your main concern?

○ a. Overall shared pool size

○ b. Library cache

○ c. Data dictionary cache

# Question 36

When is free list contention likely to occur?

○ a. When applications explicitly lock tables

○ b. When there is insufficient space in the shared pool

○ c. When an application has many inserts and deletes performed on tables

# Question 37

A deadlock is detected in statement B of a large transaction containing statements A and B. What is the state of the transaction?

○ a. Statement A is rolled back and an error message is generated for statement B.

○ b. Statements A and B are rolled back, and an error message is generated for the transaction.

○ c. The transaction is rolled back.

○ d. Statement B is rolled back, and an error message is generated for the transaction.

# Question 38

You issue the following command:

```
ANALYZE TABLE nuclides ESTIMATE STATISTICS
    SAMPLE 30 PERCENT;
```

Which column of the **DBA_TABLES** view can you query to see the number of migrated rows in the **nuclides** table?

- ○ a. **CHAIN_CNT**
- ○ b. **BLOCKS**
- ○ c. **AVG_ROW_LEN**
- ○ d. **NUM_ROWS**

# Question 39

What does Oracle use to manage the SQL and PL/SQL in the library cache?

- ○ a. LRU algorithm
- ○ b. Clusters
- ○ c. User global area (UGA)
- ○ d. Database buffer cache
- ○ e. Program global area (PGA)

# Question 40

Which view is used to detect the actual row that is causing lock contention?

- ○ a. **V$ROWCACHE**
- ○ b. **V$LOCK**
- ○ c. **V$SYSSTAT**
- ○ d. **V$SESSION**

# Question 41

What is one characteristic of a DDL lock?

○ a. It allows other processes to access the object being locked.

○ b. It allows other processes to access the row being locked.

○ c. It probably will not cause contention.

○ d. It can cause contention if used carelessly.

# Question 42

What is the purpose of the **SHARED_POOL_RESERVED_SIZE** initialization parameter?

○ a. To set the size of the shared pool

○ b. To set the minimum size of a reserved section of the shared pool

○ c. To set reserved areas of the shared pool for large packages

○ d. To prevent the release of cursor areas from the shared pool

# Question 43

What happens when the work being done is copied to the buffer on a single-CPU computer?

○ a. The latch times out.

○ b. The redo allocation latch is released.

○ c. Nothing; work is not copied to the buffer on single-CPU computers.

○ d. Nothing; work is not copied to the buffer cache until another process requests the latch.

# Question 44

Which latch statistics column in the report.txt file shows that tuning is required if it displays a high percentage?

○ a. **SLEEPS**

○ b. **HIT_RATIO**

○ c. **GETS**

○ d. **SLEEPS/MISS**

# Question 45

Which initialization parameter determines whether Oracle will bypass the buffer cache when sorting?

○ a. **SORT_AREA_RETAINED_SIZE**

○ b. **SORT_AREA_SIZE**

○ c. **SORT_DIRECT_WRITES**

○ d. **SORT_WRITE_BUFFER_SIZE**

# Question 46

You have an OLTP system and notice that your **DATA** tablespace keeps becoming fragmented. What is the probable cause?

○ a. Rollback segments were placed in the **DATA** tablespace.

○ b. Your **DATA** tablespace is too small for the load it is carrying.

○ c. This is nothing to worry about because it is normal for Oracle.

○ d. Tables are automatically shrinking as data is deleted from them.

# Question 47

When a redo copy latch is needed, which type of request is made?

○ a. **WILLING_TO_WAIT**

○ b. **BUFFER**

○ c. **IMMEDIATE**

○ d. **ALLOCATION**

# Question 48

Which process is responsible for placing blocks in the database buffer cache?

○ a. SMON

○ b. PMON

○ c. DBWn

○ d. User-server processes

# Question 49

What is the purpose of the database buffer cache in the SGA?

○ a. To store shared SQL and PL/SQL

○ b. To store data dictionary information

○ c. To store copies of data blocks that can be shared by all users

○ d. To store transaction data before it is copied to the redo logs

# Question 50

You query the **V$LIBRARYCACHE** view. Which column contains the executions of an item stored in the library cache?

○ a. **RELOADS**

○ b. **PINS**

○ c. **INVALIDATIONS**

○ d. **GETS**

# Question 51

Which views can you query to evaluate the effect of an increase or a decrease in the size of the database buffer cache? [Choose two]

❑ a. **V$CACHE**

❑ b. **V$FILESTAT**

❑ c. **X$STATS**

❑ d. **V$RECENT_BUCKET**

❑ e. **V$SYSSTAT**

# Question 52

If you are using parallel query mode, what can you do to improve performance when querying large tables?

○ a.  Use Oracle table partitioning to stripe the tables

○ b.  Increase the shared pool size

○ c.  Increase the redo log size

○ d.  Decrease the degree setting for the tables

# Question 53

If you query the **V$RECENT_BUCKET** virtual table, which value will the **COUNT** column display?

○ a.  The number of blocks in the database buffer cache

○ b.  The number of additional cache hits gained by adding additional buffer cache blocks

○ c.  The number of reads in the database buffer cache

○ d.  The number of buffers added to the database buffer cache

# Question 54

Your SQL statements are properly tuned, yet performance is still slow. What might improve performance?

○ a.  Increasing the redo log size

○ b.  Increasing the sort area size

○ c.  Increasing the number of database block buffers

○ d.  Decreasing the sort area size

# Question 55

In which state should the operating system be when using direct writes?

○ a.  Optional background processes cannot be running.

○ b.  I/O should be well tuned.

○ c.  The system should have adequate disk and memory resources.

○ d.  Data files must be sized appropriately.

# Question 56

What is one characteristic of the **MTS_LISTENER_ADDRESS** initialization parameter?

○ a. It configures the number of dispatchers used in the database.

○ b. It must contain the same value as its counterpart in listener.ora.

○ c. It configures the number of servers used in the database.

○ d. It creates the name for the MTS service process.

# Question 57

What is one purpose of the **SET TRANSACTION** command?

○ a. To control redo for a large transaction

○ b. To create a transaction

○ c. To modify a transaction

○ d. To change a system parameter

# Question 58

Which copies of a single database block can be found in the database buffer cache at all times? [Choose two]

❑ a. Deleted copy

❑ b. Read-consistent copy

❑ c. Backup copy

❑ d. Current copy

# Question 59

You run the UTLBSTAT.SQL script and then shut down and restart the instance. What will you need to do next to generate a tuning report?

○ a. Rerun UTLBSTAT.SQL

○ b. Run UTLESTAT.SQL

○ c. Run UTLBSTAT.SQL and UTLESTAT.SQL

○ d. Run UTLESTAT.SQL and UTLBSTAT.SQL

# Question 60

What is one benefit of using bitmapped indexes in a decision support system (DSS)?

○ a.  They use very little space.

○ b.  They must be ordered.

○ c.  They are great for small tables.

○ d.  They work well on columns of high cardinality.

# Question 61

What is one purpose of the alert_*<SID>*.log file?

○ a.  To store information about a process's SQL statement

○ b.  To track alerts issued by Oracle about your release

○ c.  To provide information about database events

○ d.  To track user login attempts

# Question 62

Why should you be sure that the **DB_BLOCK_SIZE** parameter is set correctly when creating a database?

○ a.  If it is too large, database performance will suffer.

○ b.  If it is too low, excessive amounts of memory might be used.

○ c.  It requires a rebuild of the database to change.

○ d.  This is set automatically, so you do not need to worry about it.

# Question 63

Where are only before images of data blocks stored?

○ a.  In rollback segments

○ b.  In redo logs

○ c.  In data files

○ d.  In indexes

# Question 64

When should sorts be done in memory?

○ a. Whenever possible

○ b. When there is insufficient temporary tablespace room

○ c. When **SORT_DIRECT_WRITES** is set to **TRUE**

# Question 65

Which parameter should be set prior to running the UTLBSTAT.SQL script?

○ a. **AUDIT_TRAIL**

○ b. **SQL_TRACE**

○ c. **TIMED_STATISTICS**

# Answer Key

| | | | |
|---|---|---|---|
| 1. a | 18. c, e | 35. b | 52. a |
| 2. a | 19. c | 36. c | 53. b |
| 3. c | 20. c | 37. d | 54. c |
| 4. d | 21. a | 38. a | 55. c |
| 5. c | 22. d | 39. a | 56. b |
| 6. c | 23. c | 40. d | 57. a |
| 7. d, e | 24. c | 41. c | 58. b, d |
| 8. a | 25. d | 42. c | 59. c |
| 9. c | 26. b | 43. b | 60. a |
| 10. c | 27. b | 44. d | 61. c |
| 11. b | 28. b | 45. c | 62. c |
| 12. d | 29. d | 46. a | 63. a |
| 13. b | 30. d | 47. c | 64. a |
| 14. d | 31. c | 48. d | 65. c |
| 15. c | 32. a | 49. c | |
| 16. a | 33. a | 50. b | |
| 17. b | 34. a | 51. d, e | |

# Question 1

The correct answer is a. The **V$CACHE** view is created when the catparr.sql script is run to install required support objects for an Oracle Parallel Server. The **V$CACHE** view tracks currently cached objects. Answer b is incorrect because **V$CACHE** tracks only currently cached objects, not historical data on cached objects. Answer c is incorrect because **V$CACHE** tracks cached objects, not objects waiting to be cached. Answer d is incorrect because the smaller the object, the more likely it is to be cached; no objects are too small to be cached.

# Question 2

The correct answer is a. Because objects are created with a specific number of free lists and free list groups, if an insufficient number is specified, processes might contend for these objects during periods of high insert activity. Note that the question specifies periods of high insert activity. Answer b is incorrect because the question specified insert activity; if the second half of the question had mentioned update activity as well, row chaining would be an issue, but because the question restricts the answer to insert activity, row chaining is not an issue. Answer c is incorrect because blocks cannot fragment. Answer d is incorrect because, again, you are asked about periods of high insert activity. Insert activity can result in unbalanced B-tree structures but not in index fragmentation.

# Question 3

The correct answer is c. Adding a proper index can dramatically increase the performance of SQL statements. Answer a is incorrect because redo header waits deal with the redo logs and their size and availability and have nothing to do with indexes. Answer b is incorrect because even with proper indexes, if the memory shortage is causing performance problems, adding indexes will not help. Answer d is incorrect because undo header waits involve rollback segment problems, not indexes.

# Question 4

The correct answer is d. A **SLEEPS** indication means that a wait occurred; the latch has not been missed until the process times out while waiting. Answer a is incorrect because a missed lock is indicated by the **MISSES** column.

Answer b is incorrect because whether a latch is received immediately is indicated by the **IMMEDIATE_GETS** column. Answer c is incorrect because a missed latch is shown by the **IMMEDIATE_MISSES** column.

# Question 5

The correct answer is c. One thing to watch for on the exam is this type of question, which seems to confuse tables and tablespaces. Because most data file placement is done by hand for tablespaces, it makes little sense to say "striping tablespaces by hand." The process of striping a table in Oracle8 involves creating a tablespace with several data files on separate drives and then creating a table with multiple extents in which each extent is either deliberately placed or sized to force placement into the multiple data files. Answer a is incorrect because the striping of tables is not covered in the OFA (Optimal Flexible Architecture) documentation. Answer b is incorrect because optimizing file placement deals with balancing I/O across the disk farm and does not involve table striping. Answer d is incorrect because, although absolutely correct sizing estimates are good to have, they would not lead you to allocate extents by hand.

# Question 6

The correct answer is c. TM always stands for *table lock*. Answer a is incorrect because exclusive locks have *X* somewhere in their names. Answer b is incorrect because share locks have *S* somewhere in their names. Answer d is incorrect because row locks have *R* somewhere in their names.

# Question 7

The correct answers are d and e. The **MISSES** and **GETS** columns are the only columns in the **V$LATCH** view that apply to **WILLING_TO_WAIT** requests. Therefore, answers a, b, and c are incorrect.

# Question 8

The correct answer is a. If SQL statements are not well written, effective low-level application tuning to improve performance might not be possible. The use of functions in joins on the right side of the condition, the use of unneeded distincts or uniques, and so on can prohibit proper low-level tuning. Answer b is incorrect because Oracle SQL provides a richer set of functionality in most cases than SQL92. Answer c is incorrect because even the best-written applications can have their performance improved by low-level tuning.

## Question 9

The correct answer is c. Anytime you see the term **UNDO**, think *rollback segment*. Because the indication is **UNDO HEADER**, it is showing contention for header blocks. Therefore, it is actually saying that rollback header block contention is occurring. Answer a is incorrect because an extent shortage is indicated by **UNDO SEGMENT** waits and would also be signaled by failure-to-extend errors involving the rollback segments. Answer b is incorrect because LRU latch contention is indicated by LRU latch, not **UNDO**, indications. Answer d is incorrect because if there were an excessive number of undo header blocks, you would not have waits for them.

## Question 10

The correct answer is c. The library cache area of the SGA is used to store shared SQL and PL/SQL. Answer a is incorrect because this is the function of the data dictionary cache, which is a separate section of the shared pool from the library cache. Answer b is incorrect because this is the function of the database buffer pool, which is a separate section of the SGA from the shared pool, which contains the library cache. Answer d is incorrect because this is the function of the sort areas provided as a separate section of the shared pool (in multithreaded servers) or as a part of the user's memory area in multithreaded server (MTS) mode databases.

## Question 11

The correct answer is b. When the UTLBSTAT and UTLESTAT utility scripts are run, the result is the report.txt file. This file gives the delta numbers between the initial statistics gathered and stored by UTLBSTAT.SQL and the final set gathered by UTLESTAT.SQL. The UTLESTAT.SQL script actually writes the report. Answer a is incorrect because this statement describes the alert_<*SID*>.log file. Answer c is incorrect because this statement describes the purpose of the UTLBSTAT.SQL script. Answer d is incorrect because this statement describes the purpose of the UTLESTAT.SQL script.

## Question 12

The correct answer is d. If your initialization parameters are set so that checkpoints occur only on log switches, increasing the size of your redo log group members will decrease the number of checkpoints performed. Answer a is incorrect because using fewer groups of the same size will result only in more redo log contention, not in fewer checkpoints. Answer b is incorrect because smaller redo log group members will result in more frequent checkpoints. Answer c is incorrect because simply adding redo log groups might reduce log contention, but if they are the same size as previous groups, the frequency of log switches will remain the same.

# Question 13

The correct answer is b. The first statement to detect a deadlock is rolled back. Answer a is incorrect because a transaction can have multiple statements, and a statement is what triggers a deadlock condition and causes itself to be rolled back. Answer c is incorrect because a deadlock is resolved by rolling back, and only statements and transactions, not rows, are rolled back. Answer d is incorrect because, again, the resolution occurs at the statement (logical) level, not at a table or a row (physical) level.

# Question 14

The correct answer is d. Because of the dynamic way in which rollback segments grow and shrink (if OPTIMAL is set), their tablespace tends to become fragmented. As long as all the rollback segments have identical values for NEXT, this is not a problem because any rollback segment can then use any released segment from any other rollback segment. Answer a is incorrect because tables, indexes, and clusters are user-created objects, and you should store rollback segments only with other rollback segments. Answer b is incorrect because all triggers are stored in tables in the data dictionary. Answer c is incorrect because storing temporary segments with rollback segments could result in space problems as both extend and contract dynamically. Temporary segments should be stored away from all other objects, including rollback segments.

# Question 15

The correct answer is c. Because of the answers provided and because you are given no other criteria to judge against, you should select the highest value.

# Question 16

The correct answer is a. The shared pool being sized too small can cause heavy I/O in the system tablespace, as object definitions are constantly being reread from the data dictionary tables. Answer b is incorrect because excessive checkpointing is caused by either having improper initialization file values or having redo log group members that are too small. Answer c is incorrect because undo header contention is caused by having too few rollback segments. Answer d is incorrect because latch contention is caused by processes contending for latches, not by having too small of a shared pool.

## Question 17

The correct answer is b. Decision support systems use many full-table scans to produce their rollups and reports, and large block sizes facilitate full-table scans. Answer a is incorrect because a block size must be a multiple of the operating system block size and in the range of 2K, 4K, 8K, 16K, and so on. Answer c is incorrect because 4K is not the maximum value for any platform that Oracle is ported to. Answer d is incorrect because the minimum value for a platform would be insufficient to support full-table scans and therefore would produce excessive disk I/O. Answer e is incorrect because this parameter is set manually or will default to a low value, not a maximum value.

## Question 18

The correct answers are c and e. The DBMSAPIN.SQL and PRVTAPIN.PLB scripts create the **DBMS_APPLICATION_INFO** package. Answers a and b are incorrect because the UTLESTAT.SQL and UTLBSTAT.SQL scripts are used for tuning, not for creating packages. Answer d is incorrect because CATALOG.SQL is used to create views, not packages.

## Question 19

The correct answer is c. Only transactions using DML statements use rollback segments; therefore, only **INSERT, UPDATE, DELETE,** and some forms of **SELECT** generate rollback. Because only DML generates rollback, only processes using DML will be assigned rollback segments. Answer a is incorrect because the value of the **DB_BLOCK_BUFFERS** parameter determines the size of the database buffer cache but has nothing to do with rollback segments. Answer b is incorrect because only processes using DML use rollbacks. Answer d is incorrect because the number of indexes has nothing to do with the number of rollback segments.

# Question 20

The correct answer is c. In the scenario presented here, I/O has most likely become unbalanced because the data files have been carelessly placed on the system. Answer a is incorrect because the question states that the application is already well tuned, and adding data files does not affect application tuning. Answer b is incorrect because you can assume that memory was tuned when the application was tuned, and as long as your sorts and data-use patterns have not changed, your memory tuning should not change; besides, everything in the question points to a physical tuning issue. Answer d is incorrect because the question does not discuss excessive waits, which is the only indication that latches need tuning. Answer e is incorrect because the question states that the application is properly tuned, and all that has been added are data files.

# Question 21

The correct answer is a. A high **GET_MISS/GET_REQ** ratio indicates that the shared pool is aging objects out when they are still being requested. This indicates that the shared pool size is too small. Answer b is incorrect because a larger, not a smaller, shared pool is indicated. Answer c is incorrect because pinning objects will not affect the aging of objects because of a too-small shared pool size. Answer d is incorrect because redo log buffers have nothing to do with a high **GET_MISS/GET_REQ** ratio.

# Question 22

The correct answer is d. The **V$SORT_SEGMENT** view is the only view that shows information on temporary tablespaces and their relationship to sort extents. Answer a is incorrect because **V$SQLTEXT** shows the text of currently active SQL and PL/SQL objects. Answer b is incorrect because **V$DB_OBJECT_CACHE** has information on the shared pool but not on the temporary tablespace. Answer c is incorrect because **V$TYPE_SIZE** shows the size information for different type structures used in Oracle8.

# Question 23

The correct answer is c. Application tuning is where you get most of the gain in all your tuning efforts. From 70 to 90 percent of all tuning gains come from tuning the application and its SQL. Answer a is incorrect because I/O tuning might contribute 10 percent of performance gains during tuning, assuming that even a minimal attempt has been made to place files correctly. Answer b is incorrect because design, although important, can contribute only so much to tuning if the SQL and other aspects are not properly implemented. Answer d is incorrect because although proper tuning of memory structures is the second-largest area for performance gains, application tuning is still number one. Only 20 to 30 percent of performance gains come through memory tuning in most systems, assuming that even a minimal attempt has been made to size memory structures. Answer e is incorrect because most contention issues are resolved internally with Oracle, and tuning contention accounts for only 5 to 10 percent of performance gains.

## Question 24

The correct answer is c. Increasing the **SORT_AREA_SIZE** value allows larger sorts to occur in memory. The more sorts that happen in memory, the fewer that are sent to disk. Answer a is incorrect because **SORT_AREA_ RETAINED_SIZE** sets the size of a process's retained sort area size, not the size of the sort that can be done. Answer b is incorrect because decreasing **SORT_AREA_SIZE** increases the number of disk sorts. Answer d is incorrect because **SORT_AREA_RETAINED_SIZE** does not govern the size of the sort that can be done in memory.

## Question 25

The correct answer is d. Any **SELECT** that uses a **DISTINCT** requires a sort. The other statements shown do not require sorts. Therefore, answers a, b, and c are incorrect.

## Question 26

The correct answer is b. Improperly written SQL statements are the number one cause of poor performance. The question states that users are having problems with ad hoc queries, which are notorious for being poorly written. Answer a is incorrect because, other than a few database and initialization parameters, you have little control over the PGA size. Answer c is incorrect because generally I/O is one of the last things you need to tune and is usually one of the last things you need to check in a tuning problem. Answer d is incorrect because further adjusting a properly sized SGA (memory) accounts for very little performance gain for ad hoc queries. The question states that ad hoc queries, not general application performance, are the users' source of complaint, so further tuning of the SGA is not warranted.

## Question 27

The correct answer is b. New dispatchers are activated as soon as they are needed. Answer a is incorrect because Oracle will start new dispatchers only as they are needed. Answer c is incorrect because the starting and killing of dispatcher processes is dynamic up to the maximum allowed number, as specified by the **MTS_MAX_DISPATCHERS** initialization parameter, and down to the value of the **MTS_DISPATCHERS** parameter. Answer d is incorrect because the starting and stopping of dispatcher processes is database controlled, not SQL*Net controlled.

## Question 28

The correct answer is b. Any use of **SORT BY, ORDER BY,** or **DISTINCT** will cause a sort in a **SELECT** statement, and answer b is the only answer that has none of these. Therefore, answers a, c, and d are incorrect.

## Question 29

The correct answer is d. The **DBMS_SHARED_POOL** package was created specifically to help DBAs manage the shared pool by providing packages that allow monitoring shared pool usage and pinning objects in the shared pool. Answer a is incorrect because this is a function of the standard.sql script. Answer b is incorrect because this is a function of the dbmsstdx.sql script. Answer c is incorrect because this is a function of the diutil.sql script.

## Question 30

The correct answer is d. The SQL*Trace facility is used to generate traces of user sessions that can be analyzed to pinpoint performance problems with SQL statements. Answer a is incorrect because this is the purpose of the UTLBSTAT.SQL and UTLESTAT.SQL scripts. Answer b is incorrect because this is the purpose of the TKPROF utility. Answer c is incorrect because this is the purpose of the Explain Plan utility.

## Question 31

The correct answer is c. A TM lock is a general table lock, a UL lock is a breakable parse lock, and a TX lock is an exclusive table lock, all of which are most generally obtained by user applications. Answer a is incorrect because a

UL lock is a lock on an object involved in an SQL statement, not a table. Answer b is incorrect because TX is an exclusive lock. Answer d is incorrect because these are not internal lock types.

## Question 32

The correct answer is a. Tuning memory will give the next-largest jump in performance after application tuning. Answer b is incorrect because I/O tuning generally contributes only half the performance gains of memory tuning. Answer c is incorrect because only minimal performance gains are realized through contention tuning, and it is usually the very last thing tuned. Answer d is incorrect because changing the application design will negate nearly all previous tuning efforts, and you will need to restart your tuning effort. By the time you do application tuning, the design is usually fixed, and it will be difficult, if not impossible, to change.

## Question 33

The correct answer is a. Oracle Expert uses internal Oracle tools to examine tables, indexes, and tablespaces to provide you with a set of steps and suggestions to improve the configuration of your database. Answer b is incorrect because performance monitoring is the job of the Oracle Performance Pack. Answer c is incorrect because monitoring tablespaces is the job of the Oracle Tablespace Manager. Answer d is incorrect because monitoring user sessions that are using the most resources is the job of the Oracle TopSessions monitor.

## Question 34

The correct answer is a. The Oracle Trace tool allows you to trace sessions of the entire database to monitor for events that occur inside the application. Answer b is incorrect because Oracle Expert is used for tuning and configuration suggestions. Answer c is incorrect because Oracle Tablespace Manager is used to monitor tablespaces. Answer d is incorrect because Oracle Performance Manager is used to monitor Oracle performance, not events.

## Question 35

The correct answer is b. The main concern with sizing the shared pool is ensuring that you have an adequately sized library cache. A library cache miss is an expensive performance hit because it involves reading from disk and reparsing

SQL or PL/SQL. Answer a is incorrect because a shared pool that is made too large can adversely affect other memory structures while not appreciably improving library cache hit ratios past a certain point. Answer c is incorrect because Oracle manages the sizing of the data dictionary cache as needed.

# Question 36

The correct answer is c. Free lists maintain a list of blocks that can have inserts performed on them. If an insufficient number of free lists exists, contention will occur on systems in which multiple processes perform inserts and deletes against the same data block. Answer a is incorrect because explicit table locking can result in deadlocks but not in free list contention. Answer b is incorrect because although too small a shared pool can result in shared pool thrashing and library and dictionary cache misses, it cannot cause free list contention.

# Question 37

The correct answer is d. Remember that deadlocks are resolved at the statement level by having the statement that detects the deadlock roll back. Answer a is incorrect because statement A did not detect the deadlock. Answer b is incorrect because this might occur, but you cannot determine this from the information given; all you can say for sure is that statement B will be rolled back and an error will be generated. Answer c is incorrect because only statement B is rolled back; this might cause the entire transaction to roll back, but you do not have enough data to determine this.

# Question 38

The correct answer is a. The **CHAIN_CNT** column is loaded with the number of chained rows when an analysis is done on the table. Answer b is incorrect because **BLOCKS** gives the size of the table in blocks. Answer c is incorrect because **AVG_ROW_LEN** contains information on average row length. Answer d is incorrect because **NUM_ROWS** gives the count of rows in the table.

# Question 39

The correct answer is a. Assuming that enough memory is available, the shared pool is managed by an LRU algorithm that ages old SQL and PL/SQL out of the pool. Answer b is incorrect because clusters constitute a physical structure and have nothing to do with the shared pool. Answer c is incorrect because the

UGA is a structure, not a management tool. Answer d is incorrect because the database buffer pool is another structure in the SGA and is not used in shared pool management. Answer e is incorrect because the PGA is a memory structure and is not used to manage the shared pool.

## Question 40

The correct answer is d. The **V$SESSION** view has statistics that are used to show not only that lock contention is occurring but also which row is causing the problem. Answer a is incorrect because the **V$ROWCACHE** view is used to monitor the data dictionary cache and has nothing to do with locks. Answer b is incorrect because although **V$LOCK** is used to monitor locks, it contains only object-level, not row-level, identification. Answer c is incorrect because **V$SYSSTAT** monitors system statistics but has few statistics on locking.

## Question 41

The correct answer is c. Answer a is incorrect because this is a property of a share lock, not a DDL lock. Answer b is incorrect because this is a characteristic of a row-share lock, not a DDL lock. Answer d is incorrect because a DDL lock is controlled internally, and users do not control its use.

## Question 42

The correct answer is c. The **SHARED_POOL_RESERVED_SIZE** initialization parameter is used to set reserved areas of the shared pool for large packages. Answer a is incorrect because this is the purpose of the **SHARED_POOL_SIZE** parameter. Answer b is incorrect because this is the purpose of the **SHARED_POOL_RESERVED_MIN_ALLOC** parameter. Answer d is incorrect because this is the purpose of the **CURSOR_SPACE_FOR_TIME** parameter.

## Question 43

The correct answer is b. Answer a is incorrect because latch timeouts happen to processes waiting for the latch. Answer c is incorrect because work is copied to the buffer on all computers. Answer d is incorrect because the work is copied as soon as it is done and the latch is freed.

# Question 44

The correct answer is d. The **SLEEPS/MISS** column showing a high percentage indicates that a large number of timeouts is occurring and that tuning is required. Answer a is incorrect because **SLEEPS** does not show a percentage value. Answer b is incorrect because **HIT_RATIO** should be as high a percentage as possible. Answer c is incorrect because **GETS** is not reported as a percentage.

# Question 45

The correct answer is c. If **SORT_DIRECT_WRITES** is set to **TRUE**, any sort requiring a disk sort will bypass the buffer cache and use sort buffers assigned to each process to write directly to disk. This requires more memory and more disk space than normal writes through buffer cache sorting. Answer a is incorrect because **SORT_AREA_RETAINED_SIZE** is used to specify the size of the retained sort area in memory for a process. Answer b is incorrect because **SORT_AREA_SIZE** is used to size the overall sort area assigned to each process. Answer d is incorrect because **SORT_WRITE_BUFFER_SIZE** is used only to size the sort write buffers, and it is not used if **SORT_DIRECT_WRITES** is not set to **AUTO** or **TRUE**.

# Question 46

The correct answer is a. If rollback segments are placed in the same tablespace as data, their dynamic growth and shrinkage can cause fragmentation of the data tablespace. Another possible cause is the use of a data tablespace as a temporary tablespace for users. Answer b is incorrect because a too-small data tablespace will result in application errors of the "unable to allocate extent" type, not fragmentation. Answer c is incorrect because this is not normal for Oracle. Answer d is incorrect because although tables will grow automatically, they do not shrink automatically.

# Question 47

The correct answer is c. A request for a redo copy latch is always an **IMMEDIATE**-type request. Answer a is incorrect because a redo copy latch is always an **IMMEDIATE** request, not a **WILLING_TO_WAIT** request. Answer b is incorrect because you are requesting a latch, which might cause a buffer request when the work is done, but first you must get the latch. Answer d is incorrect because an **IMMEDIATE** request, not an **ALLOCATION** request, is made for a redo copy latch.

# Question 48

The correct answer is d. The only process in Oracle that reads disk blocks into the buffer is the user-server process. Answer a is incorrect because SMON is responsible for system monitoring and instance cleanup as well as coalescing free space in tablespaces; however, it does not place data in the buffer cache. Answer b is incorrect because PMON is responsible for process monitoring and cleanup but does not write disk data into the buffer cache. Answer c is incorrect because DBWn writes dirty buffers to disk and performs check-pointing activities but never reads data into the buffers.

# Question 49

The correct answer is c. With some exceptions (such as direct loads and some sorts), data that comes from or goes to Oracle databases flows through the buffer cache. Answer a is incorrect because the shared pool stores shared SQL and PL/SQL. Answer b is incorrect because the data dictionary cache stores data dictionary information. Answer d is incorrect because the redo log buffers store the transaction data before it is copied to the redo logs.

# Question 50

The correct answer is b. The **PINS** column of the **V$LIBRARYCACHE** view shows the number of times an item in the shared pool was executed. Answer a is incorrect because **RELOADS** shows the number of times a requested item had to be reloaded after being aged out by the LRU; excessive **RELOADS** shows a need to increase the size of the shared pool. Answer c is incorrect because **INVALIDATIONS** shows how many times an item in the shared pool was marked invalid because of changes in the objects that the item refers to. Answer d is incorrect because **GETS** shows the number of times requests were made for the object; in an ideal setup, **GETS** and **PINS** should be nearly identical.

# Question 51

The correct answers are d and e. The **V$RECENT_BUCKET** view is created when **DB_BLOCK_LRU_STATISTICS** is set to **TRUE** and **DB_BLOCK_LRU_EXTENDED_STATISTICS** is set to a positive number. The view stores the number of hits gained by adding buffers up to the number specified. The **V$SYSSTAT** table contains the statistics used to calculate the hit ratio, which tells how effectively the cache area is utilized. Answer a is incorrect because **V$CACHE** stores data about currently cached objects. Answer b is incorrect because **V$FILESTAT** contains I/O statistics about database files, not buffer cache areas. Answer c is incorrect because **X$STATS** probably does not exist.

# Question 52

The correct answer is a. By striping the tables, you improve the efficiency of a parallel query by reducing I/O contention. Answer b is incorrect because an increase of the shared pool size will not affect query speed in this situation. Answer c is incorrect because an increase in the redo log size will not affect query speed in this situation. Answer d is incorrect because a decrease in the degree of parallel will reduce, not increase, performance.

# Question 53

The correct answer is b. The **COUNT** column will display the number of additional cache hits gained by adding additional buffer cache blocks Answer a is incorrect because no column in **V$RECENT_BUCKET** shows this value. Answer c is incorrect because no column in **V$RECENT_BUCKET** shows this value. Answer d is incorrect because no column in **V$RECENT_BUCKET** shows this value. If you issue a count against the entire table, not specifying a summation (for example, **SELECT COUNT(*) FROM V$RECENT_ BUCKET**), you can find out how many additional buffers it is projecting hits for, but that is all.

# Question 54

The correct answer is c. Many default items, such as the maximum size of cached tables and whether direct sort writes are performed (if **SORT_ DIRECT_WRITES** is set to **AUTO**), are based on the size of the data buffer area, which, of course, is based on the number of database block buffers (**DB_BLOCK_BUFFERS**) and the size of the database blocks (**DB_ BLOCK_SIZE**). In addition, the more buffers in the database buffer cache, the less contention and the higher the hit ratio, all of which translate into better performance. Answer a is incorrect because the need for increasing the redo log size is indicated by excessive log switches causing excessive checkpointing activity; because this has not been indicated in the question, you must assume that this is not occurring. Answer b is incorrect because a need for increasing the sort area size is indicated by a large number of disk sorts; again, because the question did not mention this, you must assume that this is not occurring. Answer d is incorrect because generally a decrease in the sort area size will result in less, not more, performance.

## Question 55

The correct answer is c. Sort direct writes bypass the database base buffer caches when performing disk sorts. To bypass the data buffers, each user is given his or her own set of sort write buffers to use when writing to disk. Giving each user his or her own buffers will usually result in more memory being required for Oracle usage overall. In addition, depending on how the sort direct write option uses the disk, more temporary space will be required. Answer a is incorrect because sort direct writes do not care which background processes are running. Answer b is incorrect because the only prerequisite for using sort direct writes is the one mentioned in answer c. However, be careful if this question appears on the exam because the original version of the exam considered this the correct answer (though the powers that be now know that it is incorrect). Answer d is incorrect because sort direct writes do not depend on data file sizing.

## Question 56

The correct answer is b. If the addresses listed in the listener.ora and init<*SID*>.ora files do not match, the users will receive dedicated rather than shared connections. The entries must be identical. For example, if the actual IP address is used in one and the host name as used by your domain name server is used in the other, connections will be dedicated. Answer a is incorrect because this describes the **MTS_DISPATCHERS** and **MTS_MAX_DISPATCHERS** initialization parameters. Answer c is incorrect because this describes the **MTS_SERVERS** and **MTS_MAX_SERVERS** initialization parameters. Answer d is incorrect because this describes the **MTS_SERVERS** parameter.

## Question 57

The correct answer is a. Using **SET TRANSACTION USE ROLLBACK SEGMENT** seg_name, you can force a transaction to use any rollback segment you desire. Remember that you must issue a **COMMIT** command before issuing **SET TRANSACTION** to set the rollback segment usage to force any previous transaction to close and that the command must be the first command in the transaction. Answer b is incorrect because transactions are created automatically or by using the **BEGIN** and **END** commands or the **COMMIT** command. Answer c is incorrect because a transaction cannot really be modified—it either is or is not. Answer d is incorrect because any session-related system parameters are changed with the **ALTER SESSION** command, not the **SET TRANSACTION** command.

## Question 58

The correct answers are b and d. The read-consistent and current copies of a database block are maintained in memory at all times. When a block is read into memory and subsequently modified, a second copy of the block with the original data is maintained until the data is committed back to the database. This ensures that a read-consistent version of the data is always available to other transactions. Answer a is incorrect because once a delete action is committed, there is no need for the deleted block's information; before a delete is committed, you have the current and read-consistent copies in the buffers. Answer c is incorrect because there is no such thing as a backup copy of a block.

## Question 59

The correct answer is c. If a restart of the database occurs between the time you run UTLBSTAT.SQL and the time you run UTLESTAT.SQL, the statistical data contained in the report.txt output will be bad. To get a proper tuning report in the case of a database restart, you must run both UTLBSTAT.SQL and UTLESTAT.SQL, in that order. Remember that the report generated by UTLESTAT.SQL calculates a delta set of statistics and that the statistics in the base tables are always from the startup of the instance. Answer a is incorrect because simply rerunning UTLBSTAT.SQL will not generate a tuning report. Answer b is incorrect because although running UTLESTAT.SQL will generate a tuning report, the information contained in the report will be invalid. Answer d is incorrect because the scripts are in the incorrect order; you must always run UTLBSTAT.SQL before you run UTLESTAT.SQL.

## Question 60

The correct answer is a. Because bitmapped indexes map values in the column to bits and store only the bit values, storage is reduced by several orders when bitmapped indexes are used. This is the only one of the answers given that is a benefit of using bitmapped indexes. Answer b is incorrect because bitmapped indexes do not need to be ordered; in fact, because they are used for columns of low cardinality, ordering would not make much sense. Answer c is incorrect because bitmapped indexes are actually great for large tables, which are prevalent in DSSes. Answer d is incorrect because bitmapped indexes work well on columns of low, not high, cardinality.

## Question 61

The correct answer is c. The alert_<*SID*>.log file stores information about errors and events (for example, startup, shutdown, and log switches as well as DDLs issued against the database) that occur against the database. Answer a is incorrect because process SQL statements are tracked through trace files, not the alert log. Answer b is incorrect because no file tracks alerts issued by Oracle Corporation. Answer d is incorrect because this is accomplished with the internal audit tables in Oracle, not through the alert log.

## Question 62

The correct answer is c. **DB_BLOCK_SIZE** is used to initialize all data files in the system. If the block size is changed, the database files will not be readable, so to change the block size you need to export all data, drop and rebuild the database, and import the data back into the data files. Answer a is incorrect because Oracle recommends setting the parameter to a large value, and this usually improves performance. Answer b is incorrect because setting the parameter too low results in less, not more, memory being used. Answer d is incorrect because Oracle does not automatically set this parameter. The standard default value for a block size is 2048, which is too small for most applications.

## Question 63

The correct answer is a. The purpose of the rollback segment is to allow for the rollback of transactions. Rollback of transactions is possible only if before images of database blocks are stored in the rollback segments. Answer b is incorrect because redo logs store transaction information for redoing transactions, not information on how to roll them back. Answer c is incorrect because data files are the source of data, not repositories of transient data. Answer d is incorrect because indexes store current fixed values, not transient values.

# Question 64

The correct answer is a. Memory sorts are performed using reads and writes measured in microseconds, whereas disk sorts are done at millisecond read-write speeds at best. Memory sorts are always faster than disk sorts, so they are the preferred sorting mechanism. Answer b is incorrect because disk sorts, being slower, are not the preferred method of sorting, so performing sorts in memory is always a good idea regardless of the amount of space in your temporary tablespace. Answer c is incorrect because **SORT_DIRECT_WRITES** determines how large sorts are written to disk, not whether they should be done in memory.

# Question 65

The correct answer is c. If the **TIMED_STATISTICS** parameter is not set prior to running UTLBSTAT.SQL, time-based statistics will not be properly collected. Answer a is incorrect because **AUDIT_TRAIL** only turns on auditing, which is not used by UTLBSTAT.SQL. Answer b is incorrect because **SQL_TRACE** turns on tracing across the entire database and has nothing to do with UTLBSTAT.SQL.

# Glossary

**ACCEPT**—A SQL*Plus command that enables a SQL program to prompt a user for a variable at runtime and accept an input.

**alert log**—Used to record database-level errors and alerts. All database-structure–effecting commands are logged, as are some optional events, such as redo log switches. Alternatively known as the alert_*<SID>*.log, where *SID* corresponds to the SID of the database.

**ALTER**—A Data Definition Language (DLL) command that is used to change database objects.

**analysis**—The step in the system development process where the users' needs are gathered and analyzed to produce documentation used to design a program system.

**ANALYZE**—A DDL command that causes the database to gather or drop statistics on tables, clusters, or indexes.

**application error**—An error that occurs whenever an application issues an improper command to the database, resulting in an error condition or undesired effect on the database.

**archive log**—An archive copy of the redo log. The archive log is used to recover to an earlier point in time or to roll forward from a backup to the present time.

**ARCHIVELOG mode**—A database can be in either **ARCHIVELOG** or **NOARCHIVELOG** mode. In **ARCHIVELOG** mode, the database copies filled redo logs to an archive destination, thus allowing for full recovery to point of failure or to a previous point in time.

**attribute**—A detail concerning a thing of significance (entity). For example, a PERSON entity may have the attributes of name, address, and birth date.

**audit trail**—In Oracle, a defined set of actions that are specified to be audited using system audit tools. For example, you can audit connects to the database.

**AUTOTRACE**—A SQL*Plus command that causes all SQL statements to be traced.

**BACKGROUND_DUMP_DEST**—An option that is placed in the initialization file (init<*SID*>.ora) and specifies the location where the trace files for all background processes and the alert_<*SID*>.log are placed.

**backup**—The process of taking a physical or logical copy of the database to allow for archival or for disaster recovery purposes. Alternatively, a mode into which the tablespaces in a database can be placed to allow online backups.

**buffer**—In Oracle, a memory area used to hold data, redo, or rollback information. Usually the buffers are specified using the **DB_BLOCK_BUFFERS**, **DB_BLOCK_SIZE**, and **LOG_BUFFER** initialization parameters.

**cache**—A memory area that is self-managing and is used to hold information about objects, locks, and latches. The caches are usually contained in the shared pool area of the system global area (SGA) and are preallocated as far as size, based on internal algorithms that control how the shared pool memory is allocated.

**cardinality**—A term used in relational analysis to show how two objects relate; it tells how many. For example, "A person may have zero or one nose" shows a cardinality of zero or one. "A person may have zero, one, or many children" shows a cardinality of zero to many. And, "A person has one or many cells" shows a cardinality of one or many. In reference to indexes, cardinality shows how many rows in the indexed table relate back to the index value. A low cardinality index, such as a person's sex (M or F) should be placed in a bitmapped index if it must be indexed, whereas a high cardinality value, such as a person's social security number or employee ID, should be placed in a standard B-tree index.

**chaining**—The process in which a database entry is split between two (or more) database blocks. Chaining usually happens with either **varchar2** or **number** fields that grow too large to fit inside the available free space in a block due to **UPDATE** activity.

**checkbox**—Part of a GUI interface that allows a mouse click to be registered visually as a checkmark or other mark indicating a selection from a list of values or answers.

**checkpoint**—A process where the DBWn or optional CHKP process writes SCN and transaction information into all data file headers to synchronize the database.

**cluster**—A database structure made up of one or more tables that jointly store key values in the same physical database blocks. Clusters allow for rapid retrieval of clustered data but may cause problems to tables that undergo frequent **INSERT** or **UPDATE** activity.

**column**—Part of a table's row. A column will have been mapped from an attribute in an entity. Columns have data types, and may have constraints mapped against them.

**COMMIT**—A Data Manipulation Language (DML) command. A **COMMIT** marks a transaction as completed successfully and causes data to be written first to the redo logs and then, once DBWn writes, to the disk. A **COMMIT** isn't complete until it receives word from the disk subsystem that the redo log write is complete. Committed data cannot be rolled back using the **ROLLBACK** command, and must be removed using more DML commands.

**complete media recovery**—The process involving use of archive logs, redo logs, and rollback segments allowing an Oracle database to be completely restored to the time of a media failure.

**CONNECT**—A Server Manager (SVRMGRL), SQL*Worksheet, or SQL*Plus command that enables a user to connect to the database or to a remote database.

**contention**—When two or more processes compete for the same resource, such as a table, a latch, or memory. Contention results in database wait events and slow performance.

**control file**—The Oracle file that contains information on all database files and maintains Systems Change Number (SCN) records for each. The control file must be present and current for the database to start up properly. Control files may be mirrored; mirrored copies are automatically updated by Oracle as needed. The control file provides for maintenance of system concurrency and consistency by providing a means of synchronizing all database files.

**conventional path load**—The most used form of SQL*Loader database load. A conventional path load uses DML statements to load data from flat operating system files into Oracle tables.

**CREATE**—A DDL command that allows creation of database objects.

**data dictionary**—A collection of C structs, tables, and views that contain all of the database metadata (information about the database's data). The data dictionary is used to store information used by all database processes to find out about database data structures.

**database buffer cache** —This cache is defined by the **DB_BLOCK_SIZE** and **DB_BLOCK_BUFFERS** initialization parameters. All data that enters or leaves the database passes through the database buffer cache.

**DBMS_APPLICATION_INFO**—An Oracle-supplied stored PL/SQL package of procedures and functions. It allows for tracking of application status and performance through application coded calls to the package contents that result in data being sent to the **V$SESSION** dynamic performance view.

**DBVERIFY**—An Oracle-supplied database verification tool. **DBVERIFY** is used to check the internal consistency of Oracle database data files.

**DDL (Data Definition Language)**—An SQL statement used to create or manipulate database structures is classified as DDL; examples are **CREATE**, **ALTER**, and **DROP** commands.

**deadlock**—A deadlock occurs when a process is holding an exclusive lock on a resource, such as a table, that is required by another process. The process that detects the deadlock is rolled back to resolve the deadlock automatically. Deadlocks usually result from improperly specified application-coded explicit locking.

**DELETE**—A DML command used to remove data by rows (generally speaking) from the database tables.

**DESCRIBE**—A SQL*Plus or Server Manager command that is used to retrieve information on database structure. Any stored object (except triggers) can be described.

**dictionary cache** —An internal component of the shared pool section of the SGA. The dictionary cache is used to track data dictionary items such as latches, tables, indexes, and so on. The dictionary cache is automatically sized based on internal algorithms, taking into account the values of various initialization parameters and rationing them to the size of the shared pool.

**direct path load**—In SQL*Loader, this disables all triggers, constraints, and indexes and loads data directly into the table by prebuilding and then inserting database blocks. It does not use DML commands. There are conventional and direct path loads in SQL*Loader.

**discarded records**—A record that SQL*Loader rejects for loading based on internal rules for data validation and conversion.

**disk sort**—This occurs when the size of a sort request exceeds the **SORT_AREA_SIZE** specified memory size. Generally, disk sorts take orders of magnitude longer than the equivalent memory sort and should be avoided if possible.

DISTINCT SELECT—A SELECT that uses either the DISTINCT or UNIQUE operator to force no duplicate entries to be returned by a SELECT. All DISTINCT SELECT operations result in sorts and should be avoided if possible.

DROP—A DDL command used to remove database objects.

DSS (decision support system)—A general type of database. Usually DSS systems use a number of large SELECT operations and perform multiple full table scans.

dynamic SQL—SQL used to build SQL. Essentially, queries are issued against data dictionary tables using embedded literal strings to build a set of commands. Usually, dynamic SQL is used to automate a long series of virtually identical commands against similar types of database objects. An example would be creating a script to disable or enable all triggers for a set of database tables using the DBA_TRIGGERS table and a single SQL statement.

entity—In relational modeling, a thing of significance. Examples of entities are PERSON, CAR, and EXPENSE. Entities are singular in nature and are mapped to tables. Tables contain entities.

ERD (entity relationship diagram)—A pictorial representation using a standard symbology and methodology (such as Chen or Yourdon) of a relational database.

Explain Plan—The Explain Plan facility is incorporated into the SQL*Plus engine and the TKPROF utility. In SQL*Plus, Explain Plans are generated either automatically if AUTOTRACE with the EXPLAIN option is set to ON, or manually by means of the EXPLAIN PLAN command. Explain Plans show the method Oracle will use to execute a specified SQL command (usually SELECT). The Explain Plan function doesn't execute the specified query, but provides the execution plan for review and tuning.

foreign key—A value or set of values mapped from a primary or parent table into a dependent or child table used to enforce referential integrity. A foreign key, generally speaking, must be either NULL or exist as a primary key in a parent table.

free list—A segment header structure that allows for tracking of blocks that are updatable or can be inserted into. To be on a freelist, a block must have more than or equal to the percentage of free space specified by PCTFREE.

full database export—The export utility exp allows for the creation of a logical database copy. A full export is one where all users' (schemas') grants, constraints, and other database items are logically copied into an export-formatted file. The export also allows for table and schema- (user-) level logical copies and for incremental and cumulative exports as well.

**function**—One of several structures. An *implicit function* is one that is provided as a part of the SQL language. An *explicit function* is one that is created by the user using PL/SQL. A function must return a value and must be named. As a part of the SQL standard, a function cannot change a database's or package's state, but can only act on external variables and values.

**GET**—A SQL*Plus command that loads SQL or PL/SQL commands from an external operating system file into the SQL*Plus command buffer.

**get**—A successful acquisition of a database resource.

**high-water mark**—Oracle keeps track of the highest level at which a database table is utilized, which becomes the high-water mark for that table. A table can only reclaim empty space between currently filled blocks and the high-water mark through a rebuild or truncation process. To accurately get a reading on how much space is actually used in a table, you must count the blocks used (by parsing and counting the block IDs from the **ROWID**s) and not simply perform a count of used extents, because used extents are counted up to the high-water mark.

**hint**—An explicitly stated "suggestion" to the Oracle optimizer embedded into a SQL statement as a comment.

**hit ratio**—A calculated ratio of the number of times an attempt to obtain a resource was successful against the total number of times the resource was requested.

**hybrid system**—A database that combines one or more generic types of database, such as a DSS (decision support system) and an OLTP (online transaction processing) system.

**incomplete media recovery**—This happens when one or more of the files required for a media recovery are damaged or not available. The loss of the online redo log or rollback segment, or loss of all copies of the control file, result in the need for an incomplete media recovery.

**index**—A structure that enhances data retrieval by providing rapid access to frequently queried column values. Indexes can be either *B-tree structured* or *bitmapped*. The two general types of index are *unique* and *nonunique*. A unique index forces all values entered into its source column to be unique. A nonunique index allows for repetitive and null values to be entered into its source column.

Generally speaking, a column with high cardinality should be indexed using a B-tree type index (standard, default type of index), whereas low cardinality values should be indexed using a bitmapped index.

INITIAL—A storage parameter that sets the size in bytes (no suffix), kilobytes (K suffix), or megabytes (M suffix) of the INITIAL extent allocated to a table, index, rollback segment, or cluster.

INITRANS—A storage parameter that reserves space in the block header for the transaction records associated with a table's blocks.

INSERT—A DML command that enables users to place new records into a table.

instance failure—Occurs when one or more of the Oracle base instance processes (DBWn, SMON, PMON, LGWR, and so on) fails, causing the instance to crash (shutdown abnormally). Almost all instance failures are recovered automatically by Oracle upon instance restart.

latch—A low-level locking mechanism usually used to protect internal database resources, such as memory.

library cache —An alternative name for the shared pool.

lock—A high-level construct used to protect hard system resources, such as tables, clusters, stored objects, or indexes.

lock-tree—A simple diagram showing which locks are waiting for other locks.

LOG_BLOCK_CHECKSUM—An initialization parameter that forces the checking of the block checksums as a precaution against database corruption. If any corruption is found, it usually generates an alert log message, a trace file, a core dump, and an instance crash.

logical backup—Files generated by the EXPORT facility of Oracle that contain DDL and DML commands used to rebuild all or part of the database. The operative word in this explanation is *rebuild*. The logical copy of the database can only be recovered by use of the IMPORT facility, which is also provided by Oracle.

MAXEXTENTS—Sets the maximum number of extents an object can grow into. The MAXEXTENTS value can be altered up to the maximum number of extents allowed based on block size.

MAXTRANS—A companion to the INITRANS storage parameter. MAXTRANS sets the maximum number of transactions that can access a block concurrently.

**media failure**—Occurs when one or more of the physical disks in your facility fail (mechanically or electronically). A media failure always requires a database recovery if it involves active database files. Also known as a *disk failure*.

**memory sort**—A sort performed in the user's allocated sort area in the computer's memory. If possible, you should strive for all sorts to be done as memory sorts because they are orders of magnitude faster than disk sorts. If a sort is smaller than the specified **SORT_AREA_SIZE** parameter in the initialization file, the sort is done in memory.

**migration**—*See* chaining.

**mirroring**—A simple form of RAID in which one disk or set of disks is made either by software or hardware to exactly mirror an original or active set. Usually, mirroring is accomplished by simultaneous writes to both disk sets. Mirroring protects against media failure.

**miss**—Occurs when a database resource is requested but is not made available within a specified time period.

**multithreaded server (MTS)**—In Oracle, the process that allows multiplexing of database connections. In Oracle, the MTS system consists of a listener process, one or more dispatcher processes, and multiple server processes. This multiplexing of database connections allows more users than would normally be serviced to use the database and is especially useful on systems short on physical memory.

**NEXT**—Storage parameter that specifies the size in bytes (no suffix), kilobytes (K suffix), or megabytes (M suffix) of the **NEXT** extent allocated to a table, index, rollback segment, or cluster. The **NEXT** parameter is used with the **PCTINCREASE** parameter to determine the size of all extents after the **INITIAL** and **NEXT** extents.

**object auditing**—The specification of auditing options that pertains to database objects rather than database operations.

**OLTP (online transaction processing)**—These systems usually have multiple small, simultaneous transactions involving **SELECT, INSERT, UPDATE,** and **DELETE** operations. An example of an OLTP system would be an order-entry system.

**Optimal Flexible Architecture (OFA)**—A standard, authored by internal Oracle Corporation experts, that tells how to optimally configure an Oracle database.

**optimizer**—The section of the database engine that decides the best methods to use to resolve queries against the database. In Oracle, there are two possible optimizers—rule-based and cost-based. Generally, rule-based optimizers are easier to tune for because they are easily predictable if you know their rule context. Cost-based optimizers are harder to tune for because the optimization methodology may change based on database table and index statistics.

**ORAPWD**—A generalized term for the Oracle Password Manager that creates and is used to maintain the external password file. The external password file is used to tell the Oracle Enterprise Manager and Server Manager who is authorized to perform DBA functions against a specific database.

**ORDER BY SELECT**—A **SELECT** statement that uses the **ORDER BY** clause to override any implicit ordering a query would perform. An **ORDER BY SELECT** always performs a sort operation and thus should be avoided if possible.

**outside join**—A type of join where data not meeting the join criteria (that is, the join value is **NULL**) are also returned by the query. An outside join is signified by using the plus sign inside parentheses (+) to indicate the outside join value beside the join column for the table deficient in data.

**package**—A stored PL/SQL construct made of related procedures, functions, exceptions, and other PL/SQL constructs. Packages are called into memory when any package object is referenced. Packages are created or dropped as a unit.

**parallel recovery**—When using Oracle Parallel Server, parallel recovery allows for more than one instance in a parallel database to perform recovery operations simultaneously against the shared database.

**parallelism**—The number of explicitly configured parallel query slaves that will be assigned against a specific database object. Parallelism is also referred to as **DEGREE**. A query that uses parallelism will generally outperform a non-parallel query if the proper resources are available.

**partitioning**—The physical separation of a single table or index into two or more partitions based on the value of a column key.

**PCTFREE**—Used in an Oracle block to determine the amount of space reserved for future updates. Too low of a **PCTFREE** can result in row-chaining for frequently updated tables, and too high a value requires more storage space.

**PCTINCREASE**—Determines what percentage each subsequent extent after **INITIAL** and **NEXT** grows over the previously allocated extent.

**PCTUSED**—Determines when a block is placed back on the free block list. Once used space in a block drops below **PCTUSED**, the block can be used for subsequent new row insertion.

**Performance Pack**—An optional software package that can be purchased from Oracle to allow for monitoring and tuning of the Oracle database.

**PGA (process global area)**—Represents the memory area allocated to each process that accesses an Oracle database.

**physical backup**—A backup that is performed through operating system backup commands or routines. It consists of full copies of the actual database files. Using only physical backups, you can recover to the time of the backup. Using physical backups and archive logs, you can recover to point of failure. Physical backups are either *hot backups* taken with the database in backup mode but still active, or *cold backups* taken with the database shutdown.

**primary key**—In a relational database, the unique identifier for a table. A primary key must be unique and not null. A primary key can either be *natural* (derived from a column or columns in the database) or *artificial* (drawn from a sequence).

**private**—Refers to either rollback segments or procedures and functions. A private rollback segment (the ones generally recommended for use) must be specifically brought online either through manual commands or through use of the **ROLLBACK_SEGMENTS** initialization file parameter. For procedures and functions, a private procedure or function is one only addressable from within a master package or procedure that is usually fully contained within the structure of the calling package or procedure.

**privilege auditing**—Auditing of what privileges are granted and by and to whom.

**procedures**—Stored PL/SQL objects that may, but aren't required to, return a value. Procedures are allowed to change database or package state. Procedures can be placed into packages.

**process failure**—What occurs when a user process terminates improperly. Oracle will automatically roll back a process's transactions and reclaim its memory if it detects a failed process.

**production**—The final stage of the system development cycle. The production stage corresponds to normal maintenance and backup and recovery operations against a developed system.

**profiles**—Sets of resource allocations that can be assigned to a user. These resources are used to limit idle time, connect time, memory, and CPU usage.

**PROMPT**—A SQL*Plus command used to pass a string out of a SQL script to the executing user. The **PROMPT** command can be used with the **ACCEPT** command to prompt for values needed by the script.

**public**—Refers to either rollback segments or procedures and functions. A public rollback segment (the ones generally not recommended for use) are brought online automatically based on a ratio of the initialization parameters **TRANSACTIONS/TRANSACTIONS_PER_ROLLBACK_SEGMENT**. A public procedure or function is one addressable from outside of a master package or procedure.

**RAID (Redundant Array of Inexpensive Disks)**—RAID is usually specified by a level: 0 through 5 or a combination, such as 0/1 (striped and shadowed [or mirrored]). Usually you will only see RAID 0, RAID 1, RAID 0/1, and RAID 5.

**raw devices**—In Unix, these are used when you want to bypass the internal Unix buffering systems. Generally, raw devices, or *file systems*, will perform faster than a standard or "cooked" Unix file system. Raw file systems must be used if you utilize Oracle Parallel Server on most Unix boxes.

**read-only tablespaces**—A tablespace that has been altered into read-only mode. No redo or rollback is generated against a read-only tablespace, because, as the name implies, you cannot insert, update, or delete data from a read-only structure. Read-only tablespaces are backed up when they are placed in read-only state and then never (as long as the tablespace isn't placed back into normal mode) backed up again.

**RECOVER**—A command used in Server Manager to explicitly perform database recovery operations.

**redo**—Placed inside of redo logs. Redo information is any information that allows transactions to be redone in the event of a failure. The opposite of redo is undo or rollback data, which allow uncommitted transactions to be undone or rolled back.

**redo allocation latch**—Small transactions are copied into the redo logs using this. On single CPU systems, the redo allocation latch may be the only way to copy transaction data into the redo logs.

**redo copy latch**—Large transactions are copied on these into the redo logs. Generally, redo copy latches are used on multiple CPU systems.

**redo log buffer**—A memory structure inside the SGA that buffers writes to the redo logs. The redo log buffer is sized as a product of the **LOG_ARCHIVE_BUFFERS** and **LOG_ARCHIVE_BUFFER_SIZE** initialization file parameters.

**redo logs**—External database files that store information on all database-changing transactions. Redo logs are combined in groups of at least one redo log each, and each database must have at least two groups assigned to be able to start up. Usually there are two redo logs per group and, if **ARCHIVELOG** mode is set, a minimum of three groups assigned to the instance.

**referential integrity**—The process by which a relational database maintains record relationships between parent and child tables via primary key and foreign key values.

**rejected records**—In SQL*Loader, records that don't meet load criteria for the table being loaded either due to value, data type, or other restrictions.

**relationship**—A named association between two things of significance. For example, if you say that a wheeled vehicle has one or many wheels, *has* is the relationship. Or, if an employee works for one or more employers, *works for* is the relationship.

**report.txt**—Generated by the UTLESTAT.SQL script. The report.txt file is a collection of "delta" or difference reports based on data previously stored by use of the UTLBSTAT.SQL script. The UTLBSTAT.SQL and UTLESTAT. SQL scripts are located in the $ORACLE_HOME/rdbms/admin directory and the report.txt file is usually generated there as well.

**resources**—The database and system resources that are controlled by using a profile.

**restore**—The process by which database files are brought back from an archive location or backup site.

**roll-forward operation**—Accomplished automatically by an Oracle database during recovery operations. In a roll-forward operation, the transactions stored in the redo logs, and sometimes the archived redo logs, are applied to the database in order. Once a roll forward is accomplished, the rollback segments are used to remove any uncommitted transactions in a rollback operation.

**ROLLBACK**—A DML command used to undo database changes that have not been committed. This is also used to describe the operation performed after a roll forward during recovery of a database. A rollback during recovery consists of removing uncommitted transaction changes from the database.

**rollback segment**—A database object that contains records used to undo database transactions. Whenever a parameter in the database refers to **UNDO**, it is actually referring to rollback segments.

**row-level lock**—A row-level lock is the lowest level of locking utilized by the Oracle database. Row-level locking is usually implicit in nature and allows the maximum flexibility in locking options.

**SAVE**—A SQL*Plus command used to store command buffer contents in an external operating system file.

**SCN (system change number)**—A number assigned to a specific transaction. The SCN is used to track a transaction throughout its life, even once it has been transferred to the archive log. The most current SCNs that apply to the system data files are tracked in the data file headers and in the control files.

**SELECT**—A DML command used to retrieve values from the database.

**SEP (sort extent pool)**—An area of the SGA that tracks all available sort extents for the temporary tablespaces. The SEP is not initialized until the first sort operation requiring disk space is initialized.

**Server Manager line mode**—The Server Manager has a GUI mode and a line mode. In line mode, all commands are entered at the command line.

**SET**—A SQL*Plus command used to change the values of SQL*Plus environment parameters, such as line width and page length.

**SGA (system global area)**—Consists of the database buffers, shared pool, and queue areas that are globally accessible by all database processes. The SGA is used to speed Oracle processing by providing for caching of data and structure information in memory.

**shared pool**—A section of the SGA that contains the data dictionary cache, shared SQL area, and in some cases, the response queues.

**SHOW**—A SQL*Plus command that is used to show the value of a variable set with the **SET** command.

**SHUTDOWN**—A Server Manager command used to shut down the database. **SHUTDOWN** has three modes: **NORMAL, IMMEDIATE,** and **ABORT. NORMAL** prohibits new connection waits for all users to log off and then shuts down. **IMMEDIATE** prohibits new connections, backs out uncommitted transactions, and then logs users off and shuts down. **ABORT** shuts down immediately, and not gracefully.

**sleeps**—Occur when a latch or lock on a system resource is requested and the resource is not available. The process making the request "sleeps" until the resource is available or a timeout happens, whichever comes first.

**sort direct writes**—Define that writes to a sort segment bypass the SGA buffer pool and instead are routed directly though a set of sort direct write buffers held by each process. Sort direct writes should not be used unless the system has sufficient disk and memory resources.

**spin**—One CPU cycle. The default wait time for latches or locks is defined by the initialization variable **SPIN_COUNT** on many platforms. You can reduce the number of misses by increasing the **SPIN_COUNT** setting, but performance may degrade.

**SPOOL**—A SQL*Plus command that is used to send SQL*Plus output to either a printer or a file.

**SQL buffer**—A memory area used to store the last SQL command. The SQL buffer can only store the last command executed, unless it is loaded with the **GET** command. A SQL*Plus command such as **SET**, **DESCRIBE**, or **SPOOL** is not placed in the SQL buffer.

**SQL*Trace**—Allows user and system processes to create trace files that can then be studied later to determine what SQL statements need tuning.

**standby database**—A duplicate database that is maintained in **RECOVERY** mode. An automatic process copies the archived redo logs from the active database to the standby database and applies them, thus keeping the databases in sync.

**STARTUP**—A Server Manager command used to start up the database. A database can be started in one of several modes: **MOUNT, NOMOUNT, OPEN, EXCLUSIVE**, or **PARALLEL**.

**statement auditing**—Audits statement actions such as inserts, updates, and deletes.

**statement failure**—This occurs if a transaction statement is improperly terminated either due to an error or a manual action. A statement failure results in an automatic rollback of the statements actions if required.

**STORAGE**—What Oracle uses to determine current and future settings for an object's extents. If a storage clause isn't specified, the object's storage characteristics are taken from the tablespace default **STORAGE** clause.

**strategy**—In this step of the system development cycle (usually paired with the analysis step), the overall methodology for the rest of the development effort is mapped out.

**striping**—The process where either disks, tablespaces, or tables are deliberately fragmented and placed across several disks to improve performance or allow for larger files. In disk striping, the process is usually done automatically by a disk management system such as VERITAS and is invisible to the casual user.

**table**—The structure used to store data in an Oracle database. Entities map to tables in relational databases.

**table-level lock**—An explicitly defined lock, because Oracle doesn't practice lock escalation (only lock conversion). A table-level lock locks an entire table and will result in deadlocks if not used properly.

**table mode export**—An export that only makes a logical copy of one or more tables and their related objects such as triggers, constraints, indexes, and grants.

**temporary tablespace**—A tablespace that is used for temporary (sort) segments only. A permanent tablespace can contain either permanent or temporary segments, whereas a tablespace that has been designated by either the **CREATE TABLESPACE** or **ALTER TABLESPACE** commands as a temporary tablespace can only contain temporary segments. A user can be assigned either a temporary or permanent tablespace as his designated temporary (sort) tablespace.

**TIMED_STATISTICS**—The initialization file parameter that tells the Oracle kernel to record time-based statistics.

**TKPROF**—Converts the normal, difficult-to-read format of a process trace file into human-readable format. The TKPROF utility is used for tuning Oracle applications.

**transaction-level lock**—A DML lock. It is always created implicitly.

**transition**—In this step of the system development cycle, user testing is performed and support of the application moves from development to production personnel.

**TRUNCATE**—A DDL statement used to remove all rows from a table. Because it is a DDL statement, it cannot be rolled back.

**UGA (user global area)**—Used to store user-specific variables and stacks.

**UID (unique identifier)**—Uniquely identifies a row in a table and usually maps to the natural primary key value. Each entity must have a unique identifier to qualify as a relational table.

**Undo**—*See* rollback segments.

**UPDATE**—A DML command that allows data inside tables to be changed.

**user error**—An error in the database caused by a user, such as an accidental erasure or an insertion or update to a table or to the database structure itself. User errors are usually the most difficult to recover from.

**user mode export**—An export that provides a logical copy of the objects owned by a single user. This is also known as a *schema export*.

**UTLBSTAT.SQL**—The script that creates a set of tables and loads them with statistics garnered from the **V$** series of dynamic performance views. The UTLBSTAT.SQL script is usually located in the $ORACLE_HOME/rdbms/admin directory (or its equivalent). Short for *utility begin statistics*.

**UTLESTAT.SQL**—The script that reads the current values for the statistics gathered by the UTLBSTAT.SQL script and then generates the report.txt file based on the differences between the two sets of statistics. The UTLESTAT.SQL script drops all tables created by the UTLBSTAT.SQL script after the report.txt file is generated. If a shutdown occurs before the UTLESTAT.SQL script is run, both of the scripts must be run in order to generate a proper report.txt file. If you see negative results for statistics in the UTLESTAT.SQL report.txt file, this indicates that a shutdown happened between the time the UTLBSTAT.SQL and UTLESTAT.SQL scripts were run. Short for *utility end statistics*.

**V$RECOVERY_FILE_STATUS**—A dynamic performance view used to show the status of data file recovery.

**V$RECOVERY_STATUS**—A dynamic performance view used to show the status of database recovery.

**variable**—A user- or process-defined storage area used to hold a value that will probably be different each time a script or procedure is executed.

**view**—A preset select against one or more tables that is stored in the database and has no physical representation. A view is also known as a *virtual table*.

# Index

# S